T5-AVP-313

Policy Makers on Policy

For the last twenty-five years, monetary policy has been at the centre of economic debate. During this period the theory and practice of monetary policy in the United Kingdom has been transformed. This volume offers enormous insight into this transformation by collecting together the views of a broad range of leading policy makers and practitioners.

The original versions of the chapters that make up this book were given as Mais Lectures at City University. These lectures were designed to appeal to a wide audience of policy makers and practitioners and to communicate what monetary policy was, what it did and what it could achieve. As those giving the lectures were responsible for shaping and carrying out monetary policy they offer a unique insight to changes during this period.

Monetary policy is the major focus of the volume. Whilst a wide range of positions are explored, a consensus about the objectives of economic policy, and how to achieve them, does emerge and the volume charts a shift in emphasis from short-term demand management to low inflation and long-term stability. However, within this broad consensus several areas of possible conflict are addressed including the channels of transmission of monetary policy and the significance of international monetary developments.

Monetary policy is, none the less, not the only focus of the lectures, with some contributors exploring international economic integration; the relationship between economic and social policy; and the nature of the economic system under which we live.

Forrest H. Capie is Professor of Economic History and **Geoffrey E. Wood** is Professor of Economics at City University Business School.

Policy Makers on Policy

The Mais Lectures

**Edited by Forrest H. Capie
and Geoffrey E. Wood**

London and New York

First published 2001
by Routledge
11 New Fetter Lane, London EC4P 4EE

Simultaneously published in the USA and Canada
by Routledge
29 West 35th Street, New York, NY 10001

Routledge is an imprint of the Taylor & Francis Group

Typeset in Baskerville by RefineCatch Limited, Bungay, Suffolk
Printed and bound in Great Britain by University Press, Cambridge

British Library Cataloguing in Publication Data
A catalogue record for this book is available from the British Library

Library of Congress Cataloging-in-Publication Data
   Policy makers on policy: the Mais lectures/edited by Forrest H. Capie
and Geoffrey E. Wood.
      p. cm.
   Includes bibliographical references and index.
   1. Monetary policy.   2. Monetary policy—Great Britain. I. Title: Mais
Lectures. II. Capie, Forrest. III. Wood, Geoffrey Edward.
   HG230.3 .P637 2001
   332.4'941–dc21
                                                        2001019137

ISBN 0–415–24401–3

Contents

Notes on Contributors

Tony Blair was born on 6 May, 1953 in Edinburgh. He read law at St John's College, Oxford before practising as a barrister. Married to Cherie Booth, a barrister and Queen's Counsel, they have three sons Euan, Nicky and Leo, and a daughter, Kathryn. He is MP for Sedgefield in the north-east of England. Entering Parliament for the first time in 1983, he served in opposition as Shadow Employment Secretary and Shadow Home Secretary. Following the death of John Smith in 1994, Mr Blair was elected as his successor as Labour leader. He accelerated the modernisation of the party's constitution and policies. In 1995, he won the party's overwhelming backing to replace Clause IV with a modern statement of Labour's aims and values. Tony Blair became the youngest Prime Minister for over a century following Labour's General Election victory on 1 May, 1997.

Sir Samuel Brittan is a columnist at the *Financial Times*. His most recent books are *Capitalism with a Human Face* (Edward Elgar 1995, Fontana 1996) and *Essays, Moral, Political and Economic* (Edinburgh University Press 1998). He is an Honorary Fellow of Jesus College, Cambridge; an Honorary Doctor of Letters (Heriot-Watt University, Edinburgh); an Honorary Doctor of the University of Essex. He has been Visiting Professor at the Chicago Law School, a Visiting Fellow of Nuffield College, Oxford, and an Honorary Professor of Politics at Warwick. He has been awarded the George Orwell, Senior Harold Wincott and Ludwig Erhard prizes. He was a member of the Peacock Committee on the Finance of the BBC (1985–86). He was knighted in 1993 for 'services to economic journalism' and also that year became a *Chevalier de la Legion d'Honneur.*

Gordon Brown was appointed Chancellor of the Exchequer on 2 May, 1997. He has been Member of Parliament for Dunfermline East since 1983 and was Opposition spokesperson on Treasury and Economic Affairs (Shadow Chancellor) from 1992 to 1997. Mr Brown was born in 1951 and educated at Kirkcaldy High School and Edinburgh University where he gained first class honours and then a doctorate. He was Rector of Edinburgh University and Chairman of the University Court between 1972 and 1975. From 1976 to 1980 Mr Brown lectured at Edinburgh University and then at Caledonian

University before taking up a post at Scottish Television (1980–83). After becoming an MP, Mr Brown was the Chair of the Labour Party Scottish Council (1983–84). Before becoming Shadow Chancellor he held two other senior positions on the Opposition front bench – Shadow Chief Secretary to the Treasury (1987–89) and Shadow Trade and Industry Secretary (1989–92). Mr Brown has had a number of works published including *Maxton*, *The Politics of Nationalism and Devolution* and *Where There is Greed*. He has edited a number of books including *John Smith: Life and Soul of the Party* and *Values, Visions and Voices*.

Forrest H. Capie is Professor of Economic History at the City University Business School, London. After a doctorate at the London School of Economics in the 1970s and a teaching fellowship there, he taught at the University of Warwick and the University of Leeds. He has been a British Academy Overseas Fellow at the National Bureau, New York, and a Visiting Professor at the University of Aix-Marseille, and at the London School of Economics. He has written widely on money, banking, and trade and commercial policy. He was Head of Department of Banking and Finance at City University from 1989 to 1992, and was Editor of the *Economic History Review* from 1993 to 1999. He is a member of the Academic Advisory Council of the Institute of Economic Affairs.

Kenneth Clarke was elected Member of Parliament for Rushcliffe in Nottinghamshire at the 1970 General Election. He has been Minister for Employment, Minister for Trade and Industry, Secretary of State for Health, Secretary of State for Education and Science, Home Secretary and he was Chancellor of the Exchequer from 1993 to 1997. Since his return to the back benches, Mr Clarke has taken on various business appointments. He is Deputy Chairman of British American Tobacco plc and non-executive Chairman of British American Racing (Holdings) Limited. He is also non-executive Chairman of Alliance UniChem plc, non-executive Chairman of Savoy Asset Management plc, and a director of Foreign and Colonial Investment Trust and of Independent News and Media (UK).

Eddie George (now The Rt Hon Sir Edward George, GBE) was educated at Dulwich College and Emmanuel College, Cambridge. He graduated in economics in 1962, and joined the Bank of England on leaving university. During his career, he was posted on secondment to the Bank for International Settlements and the International Monetary Fund. He was made a Director of the Bank in 1982, responsible for monetary policy, market operations and market supervision. He was appointed Deputy Governor in 1990, and Governor in 1993 (renewed for a further five-year term in 1998). He became a member of the Privy Council in 1999, and was awarded the GBE in 2000.

Sir Geoffrey Howe (now The Rt Hon Lord Howe of Aberavon, CH, QC) served as a Cabinet Minister for all but the last three weeks of Margaret Thatcher's government: as Chancellor of the Exchequer (1979–83), Foreign and Commonwealth Secretary (1983–89), and Deputy Prime Minister. He entered the House of Lords in July 1992. He served in Edward Heath's government as Solicitor General (1970–72) and Minister for Trade and Consumer Affairs (1972–74) and was responsible for the principal legislation providing for Britain's EC membership and for the Community's 1986 enlargement and 1992 Single Market Programme. Lord Howe served as Chairman of the International Monetary Fund Interim Committee (1982–83) and attended eleven World Economic Summits (1979–89). His memoirs, *Conflict of Loyalty*, were published by Macmillan and St Martin's Press in October 1994.

Nigel Lawson (now The Rt Hon Lord Lawson PC) was Chancellor of the Exchequer from June 1983 until his resignation in October 1989. This lecture was given early on in his Chancellorship, in June 1984. His widely acclaimed memoirs, *The View from No. 11 – Memoirs of a Tory Radical*, were published in 1992.

Robin Leigh-Pemberton (now The Rt Hon Lord Kingsdown KG) was called to the Bar in 1954 and practised until 1963. In 1972 he became the Director of the National Westminster Bank Limited (and other public companies) and in 1977 was made Chairman of the National Westminster Bank. Between 1983 and 1993 he was Governor of the Bank of England. Appointed to Her Majesty's Privy Council in 1987, he received a life peerage in 1993 and in 1994 the Queen appointed him a Knight of the Garter.

Peter Lilley was born on 23 August, 1943 in Hayes, Kent and educated at Hayes County Primary School, Dulwich College and Clare College, Cambridge, where he studied natural science and economics. He was a Director of Greenwell Montagu Stockbrokers (1986–87) and has been an economic advisor in underdeveloped countries (1966–72). Mr Lilley was Member of Parliament for St Albans from 1983 to 1997 and, following boundary changes in 1997, became MP for Hitchin and Harpenden. Peter Lilley was Parliamentary Secretary to William Waldegrave and Lord Bellwin (1984), and then to the Chancellor of the Exchequer, Nigel Lawson (1984–87). His first ministerial appointment was as Economic Secretary to the Treasury (June 1987), then Financial Secretary to the Treasury (July 1989). From 1992 to 1997 he was Secretary of State for Social Security. He is the author of several publications including: *Delusions of Income Policy* (co-written with Samuel Brittan), 1977; and *Patient Power* (Demos), 2000.

Gordon Richardson (now The Rt Hon Lord Richardson of Duntisbourne KG) was appointed Governor of the Bank of England in July 1973. He had then been a Director of the Bank for six years. He was re-appointed in July 1978 for a further term of five years which ended on 30 June, 1983. Appointed to Her Majesty's Privy Council in 1976, he received a life peerage in 1983 and in April 1983 the Queen appointed him a Knight of the Garter. Lord Richardson is Honorary Chairman of the Group of Thirty, Consultative Group on International and Monetary Affairs and is a member of a number of other foundations or societies. He also holds Honorary Degrees from the Universities of Cambridge, Aston, East Anglia and from the City University. He is the Deputy High Steward of Cambridge University and is an Honorary Fellow of Gonville and Caius and Wolfson Colleges, Cambridge.

Lord Robbins (1898–1984) was a Professor of Economics at the London School of Economics for 30 years, and finally Chairman of Governors. During the Second World War he established a reputation as an administrator as Director of the powerful economic section of the Cabinet. There followed a succession of appointments that included President of the Royal Academy, Director of the Royal Opera House and the National Gallery, Trustee of the Tate Gallery, Chairman of the *Financial Times* from 1961 to 1967, and Chancellor of Stirling University. He was made a life peer in 1959. He is best known for his first book, *An Essay on the Nature and Significance of Economic Science* (1932). Other works include: *The Economic Problem in Peace and War* (1947), *Classical Political Economy* (1952) and *The Evolution of Modern Economic Theory* (1970).

Rabbi Professor Jonathan Sacks has been Chief Rabbi of the United Hebrew Congregations of the Commonwealth since 1 September, 1991. Prior to this he held the Chair in Modern Jewish Thought at Jews' College, London, having gained his rabbinic ordination from the college as well as from London's Yeshiva Etz Chaim. Educated at Gonville and Caius College, Cambridge, where he obtained first class honours in philosophy, he pursued postgraduate studies at New College, Oxford, and King's College, London. Professor Sacks has been Visiting Professor of Philosophy at the University of Essex, Sherman Lecturer at Manchester University, Riddell Lecturer at Newcastle University, and Cook Lecturer at the Universities of Oxford, Edinburgh and St Andrews; and holds honorary doctorates from a number of universities including Haifa, New York, Liverpool, St Andrews, and Yeshiva University. He is an honorary fellow of Gonville and Caius College, Cambridge, and King's College, London where he is currently Visiting Professor of Theology and Religious Studies, becoming Visiting Professor of the Hebrew University, Jerusalem in 1998. In 1990 he delivered the BBC Reith Lectures on The Persistence of Faith. He is the author of twelve books, including *Community of Faith* (1995), *The Politics of Hope* (1997), *Morals and Markets* (1999), *New Revised Edition: The Politics of Hope* (2000), *Celebrating Life* (2000) and *Radical Then Radical Now* (2000).

Hans Tietmeyer, born 1931 in Metelen, Germany, studied economics and social sciences, graduated (Dipl. Volkswirt) and gained a doctorate in economics at the University of Cologne. From 1962 to 1982 he served in the German Federal Ministry for Economics and from 1982 to 1989 in the German Federal Ministry of Finance (as Permanent Secretary) in Bonn. Between 1990 and 1993 he was a Member of the Board and from 1993 to 1999 President of the Deutsche Bundesbank in Frankfurt. Since 1997 he has been Honorary Professor for International Economic and Financial Issues at the University of Halle-Wittenberg, and after retirement as President of the Deutsche Bundesbank, he is, *inter alia*, President of the European Business School in Oestrich-Winkel and member of many advisory and supervisory boards at national and international levels. He has published three books and many articles on national and international economic policy.

Geoffrey E. Wood is currently Professor of Economics at City University, London. He has also taught at the University of Warwick, and has been with the research staff of both the Bank of England and the Federal Reserve Bank of St. Louis. He is the co-author or co-editor of ten books, which deal with, among other subjects, finance of international trade, monetary policy and bank regulation. Among his professional papers are studies of exchange rate behaviour, interest rate determination, monetary unions, tariff policy and bank regulation. He has also acted as an adviser to the New Zealand Treasury. He is Managing Trustee of the Institute of Economic Affairs and of the Wincott Foundation.

Foreword

As Lord Mayor of the City of London I am Chancellor of City University. But this is only one of the many links that bring City University into a close working relationship with the City of London. I am very conscious of the immense contribution that the University makes to this, the world's leading international financial centre, in providing well-trained and well-educated people; in offering a truly impressive range of post-graduate courses; and by its support of so many sectors of the financial city.

This is tremendously important for the continuing competitive position of the City of London as an international financial centre. The presence of the large US, Japanese and European investment banks in London brings great expertise and real potential for innovation. They are one of the main drivers of change in Europe and, in particular, they are at the forefront of the current electronic revolution in financial services.

The lectures themselves cover a wide range of views on topical financial subjects which are of great interest to the markets in the City of London, as well as to the United Kingdom generally.

I hope you find them interesting and informative.

The Rt Hon The Lord Mayor,
Alderman David Howard
April 2001

1   Introduction

Twenty-five years of monetary policy*

ESL

Forrest H. Capie and Geoffrey E. Wood

(J K)

The theory and practice of monetary policy has changed out of recognition in the past twenty-five years. The perception of how monetary policy worked in the United Kingdom has undergone a profound change. To understand how this came about it is instructive to look at the views of the leading policy makers and practitioners, and it is here that the Department of Banking and Finance at The City University played a small part.

The Department (formerly the Centre) of Banking and Finance was founded in the mid-1970s. It was established following an appeal by the 1973 Lord Mayor of the City of London, Lord Mais. He took this initiative because of what had seemed to him (and to some others) an anomaly of long standing. The University had been founded in 1894 and was the only University in the City. Yet it might as well have been in Birmingham or Leeds or Glasgow – for it neglected City-related subjects, and rather concentrated on science and engineering, including, perhaps particularly surprising given its location, aeronautical engineering. Lord Mais used the annual Lord Mayor's appeal to raise funds to rectify this, and the Department of Banking and Finance was then founded and Brian Griffiths attracted from the London School of Economics as the Department's first Professor.

The original intentions were to contribute to the education of young people, equipping them for a working life in the fields of money, banking and international finance, and to conduct research in monetary economics and monetary history. Strong links with the City and government were formed at an early date. Among the achievements of the Centre was the establishment of two important annual public lectures. One of these was called the Henry Thornton Lecture in memory of the founding father of modern monetary economics. The other was named the Mais Lecture in honour of the contribution Lord Mais had made to the founding of the Department. The first of the lectures had an academic bias. The second was designed to appeal to the wider audience of policy makers and practitioners.

Thus the idea of the second was to communicate what monetary policy was, and did, and could achieve. To that end the lecturers invited were those endowed

---

* The titles of the lecturers used in this introduction are those they had when the lectures were delivered.

with the responsibility of shaping monetary policy and carrying it out in Britain and elsewhere. These were of course the Governors of central banks, the Chancellors of the Exchequer, and Shadow Chancellors, and other leading politicians or serious commentators on the subject. On occasions lectures strayed further afield than monetary policy, to the working of the economy at large.

A representative collection of these lectures thus provides an interesting guide to the developing views on the subject over the late twentieth century. (A complete list of lecturers from inception of the series in 1978 can be found at the end of this volume.)[1]

The themes of the lectures

The principal theme is naturally monetary policy. Five of the thirteen contributions deal specifically with that subject. The two that took us furthest away from that were Sir Samuel Brittan's 'Restatement of Economic Liberalism' (1989), and the Chief Rabbi Professor Jonathan Sacks' 'Markets, Governments and Virtues' (2000). Both of these were wide-ranging lectures on the nature of the economic system under which we live. Two other lectures, by Peter Lilley (1993) and Kenneth Clarke (1994) took the opportunity to discuss, respectively, social security, and the changing nature of employment at the end of the twentieth century. Tony Blair as Leader of the Opposition set out (in 1995) the economic framework of a new Labour government. Hans Tietmeyer (1998), President of the German Bundesbank, used the occasion to give a German view of the prospects for financial and monetary integration in Europe. Gordon Brown, as Chancellor in 1999, set out the framework for full employment under a Labour government. Lord Robbins, the highly distinguished public figure in British economic and artistic life (among many other things Professor of Economics at the London School of Economics and Chairman of the *Financial Times*), was an early contributor (in 1979) on what the objectives of monetary policy had been and currently were. Sir Geoffrey Howe set out what the recently elected and radical Conservative government in 1981 were doing about inflation, and in 1984 Nigel Lawson followed that up with a consideration of the achievements of the new approach to policy that had been inaugurated. The three Governors of the Bank of England, Sir Gordon Richardson, Robin Leigh-Pemberton and Eddie George, reflected, as might have been expected, on monetary policy.

The lectures: monetary policy

The second lecture in the series, that by Lord Robbins (1979), is the most appropriate with which to start the overview of this collection's contents. For Lord Robbins used his knowledge of economic history, the history of economic thought, and economic analysis, to review the objectives and conduct of monetary policy over some half a century, including in that review some policy decisions in which he had himself participated. In particular, he was concerned with the gradual acceleration of inflation that started, albeit initially very slowly, in the 1930s.

Opinion of the proper conduct and objectives of policy had fluctuated since then. Internal policy had shifted from the preservation of the gold standard to maintaining unemployment close to, in one period, 2 per cent. 'This indeed had, in my opinion, very adverse results on conceptions of appropriate policy.' The resulting rise in inflation, culminating in the disastrous policy of Edward Heath (Prime Minister from 1970 to 1974) was very damaging and, Lord Robbins notes, was warned against in advance. Those who gave that warning were of the intellectual persuasion known as 'monetarist'; the meaning of this term Lord Robbins turns to later in his lecture.

His historical review covered largely the years of fixed but adjustable exchange rates, run under the tutelage of the IMF. This system had essentially collapsed when Lord Robbins gave his lecture. This breakdown he ascribed to incompleteness in the rules specifying when exchange rates could be changed, and an inadequately flexible exchange rate for the US dollar.

So much for his view of the past. Then Lord Robbins turned to current policy.

> The essential truth of the so-called monetarist attitude – the truth to which I should be willing to subscribe – is the contention that continuing marked disparities, either way, between the rate of change of output and the rate of change of the money supply lead to damaging changes in the value of money.

He differs from some monetarists, however, in an interesting and most prescient way: for he recognised that cost push pressures in turn put pressures on the monetary authorities, and that their resistance could not be taken for granted. Political institutions matter, in other words. Only recently has this been made explicit by other economists (such as Adam Posen, 1993)[2] who argue that the correlation between central bank independence and low inflation may depend crucially on the social and political structures which produced independence, rather than on independence in itself. Very appropriately for the lectures by three Governors of the Bank of England to which we turn in a moment, Lord Robbins concluded his review of methods for inflation control by observing that incomes policies, a fashionable measure just before he spoke, were pointless except as an emergency measure and that the control of the total of expenditure was what was crucial.

The lecture concluded with consideration of international monetary arrangements. While recognising that so long as inflation differentials persisted between currencies floating was inevitable, he was not an enthusiast for floating rates. He feared, *inter alia*, that sharp moves in them, in response to government policies, would provoke the resurgence of the 'totally illiberal system of exchange control'. He did not offer any solutions. But he did propose, as at least an interim measure for Western Europe, that the 'Commission of the Community might . . . issue a new money run in parallel with existing currencies but . . . managed so as to maintain a constant value in terms of a representative collection of commodities'.[3] In his concluding remarks, Lord Robbins restated the overwhelming importance of stopping inflation. That leads very appropriately to the lectures given by three Governors of the Bank, for they were charged with that task.

The first Mais Lecture was given, in 1978, by the then Governor of the Bank of England, Sir Gordon Richardson. The timing was fortuitous, as it was then still only quite recently that monetary policy had re-emerged as a tool of economic policy. As the Governor put it:

> We are now at an historical juncture when the conventional methods of economic policy are being tested . . . the greater emphasis on monetary policy has occasioned new initiatives in the ways of conducting it. The present is therefore a suitable time to take stock.

What did that taking stock reveal? Monetary policy had just emerged from the shadow of neglect cast over it by the *Radcliffe Report* (1959). Insofar as monetary policy mattered to the authors of that Report, it did so by affecting ease of access to finance. The money stock did not matter; interest rates had modest effects; quantitative controls over credit were the most effective monetary instrument. As the Governor observed, the Bank did not entirely share these views even at the time the Report was published. This scepticism of the Bank's undoubtedly helped reassert the importance of monetary policy; but its importance was once again brought to the fore both by the theoretical and empirical arguments of Friedman (and earlier of Keynes – unlike his disciples he never neglected the importance of money) and, perhaps most compelling, the resurgence of inflation. That fundamentally weakened the underpinning of Radcliffe Report type views. In part there was an interest, and for a time emphasis, on 'monetary targets'. That is to say, an adjusting of interest rates so as to keep a particular measure of money growing within a particular range. This was not an end in itself, but because that growth rate of money was seen as being consistent with satisfactory price level performance. As is well known, that approach to policy proved a disappointment. The relationship between money growth and prices that had been reliable for a century gave way; money growth accelerated and inflation slowed. Sir Gordon was writing before the evidence of that disappointment appeared. But his lecture did nevertheless set out some aspects of the conduct of policy which have proved of great and enduring importance, not just in the UK.

What endures in particular are two points. First, prudent monetary policy is essential to the control of inflation. Other factors can, of course, put upward pressure on prices – the Governor noted wage increases, and others such as oil prices, could be added to that list – but, as he put it 'there is an observable statistical relationship between money growth and the pace of inflation. A great deal of effort has been devoted to the study of this relationship over long time periods and in many countries; and that there is such a relationship cannot, I think, be doubted.' Or, to look at the matter another way, if money growth resists the price pressures, they will not produce inflation. It would make the task of monetary policy much easier if these pressures were removed or mitigated, and that point almost brings us to the present Governor's Mais Lecture. But before moving on, one other point that Sir Gordon made must be highlighted – for it has been key to the conduct of economic policy since that date. 'It is right that people should know what the broad lines of policy are, and that such policy should be kept on its stated course until circumstances clearly call for a reappraisal.' There should, in other words, be no attempts to manipulate the economy almost from month to month, certainly from quarter to quarter, to fine tune, as the expression was; rather policy should have a pre-announced and clear medium-to-long-term focus.

How to achieve that focus? That question was examined in the present Governor's lecture. But the world did not move smoothly from that described by Gordon Richardson to that of which Eddie George spoke. There was a period when, though it was recognised that monetary control was important, it seemed hard – on occasions almost impossible – to attain. In 1987 Robin Leigh-Pemberton discussed aspects of that turbulent episode. His lecture had as its main theme the role of the interest rate which the Bank controlled in affecting the economy. A key point was there is no direct mechanical linkage from the rate to the economy.

> Outside commentators on monetary developments sometimes create the impression that those responsible for operating monetary policy sit in front of a battery of switches and levers, each one of which will produce a precise and certain response in some area of the financial markets or directly in some more distant part of the economy. I can assure you that there is only one switch in my room, and that is the light switch.

Having made that clear, the Governor ruled out controls as a way of controlling the economy, and then went on as follows:

> The instruments we are left with then are the terms on which we provide liquidity to the banking system, government funding policy (or as some prefer long-term interest rates), and foreign exchange market intervention.

Particularly in view of the attention given from time to time (in autumn 2000, for example, as a result of the weakness of the euro) to the third, it is worth continuing the quotation:

> there are practical limits to the extent to which we can rely upon either funding policy or intervention, as well as limits to their effectiveness . . . when you come right down to it, the only effective instrument of monetary policy is the short-term interest rate itself.

How does that interest rate work? What are the mechanisms by which it affects the economy? Expectations matter.

> As in other areas of economics, behaviour in response to interest rate changes is probably influenced at least as much by people's expectations about the future . . . as by perceptions of the cost of money at any particular time.

Against that background, the Governor reviewed a variety of mechanisms. The list comprised effects on bank lending to the private sector, company borrowing, effects on wealth through the impact of interest rate changes on the value of financial assets, and the effects of interest rates on the exchange rate. His conclusion was that, although all these channels mattered, it was impossible to say precisely how much they mattered.

That is in fact an issue – the channels of transmission of monetary policy – on which our knowledge is little further advanced than it was when that lecture was given. But despite that, it has become increasingly clear, and increasingly widely accepted, that sensible monetary policy is vital to the control of inflation, and a vital prerequisite for prosperity. This wide acceptance was demonstrated very clearly just after the present government took office in May 1997.

On 6 May of that year the new Chancellor of the Exchequer created the Monetary Policy Committee (MPC) of the Bank, and gave it freedom to set interest rates. In his lecture Eddie George reflected on that change, considering it 'against the background of the monetary policy framework being developed in Europe' and 'in the context of the approach to economic management more generally in Europe and this country'. It is that last point which links this lecture so closely to that given by Sir Gordon Richardson.

The change that has taken place over the past few years is that there is now a widespread consensus, across countries and across political opinion within countries, that economic policy ought to be focused on the medium and long term rather than responding to, and trying to manage, every small fluctuation in the economy. There is consensus, too, that growth can be increased only by 'supply-side' measures – making markets more flexible and efficient – and not by boosts to demand.

Where does this lead for monetary policy?

The objective is price stability – as it was, albeit expressed slightly differently, for Sir Gordon Richardson. As the present Governor pointed out, this is in many ways, including the commitment to stability over the longer term, very like the arrangement in the euro area. But there is at least one significant difference. In Britain the government sets the target, and the Bank is charged with achieving it.

> The clear separation of responsibility for setting the inflation target (the political decision) from responsibility for achieving it (the technical decision) also helps to ensure that the government and the Bank are separately accountable for their respective roles in the monetary policy process.

On the basis of that, together with four other facts – publication of the MPC's minutes, annual review of its performance by the Court of the Bank, the quarterly publication of the Bank's inflation report, and the requirement to write a letter of explanation to the Chancellor should inflation be more than 1 per cent either side of the 2.5 per cent p.a. target – the Governor argued that 'these arrangements provide for greater transparency of, and greater accountability for, the technical monetary process than anywhere else in the world'.

Why is this good? In part because it will further understanding. Monetary policy is not an exact science. It requires judgment, and the weighing up of not always clear and sometimes conflicting evidence. Revealing the process of discussion (at least in part) will show both that mistakes are possible and that, more important, if they occur will soon be corrected. This will give confidence in the longer term sustainability of the objective.

The greater part of the lecture thus focused on the major issues of monetary policy, its objective and the institutional structure designed so as to achieve that objective. It is worth emphasising that we can properly speak of the objective – in the singular – of monetary policy in the UK. The UK's policy framework is one of the few in the world which recognises that for every objective of policy we require, except by occasional happy coincidence, an instrument of policy. The same instrument cannot do two things at the same time – just as we could not, say, have a combined accelerator and steering wheel in a motor car, used to control direction and speed at the same time. It is, indeed, notable that central banks which have more than one objective cope by generally ignoring all but one in their deeds.

The view from the Treasury

Before operational independence was granted to the Bank of England chancellors of the exchequer could be regarded as practitioners as well as designers of monetary policy. The first chancellor to set out his views on the conduct of monetary policy in one of the Mais Lectures was Sir Geoffrey Howe in 1981. He chose as his title, 'The fight against inflation'. This title was not surprising given the experience of the 1970s, when at its peak inflation had reached an annual rate in excess of 20 per cent. Howe was appointed Chancellor in the new Thatcher government of 1979 and inside a matter of months the exchange controls that had been in place for forty years were abolished. There were many other indications that the new government would be radical, but what was clear was that at its core policy would be directed against inflation. This was not because price stability was seen as a sufficient condition for economic growth, but because it had come to be accepted that it was certainly necessary. How to achieve it was the question. Regarding monetary policy as central was in a sense picking up from the outgoing Labour government, for as recently as 1977 Denis Healey, the previous Chancellor, had said, 'we cannot master inflation unless we have control of the money supply'. That was the rationale for the monetary targets that were introduced. But Howe argued that monetary targets were insufficient on their own; the new government wanted to emphasise the need for fiscal discipline to support monetary policy. And additionally, they felt the need to seek moderation in pay bargaining.

Just three years after Howe's lecture Nigel Lawson, then Chancellor, gave another, in the summer of 1984. He called it 'The British Experiment' – borrowing the phrase from those who, as he said, had been 'less than enthusiastic about it'. The experiment consisted of seeking, 'to provide the freedom for markets to work within a framework of firm monetary and fiscal discipline'. He began by citing his predecessor's lecture at some length, first to show that the policy had been vindicated, second to stress that the same policy was being pursued, and third to clear up confusion which he claimed existed over the direction of policy in 1984. He outlined how policy had been followed in the intervening period and sought to explain some of what appeared to be conflicting evidence. (He rejected out of hand the view put forward by some that inflation had been reduced by having three million unemployed.)

When the Medium Term Financial Strategy was introduced (in 1980) there were two factors at work that made it more difficult to interpret the behaviour of Sterling M3. One was the continuing impact of the abolition of exchange controls, and the other was the ending of the 'corset' (the particular controls on bank lending via the liabilities side of the balance sheet dated from the early 1970s). There were other important changes taking place in the world too and differential experience in some of the principal economies.

Lawson took some satisfaction in pointing out that restoration of fiscal discipline, that was necessary as a support for monetary policy, had not produced the dire consequences forecast by the 'economics industry'. And he argued that it was no business of government to intervene in the foreign exchange markets other than in very special circumstances. Even then he doubted if it worked.

A further ten years passed before another Chancellor gave the lecture. In 1994 Kenneth Clarke gave the Mais with the title, 'The changing world of work in the 1990s'. This was something of a departure from the strictly defined area of monetary policy that his predecessors had regarded as their territory. In part this probably reflected the success of fifteen years of anti-inflation policy and a widespread acceptance of the importance of stable prices. With that achieved, attention could turn once more to the issue of unemployment. This might have been seen as being given added urgency by the fact that the economy had just recently come out of the recession of the early 1990s when unemployment had risen sharply.

Clarke restated the objectives of the 1944 White Paper, with which he fully agreed. However, he did not accept in whole the analysis of that paper preferring to lay emphasis on the need for flexible labour markets. But his declared aim was to combine the best of the American approach to labour markets with the best of the European approach to welfare. He did, nevertheless, stress throughout the need for this to be conducted within the framework of stable prices. But in essence it was the mutually reinforcing effects of flexible labour markets and a strong welfare system that was to lead to the optimal outcome.

When the new Labour government took office in 1997 the economy was still enjoying strong growth. That continued, so that when the new Chancellor, Gordon Brown, gave his lecture in late 1999 it was perhaps opportune to discuss full employment. In setting out the conditions under which full employment could be achieved the Chancellor necessarily touched on many aspects of economic policy.

Underpinning all policy there should be 'a pro-active monetary policy and prudent fiscal policy' to provide the necessary basis for economic stability. Next there needed to be a means of improving the flow of unemployed from welfare to work. The third component was a 'commitment to high quality long term investment in science and innovation, new technology and skills'. And the fourth element was the avoidance of 'short termism in pay and wage bargaining across the private and public sectors'.

In a brief survey of British economic history since 1945 Brown found governments guilty of failure on pay, productivity, and industrial relations, and of resorting to fine-tuning. Brown also picked up on Lawson's Mais Lecture identifying it as the clearest intellectual statement of the new position in the 1980s. Yet he argued that when the 1980s and 1990s are considered, economic fluctuations became even greater. A central point with which it is difficult to argue was that in a world of free capital movements governments must pursue policies that the markets believed and trusted. This calls for transparency and accountability. On improving the flow from 'welfare to work' it was the failure to reform the welfare system that was the chief culprit. Higher productivity is needed and according to Brown the way to get it is through policies that modernise capital and goods markets. Finally, responsibility in pay-setting must be established.

Further policy issues

Peter Lilley was Secretary of State for Social Security when he delivered his lecture in 1993. It was an important statement on the intimate connection between social and economic policy. He emphasised that a vibrant economy 'could do far more to achieve the objectives of social policy than could any feasible enhancements of our welfare system'. At the same time it had to be recognised that social security has a profound impact on the economy, influencing the size of the labour force, the effort expended on work, the level of savings, and the scale of taxation and borrowing. After outlining the size, growth and likely future growth of social security spending Lilley put forward a number of propositions for debate on reform of the system. These tackled the difficult issues among others of targeting, promotion of self-provision, and means testing and its associated problems. He suggested that while there were areas where 'contracting out' was not an option, that should not prevent individuals from making provisions for themselves privately. Where it is possible to contract out (e.g. in pensions) that involves a switch from 'pay as you go' to fully funded which has beneficial effects on the economy. Lilley argued that the more provision was monopolised by the state the more damaging were the effects on work effort. Reform was essential but given the size of the task it needed to be done sector by sector. Immediate reform of the whole system was, he maintained, just not a practical option.

Hans Tietmeyer (1998) dealt with economic openness, and increasing economic integration between countries. One aspect of this, the one to which he very naturally gave considerable attention, is monetary union in Europe. This does, as he observed, represent the 'maximum of policy integration in the monetary field'. To quote again: 'There are sound economic reasons in favour of a single currency; incidentally, also sound political reasons, at least, if a more thorough-going political integration is being sought.'

> The benefits of monetary union are really it maximises the trade related benefits of economic integration. But these benefits come . . . only if the euro remains lastingly stable . . . if monetary union does not . . . trigger or exacerbate economic tensions . . . [or] . . . give rise to political tension between participating states.

He then went on to develop the conditions necessary for that benign climate to eventuate. Much emphasis was laid on the importance of subordinating fiscal policy to achieving monetary stability. There must be a 'culture of stability'.

In his postscript (written in mid-July 2000), he touches on the contrasting performance of the euro, launched since his lecture, in terms of internal and external stability. The disappointing performance on the latter front he ascribed to the 'still unresolved structural, economic and political problems in a number of member states, and the insufficiently clarified outlook for further economic and political integration in Europe'.

The lecture by Tony Blair, given (in 1995) when he was Leader of the Opposition, revealed a substantial degree of agreement between the three Conservative Chancellors who had preceded him as Mais lecturers and himself. Most notably, he developed his arguments from the starting point provided by Nigel Lawson in his 1984 lecture. He writes of Lawson's view, that monetary policy should control inflation and the real side of the economy, growth and employment, be 'left to themselves', that 'I strongly dispute this thinking'. In fact his differences from it were quite narrow. He objected in part to the way in which that framework was implemented – there was no long-term focus for monetary policy. To quote, 'though the ultimate objectives (of monetary policy) have stayed broadly the same, the framework for policy has been extremely inconsistent, with one regime after another failing to meet stated objectives'. He also objected to the remaining, albeit much diminished, political influence on monetary policy at the time he spoke.[4]

The lessons drawn from the past did not stop at that. Control of inflation is even more important than previous governments had thought, not least, he observed, because failures in macro policy can swamp improvements produced by micro-economic policy. Hence the framework for monetary policy, and for keeping its long-term focus, had to be strengthened. On fiscal policy, again stability was the objective. Partly fiscal instability was produced by problems on the supply side of the economy, and the performance of this was to be improved by micro-economic measures – not only deregulation, but by measures such as improved education. 'Long termism' extended also to proposing to reduce long-term unemployment, and, very shrewdly, to careful appraisal *and rejection* of the claim that British industry was hampered by short-termism in finance and its providers.

In the postscript to his lecture (written in summer 2000), he reviewed the success of some of the changes planned. Again emphasis was placed on macro-economic stability and on the long term. A striking feature of this lecture, and of a comparison of it with those of the three Conservative Chancellors, is the extent to which common economic ground has moved, away from short-term demand management and towards the conduct of long-term stability. These lectures show a remarkable shift in the climate of opinion.

Other perspectives

Two lectures took us quite a long way away from monetary policy: for every now and again it seemed appropriate to invite a major figure who was not closely involved in monetary policy making, or even economic policy making, to address bigger questions in economics.

The first of these was by Samuel Brittan. Samuel Brittan was Assistant Editor of the *Financial Times* in 1989 when he summarised his views on economic liberalism. He had recently published a revised version of his 1973 book on that subject. The late 1980s was a good time to consider the re-flowering of economic liberalism after a fairly long period in the twentieth century when that particular set of beliefs had been in retreat in most of the world. But Brittan complained that a chasm had opened up between the two sides of the liberal tradition – market economics had become divorced from a commitment to wider personal freedom. The debate had moved since the 1970s even and he saw this as the key feature in 1989. Following some definition of economic liberalism and an outline of its broad philosophical position he tackled some of the nitty gritty of its application in everyday economic life. He began by defending the morality of markets and drew attention to the fact that a functioning market presupposed a basis of trust and effective set of property rights, showed how economic liberalism related to mainstream economics, and discussed the problems arising increasingly from a politicised market place. He recognised that for the foreseeable future there was going to be a large role for government because of the size of the welfare state. On this he made a case for embracing social contract theory and offered suggestions as to how this might be used in reform of the welfare state. It took little space to dispose of 'businessmen's economics', before showing how the economic liberal should view the workings of the financial markets and the attempts at providing stable money and a sensible exchange-rate regime. Stable money is important. Exchange rates are more difficult to deal with but it is hard to see how to improve on flexible rates.

In the second of these wide-ranging lectures, in 2000 the Chief Rabbi Professor Jonathan Sacks spoke on 'Markets, Governments and Virtues'. In recent times it has become more popular to look outside economics for the real sources of economic growth. The rule of law and the role of property rights are just two such areas. But freedom and democracy, and the part played by religion in promoting or allowing these two to flourish, have also been given greater attention. Religion has never been missing entirely from some accounts of economic development, but Jonathan Sacks made a powerful case for the part that the Judaeo-Christian tradition had played in allowing material prosperity to emerge and grow rapidly in the west. At base, this came from the linear conception of time and the concomitant idea of progress contained implicitly in this tradition. He made a strong case for the market being the superior form of economic organisation with only limited government being tolerated. But he went further and argued that free markets were also morally superior allowing as they do the individual the greatest personal freedom in all matters. But while arguing that the market was superior he did nevertheless find fault with it in the following respect. There are some essential ingredients in markets that allow their efficient operation. These are features such as well-defined and enforceable property rights. But these, he argued, in turn depend on trust and justice and these are generated outside the market – in marriage and the family religion. Thus these virtues have to be imported from Judaeo-Christian teaching. The market is parasitic on this teaching. The market needs such a moral base as is provided in Judaeo-Christian thought. There are currently dangers, too, as western countries run the risk of losing touch with these historical religious foundations.

Conclusion

On reading these lectures, two points emerge particularly clearly. The first is how fortunate we at City University's Department of Banking and Finance have been in having such a distinguished series of lecturers each give in turn such fascinating and historically important lectures. The second is how they summarise the emergence of a new consensus – one set out, it must be noted, by Lord Robbins very early in the series – about both the objectives of economic policy and how to achieve these objectives. It was a privilege to have heard these lectures. It has been fascinating and instructive to re-read them, and it is a pleasure to make them more widely available than they have heretofore been.

Notes

1 As texts of all the lectures were not available, some had to be omitted.
2 Adam Posen 'Why Central Bank Independence does not cause low inflation: There is no institutional fix for politicians' in *Finance and International Economy*, prize winning essays from the AMEX Bank Review essay competition, Oxford: OUP, 1993.
3 Minor variations on this scheme have been proposed fairly regularly. The earliest version that we can find was set out in the 'All Saints Day Manifesto' published in *The Economist* on 1 November 1975. (See J.F. Chown, *A History of Monetary Unions* (Routledge, forthcoming) for a history of those proposals.
4 At the time we were at the stage where interest rate decisions were still taken by the Chancellor, but the Bank of England had a channel, its 'Inflation Report', to make public comments on those decisions.

Part I

2   Reflections on the conduct of monetary policy

The Rt Hon Gordon Richardson   (UK)

E31 E52
E51

I must begin by saying what a privilege and pleasure it is for me to have been invited to inaugurate this new series of lectures in the field of banking and finance which are to take place annually at The City University. It is a fitting tribute to the energy and broad interests of Lord Mais, who in 1973 as Chancellor of this University and Lord Mayor launched the appeal for funds to set up this University's Centre for Banking and International Finance, that these lectures should bear his name.

This academic occasion provides me with a welcome opportunity to speak at greater length than is usually possible – or indeed acceptable – at a public function, and I propose to use it by sharing with you some reflections on the conduct of monetary policy, as they have formed in my mind over the past five eventful years. By so doing I shall hope to contribute to the public debate on monetary policy – a debate which I whole-heartedly welcome.

The City University is an especially appropriate place for me to do so. A personal reason is that it gives me the occasion, before the departure of Dr Parkes for the University Grants Committee where his expertise in the elasticity or dynamic plasticity of academic structures will be fully tested, to discharge some part of my debt of gratitude for the Honorary Doctorate of Science conferred on me some two years ago by this University during his Vice-Chancellorship – although the moral of my lecture, that the conduct of monetary policy is an art rather than a science, might be taken to suggest that he gave me the wrong degree.

Another reason is that this University, through its relationship with the City and its institutions, established with them in the ten years of its existence, has been able to combine intellectual rigour and practical relevance in its academic approach to banking and international finance: this is one of the objectives of the Centre and finds its personification in its Director, Professor Brian Griffiths.

We are now at an historical juncture when the conventional methods of economic policy are being tested. The principles on which we have conducted economic policy since the war are having to be reassessed, because, with changing conditions, we are no longer so certain of being able to achieve what once seemed possible. At the same time, the greater emphasis on monetary policy has occasioned new initiatives in ways of conducting it. The present is therefore a suitable time to try to take stock.

What I have to say today falls conveniently under three main headings. First, I shall review the change in our ideas about monetary policy since the Radcliffe Committee reported, and will discuss the shift of emphasis towards concern with the monetary aggregates. Second, I shall attempt to consider more systematically the place of monetary policy in the management of the economy. And third, I shall review some of the problems of implementing monetary policy of management of the growth of the aggregates; of the choice of aggregate for the control variable; and the case for what are sometimes known as 'rolling targets'.

The recent development of monetary thought

It may be helpful to start with an historical perspective. We tend to forget how much our ideas change in only a few years. It makes our present ideas clearer if we see them standing in contrast to what we thought earlier; and it is salutary to have to work out why we think that we now know better than we did five or ten or twenty years ago. A convenient landmark is the Radcliffe Report published in 1959.

The change in ideas since the Radcliffe Report

The doctrine of the Radcliffe Report was always complex and is perhaps difficult to summarise fairly in today's changed climate of ideas. The Radcliffe Committee saw the monetary system more as a set of institutions supporting numerous flows of funds, than as a set of institutions providing a stock of means of payment. Monetary policy was seen as acting on total demand mainly by affecting the ease of access to finance, or what was more vaguely called the 'liquidity of the economy'. Changes in monetary policy took their effect through changes in interest rates: the latter (it was argued) altered the liquidity position of financial institutions, and this in turn affected the availability of funds to borrowers. The difference from present-day thought is illustrated by a quotation from the Report: 'The authorities thus have to regard the structure of interest rates rather than the supply of money as the centre-piece of the monetary mechanism. This does not mean that the supply of money is unimportant, but that its control is incidental to interest rate policy.'

The Committee were mainly looking, as we do not today, for quick tangible effects from monetary measures on the level of demand. The Report left a clear impression that its authors believed that monetary policy had little such effect, and that what effect it did have was not all to the good. They found it difficult to believe that 'any of the changes in interest rates' had much influence – though some effect on demand probably resulted from the 'diffused difficulty of borrowing'. But 'the really quick substantial effects', they concluded, 'were secured by the hire purchase controls' – though these had disruptive effects on particular industries. That, as they said, was 'far removed from the smooth and widespread adjustment sometimes claimed as the virtue of monetary action: this is no gentle hand on the steering wheel that keeps a well-driven car in its right place on the road'.

The Bank did not entirely share this scepticism, as its evidence to the Committee demonstrated. The Radcliffe Report failed to establish a consensus. It did, however, provide a focus for monetary debate, and one strand of the Bank's thinking – and indeed practice – which found an echo in the Report was the importance attached to operations in the gilt-edged market having a wider objective than merely financing the government – though the objective suggested was couched in terms of the long-term rate of interest rather than, as today, in terms of the monetary aggregates.

Since those days ideas about monetary policy have undergone further evolution. On the theoretical plane, arguments advanced by Keynes and later by Friedman suggesting that there might well be a stable relationship between the demand for money and the level of income and interest rates found apparent statistical verification in the late 1960s. The identification of this function appeared to provide a sound intellectual basis for monetary policy; but it left a practical choice whether the money supply or the level of interest rates should be taken as the proximate objective of policy.

What swung the argument in favour of choosing a quantity rather than a price as the best indicator of the thrust of monetary policy was the acceleration of inflation. Since 1970 not only have prices risen much faster than in the 1950s and 1960s but the rate of inflation has varied considerably from year to year. With increased inflationary expectations, interest rates also have risen greatly. We can, if we like, think of the nominal interest rate as having an 'expected inflation' component and a 'real' interest element. But we can never observe expectations, which are in any case likely both to differ from person to person, and to be volatile. The real rate of interest is an abstract construct. This has made it very difficult to frame the objectives of policy in terms of nominal interest rates.

For these reasons we were led to pay increasing attention to the monetary aggregates as a better guide – though not of course a perfect guide – to the thrust of monetary policy. In this we were not alone; a move in this direction occurred quite widely in the western world towards the end of the 1960s. This emphasis was reflected in the new approach to monetary policy put into effect in September 1971, on which I must now say a few words.

Competition and Credit Control

The aims of Competition and Credit Control were twofold. First, it was a move away from reliance on direct restrictive controls in the monetary sphere. They had remained in being far longer than appropriate for the health of the banking system, and such restraining effects as they had were being increasingly eroded. More positively, it was a move towards a system in which market forces could play a predominant role. As I have already indicated, importance was now attached to the monetary aggregates; their rate of growth was to be controlled by the market instrument of interest rates.

A change on these lines was clearly desirable and indeed overdue. Nonetheless the results over the ensuing two years have provoked serious criticism. There was rapid expansion of the monetary aggregates, and the economy did in fact expand rapidly – though in some large part no doubt because the stance of fiscal policy was strongly expansionary. And prices later started to rise rapidly – though here again other factors, including a worldwide commodity boom, have also to be taken into account. I shall not attempt to disentangle the complex strands of causation, but some points may be remarked.

The removal of earlier restrictions over the growth of bank lending allowed the banks to recapture a share of the business which controls had caused to be undertaken through non-banking channels. Such reintermediation was indeed natural, as the banks benefited from their comparative efficiency in the provision of services. In addition we had hoped that this process would go further: that some of the business undertaken by the fringe institutions which had grown up during the 1960s would be taken over by the longer established banks. In the event, however, this transfer was to some considerable degree frustrated by the more general expansion in lending which took place.

In the two years to September 1973, M3 grew at an average annual rate of about 26 per cent, compared with about a 10 per cent rise in M1. Part of the increase in broad money was possibly associated with a general preference for increased liquidity at a time of uncertainty surrounding the future course of inflation and interest rates; part undoubtedly reflected the sort of reintermediation I have touched on above; and part reflected the arbitrage which developed when companies found it profitable to borrow on their lines from the banks and on-lend in the wholesale money markets. To the extent that these factors represented shifts in the demand for money function rather than an excess creation of money, their effects on the real economy were likely to have been much less significant.

The process of reintermediation was accompanied by a number of other developments. In the financial sphere the banks – here and in many industrialised countries – were shifting towards 'liability management'. In expanding their loan books they began to pay less attention than before to the resources already available to them, since they could if necessary make up any deficiency by recourse to the wholesale money markets. This was facilitated by the encouragement of competition in the banking system in 1971. With banks increasingly prepared to compete for wholesale deposits in this way, the development of the broader monetary aggregates came increasingly to depend on interest rate relativities – between wholesale money rates, Treasury bill and local authority rates on the one hand and bank lending rates on the other – rather than on the average level of rates. In 1972 and 1973, for example, the major banks competed extremely vigorously to expand the size of their books and their individual share of the market; this helped to bring about a pattern of interest rates conducive to very rapid expansion. The Supplementary Special Deposits scheme was precisely tailored to arrest this development: after its introduction at the end of 1973 the differential between rates of interest offered on wholesale deposits and charged on loans widened and the rate of growth of wholesale deposits fell back. However it is hard to know how much this was due directly to the impact of the scheme and how much due to other factors.

The government over this period was deliberately promoting a faster rate of economic growth. To revive slack domestic activity against a background of mounting concern for unemployment, an expansionary budget in the spring of 1971 was followed by further tax reductions and increases in expenditure in July, and another reflationary budget in the following spring. The public sector borrowing requirement began to move upwards.

The monetary expansion which occurred largely resulted from the conjunction of these separate factors – reintermediation, the banks' aggressive search for new business and with it their move to liability management, and fiscal expansion. Monetary expansion must have contributed to the rapid rise in asset prices that occurred, notably in real property. It is more difficult to decide how far it caused the boom in the real economy, and the acceleration in the rate of inflation that began to set in. Some would regard the monetary development as the sole, or at least the dominant, cause; others would see it as a minor contributing factor accompanying, and in part reflecting, other more powerful forces. Despite such uncertainties about the nature and the effects of the monetary expansion, it cannot be judged other than excessive.

It had proved difficult to raise interest rates sufficiently to match the worsening inflationary environment and braking the monetary expansion by this means was in any case proving unacceptably slow to show its results. In these circumstances, after raising Minimum Lending Rate from 7.5 per cent to 13 per cent during the second half of 1973, the Bank introduced the new mechanism of Supplementary Special Deposits.

Since then emphasis has continued to be placed on controlling the growth of the monetary aggregates as a specific proximate target for policy. Only since 1976 has this taken the form of publicly declared quantitative targets. Before that it constituted an internal aim: I think it is not therefore entirely accidental that during each of the three years 1974–6 the growth of £M3 was about 10 per cent, well below the rate of expansion of national income in current prices. This was achieved during a period in which inflation, though latterly declining, was at an explosive rate and in which the financing requirement of the public sector increased notably.

The place of monetary policy in the scheme of things

I now turn to discussing the place of monetary policy in the context of economic policy generally, and what we hope to accomplish by monetary policy.

I am conscious that this aim is ambitious. This is a subject much written about and much disputed by economists and non-economists alike. Moreover a statement of view by an institution is something very different from that of an individual expert. An institution like the Bank differs in being first a collectivity, a team; in having primarily operational responsibilities; and, as such, in operating in a political environment. We hope to be sensitive to new currents of thought; yet at the same time we must exercise our judgment and not be too ready to accept every change of intellectual fashion. Formulating a line of practical policy and trying to stick to it, while yet remaining appropriately flexible amid the uncertainties of day-to-day affairs, feels very different from devising ideal solutions in the seclusion of a study.

It is, however, reasonable to expect us to seek to abstract ourselves from day-to-day pressures, and to try to systematise the philosophy that underlies our actions, though of course I have no illusions that I am stating the last word. Indeed, I hope that our critics will say why they disagree, and that thus we will together participate in a dialectic which will contribute to the evolution of a new climate of public opinion.

Monetary targets and their part in general economic policy

I will start by trying to say something about the nature of monetary targets; and go on to touch on some current issues about the proper way to conduct economic policy.

The achievement of a monetary target is not an end of policy in itself. The real objectives of policy include economic growth – in the short term, and also in the long term: and stemming from this the provision of sufficient investment for the future, and of adequate employment opportunities. They include also price stability, both as a major end in itself, and as a means to much else; and as a means if not an end, they include maintaining an appropriate relation to the rest of the world and a prudent balance of payments stance. It could be argued that monetary policy is but one instrument of policy, along with fiscal policy, exchange rate policy and, to the degree that it is possible, incomes policy; and that all such policies should be jointly set so as to achieve the desired feasible combination of final objectives, and should be adjusted from time to time as circumstances change.

In such a context, is there a place for having a target for the single instrument of monetary policy? Might this not introduce an element of undesirable rigidity – particularly inappropriate, it might be thought, for monetary policy, whose advantage has often been claimed to be that it was flexible?

To this, however, it can be replied that we should beware of over-reacting to changing circumstances, and of being over-active in economic management. Policy changes are unsettling and disturbing in themselves. It is right that people should know what the broad lines of policy are, and that such policy should be kept on its stated course until circumstances clearly call for a reappraisal. There has in any case been a reaction against frequent policy adjustments, or attempts at what has popularly been dubbed 'fine tuning' – a reaction which is part of a wider disillusion with the possibilities of economic policy and the post-war enterprise of trying to manage the economy.

This spirit of disillusion with demand management is justified up to a point, but is capable of being carried too far. To eschew demand management entirely would involve tenacious faith in the self-correcting properties of the private sector of the economy, for which the evidence is not strikingly clear. Moreover the economic functions of government have become so extensive that it is difficult to define what a neutral policy is.

What, however, does seem clear to me is that the conventional methods of demand management can only work well against a background of financial stability. In recent years the economic system has received so many shocks that the stability of the post-war world has been fractured.

Our first order of business must, therefore, be to restore confidence in the framework of the system. The crucial economic decisions, for example to undertake investment, involve an act of faith in the future. That faith has been undermined by uncertainty – uncertainty in particular about the future value of money, externally and internally. In times past other features of the economic system, such as fixed exchange rates or Gladstonian budgetary principles, were thought to provide some guarantee of stability. These restraints have now gone. The main role therefore that I see for monetary targets is to provide the framework of stability within which other policy objectives can be more easily achieved.

It is essential for this purpose that monetary targets should be publicly announced, and that the authorities' resolve be sufficient to make that announcement credible. Our acts have, I believe, given observers cause to regard our resolve as strong. This in itself has dampened fears of worsening inflation, and provided an appropriate backdrop against which we can continue the struggle to bring inflation steadily down. I would not claim that monetary policy can or should be left to fight inflation singlehandedly – I shall turn to this subject again later. But monetary targets have an important place in the relevant armoury.

Monetary targets represent a self-imposed constraint or discipline, on the authorities. This can at times seem irksome, the more so perhaps because the permissible thresholds cannot be precisely and scientifically set, involving a considerable element of judgment. Yet the layman's apparently intuitive perception of the broad relationship between monetary growth and inflation – clearer perhaps to him than to the professional who knows all the necessary qualifications – may well make it easier to explain and justify measures necessary to achieve the goal of stability but with immediately unpopular effects. We need a basis of public support and understanding of the limits to prudent action. Furthermore, quantitative monetary targets can provide a useful trigger for more expeditious policy decisions.

The main purpose of having publicly announced monetary targets is, therefore, to provide a basis for stability. Stability does not, however, imply rigidity. There can be occasions when policy needs to be adjusted because circumstances have changed. There is a case for adjusting monetary policy, as well as fiscal policy, to offset cyclical swings in the economy. In recent years, however, severe cyclical disturbances have been overlaid and accompanied by an even more menacing inflationary trend. We will not, in my judgment, be able to deal satisfactorily with the present recession until we can conquer our inflation problem, whose implications for monetary policy I now turn to discuss.

Monetary policy and inflation

There is, I think, a two-way connection between inflation and economic expansion. The common wisdom used to be that there was a trade-off: high levels of activity led to high rates of inflation, and lower levels of activity similarly to lower rates of inflation. Nowadays, with the elusiveness of what economists call the Phillips curve, this route to controlling inflation has seemed to become less sure. And yet some important part of that connection must surely remain. The governments of almost all industrial countries have acquiesced in low rates of economic expansion in the last three years. Their motives have been manifold, but a main one has been a fear of inflation; and inflation rates have fallen. And in this country, I think it is generally accepted that the practicable rate of economic expansion will depend in large part on how successful we are in moderating the pace of inflation. The connection is in part a matter of market forces – strong demand pressure would generate larger wage increases; in part semi-political – unrestrained expansion would erode the braking power of the present policy of pay restraint.

The reverse connection is that – quite apart from this connection via economic policies – inflation impedes economic expansion by inducing caution among consumers, and by making business, and in particular investment, so much less predictable. If we could reduce inflation, this would itself generate a faster expansion in the private economy. The expansion we sacrifice in order to deal with inflation is less than might appear.

One should recognise that the blame for inflation rests not on any simple cause, but rather on a multitude of political and economic pressures. Is it not clear enough that our system has a strong inflationary bias? In recent years annual wage increases have become the accepted norm, though there is no logic in this. The size of wage increases moreover depends on an unco-ordinated and to some degree competitive process in which, to say the least, the collective effect on price stability does not naturally act as a dominant consideration. Governmentally inspired efforts at pay restraint take their rationale from these circumstances. In our post-war history there has been a succession of attempts at such policies, some more successful than others; and I would guess that we are destined to continue the effort. Such policies have their obvious shortcomings and considerable attendant disadvantages. Nevertheless from the point of view of monetary policy we should welcome whatever success they can achieve, while giving them in turn all the support from monetary policy that we can devise.

I would not want to suggest that there is always a direct, simple chain of causation running from the money supply to the price-level. Indeed, it is generally recognised that inflation can, at least for a time, follow a life of its own quite independent of current or past monetary developments. The peak of recent inflation in the United Kingdom three years ago owed much both to the rise of world commodity prices in 1973 and to the repercussions this had – through the unfortunate accident of the threshold agreements then in force – on domestic wages. Equally, exchange rate movements had important effects – though I know this raises more complicated issues on which I shall comment later.

But though the causation may not be simple, there is an observable statistical relation between monetary growth and the pace of inflation. I am not here thinking of the short-term relationships which underlie the demand for money equations to which I have already referred. There has been a fair measure of success in establishing such relationships, even though the success is far from complete. I think however that what is far more important is the relationship between monetary growth and inflation over the longer term. A great deal of work has been devoted to the study of this relationship over long time periods and in many countries; and that there is such a relationship cannot, I think, be doubted. To many this provides adequate intellectual justification for establishing medium-term aims for the rate of growth of the money supply.

Some I know may still feel doubts as to how the statistical relationship between money and prices should be interpreted. Governments and central banks are often in effect under pressure to validate price increases stemming from non-monetary sources because the alternatives have seemed to be pressures on interest rates or on employment. It might then be questioned whether under such circumstances the causality could not run as much from prices to money as from money to prices.

To those who doubt on some such grounds how far monetary policy can be of help in dealing with inflation, I would venture to address a more general defence of our present line of policy. The latest issue of the National Institute Economic Review suggests for instance that the Institute is of this school. The Institute base their contention on the grounds that labour market pressures in general and unemployment in particular do not serve greatly to moderate the wage spiral, unless extremely severe. With wages in their view thus determined by non-market pressures, they argue that financial targets will either fail to bite, and thus be ineffective; or alternatively that they will have their major impact on real output. But in the same issue I note that the Institute declare that the early re-establishment of reasonably full employment would be foolhardy until a solution is found to the problem of inflation – which, from the viewpoint of the Institute, depends on the adoption of incomes policies on a permanent basis. Until then, it is implied, the pace of expansion will have to be kept down to a strictly modest pace.

I concur with this last judgment – as I have already indicated. I take the view that we cannot allow the economy to expand very vigorously until inflation has been brought down to a lower level and we have some assurance that this achievement will not be threatened by faster expansion.

A monetary target both provides an overt public expression of this need for caution, and embodies some assurance that action will be triggered if the need for it arises. In the short term if things go wrong adherence to an unchanged monetary target will be the equivalent of early restraining discretionary action. In the longer term, the commitment to monetary targets will also ensure a general degree of caution. One may therefore say that in a figurative sense to announce such a commitment is to serve notice on all those concerned, including those concerned with wage bargaining, how far the authorities are prepared to finance inflation. It will be said that those involved in wage bargaining pay no heed to the size of the monetary targets. This may be so – though I would think it better if it were not. Yet, over time, perseverance with a policy of the sort I have outlined will, I believe, have an increasingly pervasive effect. As it becomes clear to all that faster growth can only be had with less inflation, will there not be more pressure to see how this can be done?

I think one thing will be evident from what I have said. Monetary policy is often classed as an instrument of demand management: in practice, until we have made more progress with inflation, its services are likely to be pre-empted by the need to use it as an instrument against inflation. Nevertheless, it is clear also that we need a reasonable rate of expansion; and the prospect I see is not of no expansion, but of a reasonably controlled expansion.

I should now refer to the relation between monetary policy and the exchange rate. Many monetarists would I know see the chief influence of monetary policy on prices as coming via this route, and would regard a floating exchange rate as an essential concomitant of a sound monetary policy.

It will be plain that the Bank have not adopted the whole of this intellectual position. The advantages of an appreciating rate for domestic prices are evident enough. But as a recent issue of the Bank's Quarterly Bulletin made plain, we are also concerned with the effect on export prices and on the profitability of exports. Nor did we wholly accept the argument that capital inflows arising at a time when we were intervening on the exchanges to keep the rate lower than it would be on a free float must necessarily undermine the effectiveness of our monetary control. Indeed for ten months of last year – when massive inflows occurred – this was not the case. A time came however when we felt unable any longer to maintain full control over the growth of the money stock without setting the exchange rate free to float – concern about exports notwithstanding. The decision made in those circumstances emphasises our commitment, in conditions of conflict, to controlling the monetary aggregates.

The implementation of monetary policy

I should now like to turn from the broad general principles of policy to the more technical problems of implementing monetary policy in practice.

Management of the monetary aggregates

The difficulties of achieving the desired path for the monetary aggregates can be described in various ways. Let us start by considering what influences the demand for money. Given the level of national income, and neglecting temporary influences, we work on the theory that interest rates are the main determinants of the demand for money. That is the logic of our method of operating, as I have sought to describe it earlier in this lecture – we seek to manage the course of the monetary aggregate by bringing about changes in interest rates. But it is of course difficult to predict the level and structure of interest rates at which the stock of money the public wants to hold will be brought into equality with the stock the authorities would like to see being held. I need not apologise for this: the converse of this ignorance is that how interest rates will be influenced by various factors is highly uncertain, a fact of life known to all market operators.

In practice we often try to get round this difficulty by building up a forecast from, as it were, the 'supply' side. Thus we look separately at the main items which statistically speaking are the components of the money supply on a broad definition – such as the public sector borrowing requirement, sales to the public of government debt, the volume of bank lending to the private sector and external flows to the private sector. What we are in effect doing in such an exercise is to attempt to predict what the rate of monetary expansion will be if we refrain from trying to change interest rates – as a preliminary to considering the need for intervention. This may disguise, but does not really evade, the central difficulty of prediction which I have just mentioned.

We are of course kept constantly awake to this difficulty by the sheer erratic variability of the counterparts of the money stock with which we are dealing. For example, since 1974 the mean error of forecasts of the public sector borrowing requirement made at the beginning of each financial year has been of the order of £3 billion. Again, the monthly growth of bank lending frequently fluctuates from its trend by over £100 million; extreme fluctuations in recent years have been as much as three times as large as this. Moreover in the last two decades bank lending has been greatly affected by numerous types of official intervention and control; and, partly no doubt in consequence, we do not now know at all exactly how it is likely to respond to changes in economic or financial conditions.

The essence of monetary management, as I see it, is to act to offset divergences from forecast in these sources of monetary expansion – difficult to predict and control – as soon as it becomes reasonably clear that inaction is likely to undermine achievement of the monetary target. Such divergences from forecast are difficult to identify quickly, partly because of inevitable delays in statistical information about the recent past.

A corollary is, I believe, that so long as we can see our way to bring it back within a few months to the charted path, we should not be unduly concerned when monetary growth goes temporarily off course. I do not for example see much case for supposing that the temporary slow down in monetary growth last winter, or the temporary acceleration last autumn – largely influenced by massive inflows of funds from abroad – had or will have a significant effect on the development of the economy. Nevertheless, the long run is a summation of short periods; and what is above all important is that we do not allow monetary developments to diverge too long from trend.

I know that there are critics and commentators who believe that the problem of maintaining control over these short-term developments could be more satisfactorily achieved by a change in our form of operations. They argue that control over some form of high-powered or base money would be more effective in controlling monetary growth than are our present methods. This same debate is occurring in several countries between central banks and their academic critics. It is the case that most central banks, including most of those with publicly quantified monetary targets, seek to affect monetary growth by varying the general level of interest rates. The monetary authorities in the USA, in Canada and in Germany, for example, operate by this method. I would not seek to suggest however that the methods adopted by the major central banks are, *ipso facto*, right.

This is too large a subject to enter at this stage in my address, and I would hope to return to it on some future occasion. What I want to say now is that I doubt whether a move to base money control would enable control to be achieved with less variation in interest rates than at present. Indeed, the extent of interest rate variation that the system would have to tolerate might be considerably greater, in the short run at least, if base money control was to be rigorously imposed.

Choice of monetary aggregate

I turn now to the question of which of the monetary aggregates is the most appropriate series on which to set the target. If you plot the rate of growth of the alternative monetary series in the UK since 1970, particularly the series of M1 and M3, you will see that they have followed markedly differing paths. For the technically minded, the correlation of the quarterly changes in these aggregates over this period has been only + 0.1. Which series one chooses to look at can clearly affect one's interpretation of monetary developments.

The broad monetary aggregate, £M3, in terms of which our present target is expressed, has a number of advantages over its rivals. As I have already said, it can be linked to changes in certain key credit counterparts, such as the PSBR, bank lending, government debt sales, DCE and external financial flows, in a way that helps our understanding of the course of monetary developments. It has also some comparative statistical advantages; for example, it is proportionately less disturbed by transit items – somewhat arbitrarily treated as they are – than M1.

Nevertheless there are certain shortcomings in this series which call for caution in its interpretation. The velocity of M3, the ratio of incomes to broad money, has exhibited very sharp fluctuations, with a major fall during the period of adjustment to Competition and Credit Control, and subsequently a return to – or above – its previous average level. The econometric equations, estimated earlier, neither forecast nor have since adequately explained this development. It probably arose because (as I have already noted) the rate of growth of one of the major constituents of M3, wholesale deposits, depends on relative interest rates, rather than their general level.

Increases in Minimum Lending Rate and in the general level of interest rates do not of themselves bring about a shift in the relative pattern of interest rates that would serve to moderate the growth of wholesale deposits within M3. Indeed, if the increase in rates is closely connected, as it often is, with pressure on banks' liquidity, the relative pattern of rates is liable to adjust adversely, leading to even faster growth in wholesale deposits, at least temporarily. On occasions the path of M3 can be significantly influenced by changing competitive conditions within the banking industry – conditions which can change for reasons quite separate from the course of nominal incomes in the economy, or the actions of the monetary authorities.

There is also, I believe, worthwhile information to be obtained from looking at series other than M3. Over the period for which we have complete data since 1963 the relationship between movements of narrow money (M1) on the one hand and of incomes and interest rates on the other has been closer and more stable than has been the case with M3. Though for some economists that alone would be reason for putting chief emphasis on M1. I would not go that far. First, the relatively stable relationship involving M1 has been observed for a comparatively short period, during which the authorities have not given emphasis to controlling M1: this does not guarantee that the relationship would remain as stable under differing conditions, particularly if the authorities were to seek to control it more closely. Second, I value the broader descriptive analysis that reference to M3 allows, which one cannot obtain with M1.

Reasons could also be advanced for paying attention to wider liquidity series than M3. There is a high degree of substitution between some assets included in M3 and some excluded, Treasury bills and Certificates of Deposit for example. Moreover the growth and evolution of the building societies has blurred the distinction between deposits with banks and shares and deposits with building societies. This development raises a number of issues, among them the scope and coverage of any series intended to measure private sector transaction balances.

One specific proposal put to us is that we should once again provide a refurbished M2 series, which would aim to exclude wholesale deposits (whose course is so hard to predict or control) and to include retail-type time deposits. We welcome and seriously consider suggestions of this kind. However, we have certain doubts about this particular suggestion. We doubt whether the addition to the existing M1 series of seven-day deposits with the clearing banks would provide much additional information. A theoretically better split between retail and wholesale-type deposits might be obtained by grading deposits by size, over and under £50,000 for example. However not only would any such dividing line be arbitrary, but it would impose a new, onerous burden on the banks' statistical systems. Moreover, for the reasons I have already indicated, I am not sure that it would be sensible to restrict a statistic measuring private sector retail-type deposits to the banks alone, excluding similar-type deposits with building societies.

More generally there will be some information to be had from observation of virtually any financial and economic indicator. But we cannot and should not translate all such indicators into targets for policy. That would be a recipe for confusion. We need to have clear and simple targets, and I am satisfied that in the present state of the art we have chosen best in selecting £M3.

Rolling targets

Finally, I might comment on the question of how often targets should be reviewed and revised. The present monetary target was set in last March's Budget to last without review for the whole financial year. But it is open to question whether this is the optimum strategy. New information on the economy is continually becoming available and it is my view that we should reassess developments as often as sufficient information makes this worthwhile.

A drawback of the present annual targets has been the implied requirement to hit a particular number on a particular date. The various time-lags in the system make it difficult, and certainly highly undesirable, to try to offset undesired monetary movements very rapidly. Firm deadlines can force one either to try to adjust too fast to an unforeseen trend developing late in the period; or to appear to accept a failure to reach one's target. For such reasons it is for consideration whether it would not be advantageous to rebase the target before the previous target period has been fully completed.

The Federal Reserve undertakes a reassessment each quarter. I believe that for us that would be too frequent. Such a reassessment might however be undertaken along with a review of fiscal policy, for instance at the Budget and again in the autumn.

Targets operated in this way have come to be called 'rolling targets' – yet another addition to our growing dictionary of economic jargon, though perhaps a useful and expressive one. I am aware that some people fear that a move to rolling targets would permit much greater elasticity, so that over a period monetary growth could drift further and further away from a desirable medium-term trend. The ability to reassess policy at six-month intervals, however, would not necessarily entail altering course. Indeed I would hope that, more often than not, it would validate staying on the same course for an extended period. I need hardly stress again the value that I place on the importance of maintaining monetary stability.

I would not of course support the adoption of rolling targets if this implied a change of direction in our present strategy. But I could see it as a minor, but useful, technical change to our continuing policy of having publicly announced monetary targets – a policy which I have sought to defend and explain this afternoon.

In doing so, I have covered a lot of ground and will therefore spare you – and myself – the added burden of summarising what I have had to say. We have not, it is plain, adopted a wholehearted monetarist philosophy. But what we do is likely to give a monetarist a good deal of the prescription he would recommend, which may be what Mr Volcker, President of the Federal Reserve Bank of New York, implied in his phrase 'practical monetarism'. But the essence of what I have been saying is indeed very old fashioned – the predictable caution of a central banker.

3 Objectives of monetary policy

Past and present

Lord Robbins of Clare Market

E52
E31

(UK)

I

May I begin by saying how honoured I feel at being asked to deliver this lecture. I listened with rapt admiration to its inauguration last year by the Governor of the Bank of England to whose calm head and sober perspective we owe so much of what stability there has been in our distraught and deranged economy in recent years; and I know that I cannot maintain that standard. But it is a stimulus to do what is possible.

Let me first explain my intentions. It would be idle in my present position for me to discuss the technicalities of current financial problems. But it has occurred to me that some survey of the general aim and objectives of the ideas which have dominated monetary policy in this country during the last half century and some glance at present conceptions may not be outside the spirit of Lord Mais's foundation; and this I propose to attempt. My lecture will thus fall into four parts. In the first I shall consider changes of thought regarding internal financial policy since 1925. In the second I shall turn to external financial relations in the same period. Thirdly and fourthly I shall consider present problems in both these aspects. As you will realise from the nature of this programme, the treatment must be highly impressionistic. But I hope I shall avoid superficial detail.

II

I begin with the period 1925–31 when the main internal and external objectives were the same, namely to maintain the parity of the pound sterling. As I think it would now be commonly agreed that the parity chosen in 1925 was an inappropriate overvaluation, this decision involved all sorts of troubles: a disastrous coal strike, continuing unemployment, and trouble with the balance of payments. If one contemplates the vicissitudes during this period of the recommendations for policy of John Maynard Keynes, his advocacy of tariffs and his growing economic nationalism, it is easy to see in these reactions desperate attempts to escape the results of the folly of the decision of 1925. It is also easy to imagine that, if the policy had been adopted at an earlier date after the war of a return to gold at a devalued parity the history, not only of this country but of the entire western world might have been different.

Then came the Great Depression of the 1930s; and in spite of the fact that in 1931 the attempt was abandoned to maintain sterling at the 1925 parity, unemployment developed on a scale which, as a percentage of the working population, has not been seen since that day. It was in those times that the idea of government spending to offset the decline of private investment, either by way of long-term loans or an unbalanced budget, began to influence public opinion on a large scale, backed, as it was, by the sensational break with much traditional opinion regarding the capital market, in the shape of Keynes's *General Theory*. Later on these views were immensely strengthened by the palpable effect on employment of increased government spending on rearmament which, by the spring of 1939, when unemployment was still about 1,300,000 – a much larger percentage of the working force than the same figure would be now – had led Keynes to warn that movements already taking place were beginning to make the assumption of underemployment invalid.

It is against this background of inter-war experience that the celebrated *White Paper on Employment Policy*, issued under the auspices of the wartime Coalition, must be interpreted. This was a very moderate document, denounced as such by Beveridge in his *Full Employment in a Free Society* where he took as his leading principle the maxim that in the labour market demand should always be in excess of supply – a principle which, although I do not think he realised it, was clearly absolutely a recipe for non-stop inflation. But in order to understand the commitment to 'high levels of employment' which the Coalition document certainly gave, it must be realised that the opinion at that time prevalent among most economists of the English speaking world was that, after a brief restocking boom at the end of the war, the main problem would be *deflation* rather than *inflation*, and therefore that the business of government in this respect would be to sustain aggregate demand rather than to restrain it. I am quite sure that among those who were responsible for the drafting of the White Paper there was no intention of commitment to a policy of letting the value of money be determined by the demand for wages and salaries, however unrelated that might be to the value of the product.

As we know, the history of the years after the war was the reverse of the expectation on which the White Paper was based. Indeed for a very long time the percentage of unemployment was far less than even Beveridge, who had promised an average of 3 per cent if his ideas were accepted, had expected. This indeed had, in my opinion, very adverse results on conceptions of appropriate policy. An unemployment percentage often below 2 per cent had only to rise a decimal point or two, when politicians of all parties – and even the quality newspapers – would express grave apprehensions and hasten to adjust policy accordingly. At an early stage the decline in the purchasing power of money in this country brought with it all sorts of inimical tendencies as regards production and distribution, not to mention trouble with the balance of payments, all of which might have been avoided if this internal overheating of the economy had not taken place. And it is surely clear that the main *raison d'être* of the disastrous policies of the early 1970s – the Heath inflation – sprang from fears aroused by the rise in unemployment more or less inevitably caused by the stabilisation of a devalued pound which had begun under Mr Jenkins's chancellorship. It cannot be said that the government responsible was not warned of the probable consequences of what they were doing: a group of some of the best of the younger economists led by the late Harry Johnson – and including Professor Griffiths – wrote a prophetic protest to the Prime Minister of the day predicting the dangers to which he was exposing the economy. But I doubt whether their very moderate and correct analysis received any consideration whatever.

It is sometimes said that the conceptions of policy which were dominant during the period I have been discussing were appropriately to be described as Keynesian. Whether this is correct or not is not, I think, a matter which is fruitful to discuss, for there are almost as many varieties of points of view of those who are designated as Keynesians as there are persons concerned. But I think it is important to distinguish such points of view from those of Keynes himself; for to attribute to him approval of most of the errors of judgment which have led us into the pickle in which we find ourselves is to commit a grave injustice. It is true that his important and influential work, the *General Theory of Employment, Interest and Money*, has been described as essentially the economics of depression; and in my opinion there is something in this description. But to judge Keynes's outlook in the last years of his life by his prescriptions for dealing with acute deflation and not to take account of his *How to Pay for the War* which is a prescription for dealing with incipient inflation, is radically to distort the perspective. It is probably wasted effort to spend much time speculating on what a great man might have said in circumstances which had not arisen when he died. But it is my profound impression that Keynes would not have viewed with complacency the inflationary tendencies of the last quarter of a century and that, had he lived, his protests against them would have been as pronounced as his protests against the deflation tendencies of the inter-war period.

III

I now turn to considerations of external policy.

As is well known, in the days of the gold standard the division between internal and external objectives of policy was of relatively minor significance. Apart from a few currency cranks whose views carried little or no weight, the idea of a common basis for money in the western world was more or less taken for granted; and though there were numerous problems concerned with the stability of local banking systems and the size of reserves, the idea of national independence in this respect was not at all prominent. What discussion there was related to the international system as a whole. The bi-metallic controversy of the last half of the nineteenth century, in so far as it was not stoked up by the interests of the silver producers, was essentially of this nature and not so uninteresting as Oscar Wilde thought it was; and the beginnings of discussion among professional economists regarding the regulation of the future value of money was likewise principally concerned with international action. At the end of his life, Alfred Marshall wrote to Keynes that he was convinced that monetary reform, if it came, had to be international in character.

But the First World War with its recourse to unequal issues of paper money by the respective combatants and therefore with the mechanisms governing national balances of payments unrelated to a common standard, changed all that: and the attempt in 1925 to restore a sterling–dollar relationship was so frightfully botched that in some ways it made things worse. Thus concern with national policy was, so to speak, forced upon public opinion by the break-up in 1914 of the international standard and the lamentable failure to restore its effectiveness when the war was over. In the years immediately following the war Keynes saw no alternative but a return to gold. But even before 1925, in his *Tract on Monetary Reform*, he was considering independent national action to set a good example to others.

In the end the collapse of the pound sterling in 1931 and the uncertainties regarding the dollar after 1933, not to mention the troubles of these countries – the so called Gold Block – which attempted to maintain a stable relationship with gold, completed the process. It may be that such developments were inevitable; but certainly, even when the disorganisation created by uncertainties of exchange rates were generally realised and attempts were beginning to be made, via the tripartite agreement between the US, UK and France, to introduce some order into the situation, it was the co-ordination of national policies rather than the acceptance of a common standard which was the order of the day.

It is against this background of inter-war confusion and the change in outlook which accompanied it that the attempt to create a new international monetary system must be considered. Both Keynes and White, the initiators of thought in their respective centres, were intent on eliminating the disorderly relationships between different currency centres which had prevailed. In its origin the Keynes plan was the more ambitious. He actually produced a scheme for an international money which would automatically reduce the deflationary pressures attributed to the gold standard. But this ran against the alleged unwillingness of the US Congress to bear the unlimited liabilities of a creditor position which was then assumed to be likely to last forever. It also contained fewer safeguards against inflation than might have been regarded as desirable. Eventually, as we all know, there emerged the establishment of a fund of different currencies, available to its various members on rules which permitted changes of exchange outside very narrow limits only by common consent.

Now I may have a lingering personal interest in events in which as an official I played a humble role. But I confess that I still think that the agreement which brought the International Monetary Fund into being was a notable achievement – one of the few attempts at international co-operation which have had any meaning; and certainly it has built up a secretariat which, in various ways, has contributed greatly to expert discussion and advice.

Unfortunately, as regards its operations, it had various inbuilt defects which, as time has gone on, have gradually shown themselves.

First, as regards constitution, its makers did indeed avoid the fatal error of the one state one vote system which makes such utter nonsense of the Assembly of the United Nations: votes weighted according to a complicated formula were adopted. But the size and composition of the executive council were inappropriate for discussion of the degree of secrecy necessarily involved in changing the par values of important currencies. The result has been that all such changes have been decided by other methods. The reference to the council was just ritual rubber stamping.

Secondly, the rules permitting changes of rates in conditions of a fundamental disequilibrium which was inadequately defined, tended to give rise to the build-up of speculative positions long after change had become desirable, by reason either of unequal rates of inflation or changes in the terms of trade. In consequence, there developed a reaction favouring completely free floating – of which more later.

Finally, the drafting of the agreement and its interpretation by the US Congress resulted in effect that the ultimate basis of the system involved a dollar which in fact was far less susceptible of change than other currencies. The result was that, when the US position came under strain, for a long time nothing could be done about it and then eventually there was a breakdown into a system of floating rates for the main currencies – which was just what the founders of the Fund had intended to avoid.

I still think the IMF has its uses and potentialities, especially when a government which has been pursuing radically destabilising policies wishes to change course but desires to have some other institution on which to put the blame. But it would be idle to argue that there is at present any consensus whatever regarding desirable international monetary policy, such as seemed to prevail at its inception.

IV

So much for a most superficial view of the vicissitudes of opinion in regard to monetary objectives in the past half century. I now come to present conceptions of policy and, as I indicated at the beginning, I propose to treat it under the same two headings, first internal policy, neglecting external effects, and then the complications of external policy.

To begin then with internal policy. I take it that most of us are against inflation, particularly when it is so well anticipated that it no longer seems to have any favourable effects on unemployment. I know that some highly sophisticated people, especially in the United States of all places, have tried to show that it does not matter all that. But I am quite out of sympathy with this attitude. It is true that the economic system has not come to an end in Latin America, despite rates which, if not rivalling the hyper-inflation of Germany and elsewhere after the First World War, have still been very high. But democratic government there has more or less perished and some things even more important than democracy as well; and I doubt very much whether societies more complicated than those of Latin America can stand without catastrophic divisiveness degrees of inflation even considerably less. We only have to look around in our own unhappy country at the deterioration of industrial relations, the 'real' profitability of enterprise, so concealed by historic cost accounting, and the general erosion of standards of public and private honesty, to see what can be done to a hitherto stable society by rates of inflation of the kind we have experienced in the last few years.

So what? There are still some who, looking at the historic record, point out that metallic standards have never deteriorated in this way unless the subject of wilful debasement by governments. They may still be right in urging that, given the pressures on most kinds of governments, we cannot do better than this. But I am sure that, among expert opinion at least, they are a minority whatever may be the desires of a substantial proportion of the rest of humanity. Most expert opinion has, so to speak, eaten of the tree of the knowledge of good and evil as regards gold. It knows that its relative stability is largely a matter of geological and techno-logical accident; and it thinks we ought to be able to do better. A stable money which does not depend on digging metal from one place and depositing it in another is still a common aspiration among men of good will not infected by cynicism.

What then are the causes of inflation under paper moneys? Over the course of history, even modern history, probably the principal causes have been, quite sim-ply, excessive spending on the part of governments. Either because of the pres-sures of war or because of the subtler pressures of desire for growth or welfare, governments, unrestrained by the obligations of convertibility have indulged in demand inflation. Excessive creation of money and credit – these are simple matters to understand, although the necessary political mechanism for restraining them is not perhaps so simple.

In recent years, however, there have been influences which are more complex. If the terms of trade turn against an economy, say because of a cartel controlling important raw materials, then, in the absence of an increase of the supply of money and credit from some quarter or other, people have less to spend on other things and demand in such quarters falls off. But if, in compensation for this deprivation, new money and credit is created, then, failing some extraordinary increase in productivity, inflation will take place. The same sort of reasoning applies to the prices of services. If rates rise appreciably above the value of the production in respect of which they are paid, then either with constant aggregate expenditure, there is unemployment or, if new money and credit are created, you have inflation. It is, of course, true that, in either of these cases, increased expend-iture may be financed by a more intensive use of money and credit. But clearly there is a limit. It is safe to say that continuing inflation arising from increasing costs can only be mainly financed from increases in the supply of money and credit – until all confidence in the future value of the currency concerned has vanished.

This brings me to the question of monetarism. Monetarism has become a dirty word nowadays among those who positively prefer policies which ignore the effects of variations in the supply of money. It is therefore probably incumbent on anyone who insists on the importance of this factor to spell out exactly where he stands. In my judgment the essential truth of the so-called monetarist attitude – the truth to which I should be willing to subscribe – is the contention that continuing marked disparities, either way, between the rate of change of output and the rate of change in the money supply lead to damaging changes in the value of money.

Such is the extent of my agreement with the so-called monetarist point of view. Now for qualifications positive and negative – remember always that I am still dealing with internal problems ignoring international complications.

First, I repudiate the suggestion that any sane monetarist regards the influence of the supply of money as uniquely and at all times correlated with the volume of production. This accusation is frankly tilting at windmills. It is abundantly clear that, in the short period, there may be, and indeed are, fluctuations in velocity (or the demand for money) which also influence the volume of output. This has been again and again emphasised by the monetarists themselves, especially Friedman. All that is claimed is that sharp falls in the value of money are not likely to go far if the rate of increase of the money supply is held to a constant target.

So much by way of vindication of a position which is often misrepresented. There are however two respects in which I must part company with this outlook. The first relates to causation. Your true blue monetarist denies the significance of cost inflation. A rise in costs is a once for all business, he contends: and, while it may cause unemployment, it is not cumulative in its effect on the value of money. It is always the government which is to blame rather than those who demand disproportionate rates of pay and prices. Perhaps controversy in this respect is a matter of semantics. But I personally am not prepared to concede that oligopolistic demands for prices and rates of pay far exceeding the value of the product are not to be called, in common language, inflationary. I agree that, if there is no response *via* increasing the supply of money, the results are more likely to be unemployment then continuing decline in its value. But I am not prepared to exempt such claims from any part in the causation of inflation. That seems to me to put too severe a limitation on the notion of a cause: and to provide excuses for conduct which does not deserve them.

My second reserve concerns policy. A rigid monetarist denies all place in his strategy for overall stabilisation to variations of fiscal policy. I am not inclined to go as far as this. I agree that, if monetary policy conforms to the monetarist criterion, then recourse to tinkering about with the budget may be eventually unnecessary; and I am sceptical of the so-called 'fine tuning' of years past, here and in the United States. But I am certainly not prepared to pass a self-denying ordinance in this respect and to forswear in all circumstances recourse to any fiscal instruments – for instance the regulator. It is not difficult for me to conceive of practical situations in which a combination of monetary and fiscal policy is sensible.

I now turn to an entirely different conception of policy – the conception which, conceiving most of the inflations of recent years to have been started on the cost side, urges that the most effective way of dealing with this is the policy of an overall control of incomes. This is usually combined with a recommendation of overall control of prices. But since this is so obviously a political cosmetic and since, the control of public service prices apart, it so clearly complicates unnecessarily the administrative problem, difficult enough in all conscience, I leave it undiscussed.

Now let me make it clear that, so far as the sections in which the government is directly involved, there must be an incomes policy. The government is the ultimate employer; and any employer who goes into the labour market without clear conceptions of what he is prepared to pay for the various services which he purchases is clearly asking for trouble. Doubtless such plans are much more difficult to elaborate in the public than in the private sector: the myth of the bottomless purse dies hard; there is often no guidance from the market, and political considerations thrust themselves into the picture. I will not go into the question of what such considerations imply for the desirable width of government administration. All that I wish to emphasise here is that nothing that I am going to say exempts government from having a policy for wages and salaries in the sector for which they are directly responsible.

But the conception that I am discussing, the conception of a general policy for contractual incomes throughout the whole economy, nationalised industry and private enterprise, goes much further than this: and here it is necessary to make quite explicit the main points of the relevant considerations.

I will leave undiscussed the administrative difficulties involved, though those members of the audience who have been concerned either in Whitehall or in the different branches of business, will, I imagine, agree that the additional burden of interpreting and arguing about individual problems is very formidable. Indeed, in our own recent history it must have subtracted a substantial amount of time which otherwise might have been devoted to improving our not exactly brilliant record of productivity.

The central idea, as I understand it, of a general wages and salaries policy, is that if such money costs can be kept roughly in line with the value of the Gross National Product, then inflation will not take place; and policy as regards money supply and general expenditure can be devoted to maintain a reasonable level of employment. The problem was discussed at some length by Beveridge, in the book to which I have already referred, whose recommendation of a demand for labour always in excess of supply certainly raised it in a very acute form. But he preferred to rely on a rather nebulous appeal to understanding and good behaviour, leaving it to others to urge the more logical and drastic solution.

Unfortunately things do not work out that way – in theory or in practice. Even in speculation in the study it is difficult to conceive of a centrally managed incomes policy which could take into practical account the multitudinous changes in the demand for and the supply of the various kinds of labour, which is the theoretical desideratum of this conception of policy. Much more probable in practice is the setting of wooden norms, either completely general or, at best, covering widely different fields of activity, which can never be remotely near an approximation to the theoretical ideal. Moreover, hitherto in history, the imposition of wages and incomes policy has been preceded by rates of general public expenditure having markedly inflationary tendencies which set up disturbances which multiply the difficulties of achieving the ideal norm.

On top of this, in real political situations, the measures of this sort adopted have a tendency to upset, or to threaten to upset, relativities between higher and lower paid groups of producers: and this increases the difficulties of controlling the situation. In many communities people tend to attach almost as much importance to relativities as to absolute levels and often fight as hard for them. Policies which ignore such factors tend to lead to situations in which there are scarcities of some types of services coexisting with excesses of others. It is really no accident that, hitherto, attempts to control inflation arising on the cost side by measures of this sort, have sooner or later broken down, leaving behind them wreckage, both industrial and social, which takes some time to clear up.

This is not to say, however, that there is no conceivable use for wages and salaries policies in certain very limited circumstances. Consider a position in which, inflation having become something of a social menace generally recognised as such, steps are being taken, either by action on the money supply or by appropriate fiscal measures, to bring it under control. In such a position there can be little doubt that, if wage and salary demands out of harmony with the proposed reduction in the rate of inflation are achieved and the government stands firm in its anti-inflationary policy, then unemployment will tend to increase. On the contrary, if there is restraint in such quarters, either voluntary or statutory, this need not happen. This then is the genuine use of such policies, voluntary or compulsory, not to curb inflation – that is better done in other ways – but rather to prevent an increase of unemployment. Admittedly they cannot be expected to work for ever; all such policies known to me, at least in democracies, have sooner or later come to grief. Admittedly in practice they are liable to involve all the difficulties already discussed. But it is undeniable that they can have that use for short periods.

But how precarious it all is once inflation has infected the system. If, without political bias, I may allude to the episodes of last winter, I would say that the former Prime Minister, Mr Callaghan, was quite right in his suggested guideline of an average increase of earnings of 5 per cent. Given a rate of growth of GNP of 2 per cent that would have left us perhaps another year to achieve the eventual goal of the elimination of inflation. But, alas, how vain it was to expect it to happen. Two years of income restraint, imperfect as that was, was too much for the powerful producers' associations with the special legal privileges which successive governments have conferred upon them: and in fact they achieved an increase in earnings considerably more than twice that figure.

On the whole then, I am clear that the method of controlling inflation by general control of wages and salaries is one which has only limited justification in very exceptional circumstances; and even then it gives rise to false expectations. Speaking generally I am convinced that the control of aggregate expenditure in one way or another is still the main hope of restraining the alarming decline in the value of money which has been the outstanding internal menace to free societies in the years since the Second World War.

V

I now come, finally, to the problem of relations between national currencies. Here I have to be more tentative than ever, since the situation and its associated problems are changing from year to year.

Let me begin, however, with what I believe to be an incontestable proposition, namely that so long as different rates of inflation in relation to the value of output, prevail in different areas, so long fixed rates of exchange between the different currencies concerned will not be permanently viable. Small areas may link up with large areas and may avoid exchange depreciation for a time by borrowing. But, in the end, if they wish to maintain a fixed rate relationship, they have to harmonise their monetary policy with that of the parent area. As for large areas, changes may for a time be averted by concerted action by benevolent central bankers. But if unequal rates of inflation persist, eventually the rates of exchange will be affected. I do not need to quote contemporary examples.

Now advocacy of generally floating rates as an ideal rather than a remedy for a situation that has got thoroughly out of hand, has been very popular in the last quarter of a century. But I personally do not think that, even on the purely speculative plane, on which some of its advocates elect to move, this claim is generally tenable. This for two reasons: one analytical; one ideological.

The analytical reason is pretty obvious, though it is odd that it should have received so little attention. The fundamental argument for floating rates, whether correct or not, is that they provide an easier way of adjusting to changes in international demand and supply than adjustments of money incomes. How much easier to let the rate of exchange go down than to risk the impairment of industrial relations. But in the end this rests upon the assumption that the recipients of money incomes are relatively indifferent to what happens to exchange rates, which may be true – or may have been true – in very large currency areas, but is palpably not the case in small ones. This is indeed one of the chief justifications for small areas linking their currencies to the currencies of larger ones. But I doubt whether, save in the very large areas, the assumption holds that the markets for services nowadays are usually focused exclusively on money rewards and not on the real goods and services which they purchase – and these real rewards in part depend upon costs and prices in international markets. I am therefore reasonably clear that we have outlived the epoch in which governments could get away with the adverse results of internal policies, by simply relying on changes in rates of exchange.

My second reason is severely practical though it involves an element of ideology. In the long run a system of floating rates can only be maintained if it involves exchange control somewhere or other. Otherwise the anticipation of change leads to movements of funds which may be highly disequilibrating and may eventually lead to the disuse of those currencies which are expected to deteriorate fastest. Who of us would not have liked to have had our investments and pension arrangements in Swiss francs or German marks in the last twenty years or so if we had not been subject to severe penalties for doing so?

Thus, in the end, the so-called 'liberal solution' of the problem of international currency relations proves to depend on the totally illiberal system of exchange control. The freedom that it is supposed to guarantee is only the freedom for the internal government to debauch the currency – or allow it to be debauched – at the expense of the unfreedom of the citizens to preserve the value of their savings.

It is my impression that in the last few years fashionable opinion has begun to perceive that the argument for a general international system of floating rates involves considerably greater inconvenience than was earlier supposed. It will be remembered that a great cry of relief went up as what remained of an international system in the form of the Smithsonian agreements collapsed – as might have been expected. Freedom from Bretton Woods, freedom from any external obligations, what splendid prospects that opened – or seemed to open. Nowadays I suspect that responsible opinion is coming to the view that, whatever might be the case in a world in which each currency area was committed to maintaining stability in the internal value of money, and exchange markets looked after changes in the terms of trade, we are a long, long way from that. The international monetary position is highly unsatisfactory and indeed pregnant with all sorts of considerable trouble.

But where then are we to turn?

I am afraid I do not see much prospect for the re-creation or perhaps better said the creation of an international system devoted to maintaining the purchasing power of money at fixed exchange rates. I still value what remains of the IMF with its dedicated expert staff and their influence. But I do not see the special drawing rights as at present constituted as a suitable basis for such a system. I remember with some sympathy the remark of a high international expert who said that he would believe in SDRs *in that role* when his wife asked him for a necklace composed of such paper. As for possible reinforcements, I have sometimes thought of Irving Fisher's compensated gold unit as a backing, provided that it was somewhat modified in both how it was managed and in its basis. But although the popularity of gold as an investment shows that there is a considerable body of opinion which might be attracted by such a solution, such is the irony of history – it would have to confront the implacable opposition of the massed body of much American expert opinion to anything related to gold! As for an international standard directly related to stocks of commodities, although in some ways not unattractive, I should be doubtful of its successful management; especially given the present frame of mind of the less prosperous 'developing countries' who doubtless would clamour in vast numbers for representation on its management.

In my judgment, a completely international system cannot be created yet awhile, even if that were thought to be more desirable than other imperfect arrangements. But we can possibly hope to eliminate some of the elements of instability in the present international situation by some consolidation of financial arrangements among the countries of Western Europe. I agree with the view that a strong Western European currency, although not ideal, would solve many local problems in this important area; and I think that its relationship with the dollar and other currencies need not give rise to the difficulties which have recently beset the international financial situation.

But having said this about Western Europe, I would wish to add immediately that I am convinced that we need to go much beyond the present arrangements and proposals which are fashionable and thought to be advisable in this respect. I am sure that, with different rates of growth in money supply in the different Western European centres, a system of fixed exchange rates must inevitably break down: and although *ad hoc* adjustments may from time to time be possible, the fact that they may have to take place, necessarily impedes the objective of the whole system.

How can this be avoided? It is of course conceivable that, in the absence of exchange control, the most stable of the various currencies might attract so much use that it became eventually the main money of the entire area. Alternatively, it might be that the central Commission of the Community might embark on the issue of a new money parallel with existing currencies, but guaranteed to be so managed as to maintain a constant value in terms of a representative collection of commodities. This too, if allowed to be freely used for all transactions within the community, might speedily become the predominant Western European medium of exchange: and, although it has not been canvassed widely in this country, it certainly commands the support of some of the best of the younger economists on the continent.

Whatever form such a change might take, the fundamental desideratum is this: that eventually there should be one Western European money so that transactions *between* what are now areas of independent money supply should involve no more complications than at present take place with transactions *within* these areas. Confronted as we now are with states, with different historic origins and different fiscal systems, which insist that whatever happens they must retain sovereignty in every conceivable respect, this is doubtless a tall order and perhaps unlikely to happen. But, in the last analysis, I doubt very much whether eventually the different societies of Western Europe will survive unless they are prepared to readjust to some sort of federal unity – and of such unity a common money must be an important, although by no means the only, essential feature.

VI

In concluding I would like to emphasise what has been the main thought animating my remarks in the second half of this lecture which is simply that, somehow or other, inflation must be stopped, at any rate in the main western states of the world. I do not think that all problems would be solved by stable monetary conditions in such areas: we should still be confronted with the many real problems of production and distribution. But the instability of units of account creates a multiplicity of complications which ought to be unnecessary; and internal stability and orderly relations between states would be immensely facilitated if they were absent.

Let me end by quoting some words from the last sentences of a public lecture which I delivered some years ago. 'Stop the inflation', I said, 'that is the paramount need of the moment in the economic sphere: if we meet it . . . we have still a future of high promise. If we do not then I fear that our days are numbered, certainly as a great power, perhaps even as a stable society.' These words were uttered in 1951. They are still applicable. Indeed they are much more urgent: and the problems involved are much more complex.

|UK|

4   The fight against inflation

The Rt Hon Sir Geoffrey Howe QC MP

£31

£52

Introduction

I am honoured to be invited to give the third Mais Lecture. It is hard for anyone to measure up to the standard set by my two predecessors. But I recognise a certain logic in the choice. Those who instituted the lecture envisaged that it should be given either by a theoretician or a practitioner. It therefore seems natural that the central banker and the economist should be followed by an economic minister, by any standards a practitioner.

I have now been a participant in the evolution of economic policy for almost ten years. My first experience as a Cabinet minister was in the engine room of prices and incomes policy in Mr Heath's government. During five years in Opposition I continued to play a part in reformulating the strategy against inflation. And for the last two years, of course, I have been responsible for its implementation.

I hope then that I may offer you today some thoughts distilled from that experience. My approach will not be theological. I do not believe that rigid adherence to one or other 'school' of economics is the best way to respond to our economic problems. All our economic judgments must be based on an assessment of the evidence available to us at a particular point in time. My views have developed, I hope, in response to my experience; and on some subjects I acknowledge they have changed very significantly. I am perhaps not alone in this. But, as I hope to illustrate in the course of this lecture, the evolution of this government's economic strategy, for which I am now responsible, has been a logical development given the experience of recent years.

Inflation

I have chosen as my title 'The Fight Against Inflation'. This is not because inflation is the only aspect of the economy on which government should have a policy, or indeed because the conquest of inflation is our only goal. The ultimate goal must be to restore the British economy to growth and prosperity: defeating inflation is one crucial condition for that. The other is improving the performance of the economy, by making it more flexible and adaptable in its response to technological change and developments in market conditions. Both tasks are vital. But whilst the conquest of inflation may not be a *sufficient* condition for sustainable economic growth, it is, we believe, a *necessary* condition.

Some people no doubt would argue that our first priority now should be to reduce unemployment. I am equally concerned about unemployment, but I do not believe that the way to reduce it is to relax in the struggle against inflation. In the 1950s and 1960s – especially after the publication of Professor Phillips's famous article in 1958 – many people believed that there was a policy trade-off: that if you tolerated so many extra points on the inflation rate you could get so many extra points off the unemployment rate. But however strong a negative correlation Phillips found for the 100 years before 1957, more recent experience does not support the argument. In each cycle since then inflation has accelerated and unemployment has risen. The average rate of inflation under successive governments in the years to 1979 has marched remorselessly upwards: 3.5 per cent, 4.5 per cent, 9 per cent, 15 per cent. Meanwhile unemployment also rose: 300,000, half a million, three-quarters of a million, one and a quarter million.

All this has strengthened the conviction that it is not possible to reverse that trend in unemployment by stimulating demand and permitting higher inflation. The notion of a trade-off in that form no longer commands wide acceptance. If we look instead at the simultaneous upward trends in inflation and unemployment a very different conclusion suggests itself. Now that it has been shown what damage high rates of inflation can do to an economy, it has been widely accepted that the defeat of inflation is a pre-condition for the resumption of steady growth and a reduction in unemployment. Inflation is the enemy of confidence and stability. The uncertainty it creates – over future *relative* prices as well as the general price level – discourages new investment, and so undermines the vitality and competitiveness of the economy. Inflation distorts the choices of savers as to where to direct their savings, encouraging them to prefer inflation 'hedges' such as housing or antiques, to investment in productive sectors of the economy.

Moreover, the defeat of inflation is a worthwhile goal in its own right. For inflation is socially divisive. It redistributes wealth in an arbitrary way. It exacerbates tension over pay bargaining, as employees struggle to maintain their real incomes.

Living with inflation

In his lecture last year, Lord Robbins argued persuasively against those who claim that a society can tolerate persistently high levels of inflation. 'In Latin America', he observed, 'democratic government . . . has more or less perished and some things even more important than democracy as well.' I share his doubts 'whether societies more complicated than those of Latin America can stand without catastrophic divisiveness degrees of inflation even considerably less'.

Others have argued that a little inflation is a tolerable, even a good, thing. In practice I do not believe that we can learn to live with inflation in any sort of satisfactory way. That would imply that a purely technical solution was available to a problem which I am convinced is much more complex and deep-rooted.

Inevitably in an open society there is competition for real income; and in an economy where the springs of enterprise have become rather sluggish, that competition becomes sharper. Some people commend inflation in these circumstances as the device which reconciles these conflicting claims. But as people see that nominal sums of money no longer buy what they expected, the competition becomes still greater and inflationary pressure grows. Governments then have a choice between accommodating the inflationary pressure and improving the underlying workings of the economy to make more real resources available. There is no doubt in my mind that while the former may be a short-term palliative, the latter is something which eventually has to be faced.

The alternative approach was recently condemned by the Chairman of the US Federal Reserve. 'The game was up', he said, 'when the public would no longer accept nominal gains as a substitute for the real thing. Inflation, instead of being a relatively benign social solvent, is a degenerative disease.' So I do not believe that there are virtues in inflation, however low the rate. Even at 5 per cent prices double every fourteen years. And there is the ever-present danger that if some inflation is tolerated, a slight acceleration will also be tolerated, and so on until the thing is once again out of control. Give inflation an inch and it will take an ell.

I do not believe we can go on compromising with inflation. Price stability – zero inflation – *is* possible. It is not all that long since we had it in Britain, at least for a short time. Between October 1958 and May 1960 the Retail Price Index did not move by more than one point in either direction. Inflation has certainly not gone on continuously since the beginning of time. According to Deane and Cole (*British Economic Growth, 1688–1939*) the price level at the outbreak of the First World War was about in line with what it was in 1660, so far as it is possible to make a comparison. The price level did rise from time to time during that period, usually because of wars, but prices then fell back so that the trend was roughly steady. The problems have certainly become more difficult as a result of the upward trend in prices since the last war. But we should not conclude that we shall never again be able to do better than we have in the 1970s.

It follows from the damage done by inflation that alternative policies which compromise with it must be rejected. They might seem to provide short-term relief but they would not solve any of our long-run problems.

Short- and long-run causes

What then are the right weapons for the fight against inflation? This question cannot be answered until we are clear about the causes of inflation. Here I would distinguish between non-monetary influences on the price level, such as changes in commodity prices and indirect tax changes, and the slower acting influence of the rate of monetary growth. All kinds of shocks can affect prices in the short run; in some cases they may change the relationship between money and prices permanently, but the evidence suggests that over the medium term the velocity of circulation is relatively stable and predictable.

From this it follows that to control inflation on a permanent basis it is necessary to control the rate of monetary growth. One can, of course, hold down individual prices for a short time by a variety of direct controls and subsidies. From 1972 to 1974 I was the minister responsible for the design and implementation of price control. My Treasury colleague, Lord Cockfield, was Chairman of the Price Commission, which we established. And we learned, as did others, from that experience, that price controls are neither an acceptable nor an effective way of achieving a *permanent* reduction in the rate of inflation. Price controls create their own tensions, by preventing the adjustment of *relative* prices, which is essential to the proper functioning of the economy. Where prices are held down by subsidy, as has repeatedly been attempted, particularly in the case of nationalised industry prices, the burden of the subsidy rises over time and ultimately must place an excessive strain on public finance. In short, if the underlying causes of inflation are not tackled a policy of price control can only check price rises for a short time.

What is needed is a framework which permits relative prices to adjust to their market-clearing levels against the background of an overall restraint of the general price level. Such a system promotes economic efficiency and freedom.

The need for monetary policy

The framework for restraining the general price level which has been judged desirable, here and in many other countries, is control of the supply of money. In a general way this was well understood by David Hume, even before Adam Smith. There has been no sudden blinding flash on the road to Chicago. If there is too much money in circulation, prices will rise. If we do not want that to happen – and I have already explained why I am sure we should resist it – then we have to keep monetary growth under control.

Some people in Britain still imagine that this government is in some way eccentric in re-emphasing this truth. But, as Alexandre Lamfalussy of the Bank for International Settlements observed the other day, western industrial countries have been demonstrating an 'increasing, and in some cases dominant, reliance on monetary policy in fighting inflation'. The continental Europeans recognise the point very readily: they do not seem to suffer the same intensity of theological debate about monetary policy as we do in this country, or as to a lesser extent do the North Americans. Consider, for example, the evidence submitted by the Bundesbank in response to the enquiry conducted by our own Parliamentary Select Committee. They rightly insist that a sound monetary policy promotes growth. 'The Federal Government and the Bundesbank are both firmly convinced that in the long run a consistent policy of tight and stable money creates the best conditions for satisfactory economic growth.'

What is perhaps more recent is the setting of explicit monetary targets. But the evolution of such targets has been quite a natural development. When currencies were tied to the gold standard, monetary restraint was more or less automatic. If prices rose too rapidly in one country a balance of payments deficit would ensue. The country would lose gold across the exchanges, with a consequent reduction in money supply and so in ability to finance the going level of activity. The result was a strong downward pressure on inflation. The fixed exchange rate system effectively produced the same result: countries which inflated too fast had to cut demand in order to maintain the external value of their currencies and prevent the total loss of their reserves. Thus, for most of the nineteenth and twentieth centuries monetary discipline was imposed from without, via the linking of the currency to an external standard.

By the early 1970s, however, the strains imposed by inflation, disparities in economic performance and the weakness of the dollar forced the abandonment of the fixed exchange rate system. A floating rate system became necessary. And thus it also became necessary for individual countries to make explicit the implicit monetary control that had been exercised by the old system. Hence the significance of monetary targets, or – for those smaller countries which prefer this approach – the objective of keeping the domestic currency in a fixed relationship with the currency of a major economy.

In Britain the lesson was learnt rather painfully. Monetary growth was allowed to accelerate rapidly in 1972 and 1973 under the impression that, now the restrictions of the fixed exchange rate discipline were gone, this was the way to increase output. By 1975 inflation, helped by the rise in the price of oil, had risen above 25 per cent. A sterling crisis ensued in 1976. And so my predecessor, following discussions with the IMF, realised the need for monetary targets and restraint of public borrowing. By 1977 Mr Healey was prepared to say that 'we cannot master inflation unless we have control of the money supply'. And in the following year Mr Callaghan explained that: 'it was against this background' – that is to say the earlier rapid monetary growth and inflation – 'that the government took the decision to put the money supply under proper control and then to publish quantified monetary targets'.

Thus monetary targets were already an established part of British economic policy when this government took office. The important innovation that we have made is to set out these targets for a longer period ahead. If monetary policy is to provide a framework of stability for the operation of the economy, it must clearly be sustained and permanent. That is the reason for the medium-term financial strategy, which is now in its second year of operation.

The last government also taught us the lesson that, having moved to a system of monetary targets, you cannot have it both ways and also hold the exchange rate at a particular level. If any inconsistency emerges, the monetary targets have to come first. The Governor described in 1978 how this had happened in the previous year: 'A time came when we felt unable any longer to maintain full control over the growth of the money stock without setting the exchange rate free to float – concern about exports notwithstanding. The decision made in those circumstances emphasises our commitment, in conditions of conflict, to controlling the monetary aggregates.'

The similar experience of other countries suggests that international capital flows are almost always too strong to resist for very long. Not only has it proved impossible to meet a particular exchange rate objective, but domestic monetary control has been compromised by the attempt. In the end there is little alternative but to leave exchange rates to be determined by the balance of forces in the market. So despite the importance of the exchange rate – both in its influence on the rate of inflation and its effect on industry's competitiveness – there are no magical means open to the government to manipulate it. No doubt we could reduce the current nominal exchange rate by pursuing more inflationary policies. But that would not help competitiveness. The only solution to our competitiveness problem is to adjust our costs to the exchange rate, not the other way round. Our wages and prices must be directed towards those which rule internationally. I shall say more on this in a moment.

The conduct of monetary policy

Given then that the supply of money has the central place in our anti-inflation strategy what has been our experience with the policy over the last two years? The first point to make is that this has been a time of upheaval in the world economy. The 1979 increase in the world price of oil – as serious as that of 1973–4 – has created worldwide recession and increased inflationary pressures. The oil price increase has almost certainly magnified the strength of sterling. All this has made economic management over the last two years more difficult.

Inflation has, however, been coming down. It was on an upward trend when we came to office and reached a peak of nearly 22 per cent a year ago. But since then it has declined steadily. The annual increase in the RPI is down to 12.5 per cent and we forecast single figures next year. This deceleration of prices appears very clearly to have come as a response to tight financial conditions. Yet the recorded rate of growth of £M3 – our target aggregate – was well above the target range last year. This has led some – including distinguished members of this university – to criticise the authorities for maintaining an insufficiently tight monetary policy. But other indicators do not support this criticism: the behaviour of the narrower monetary aggregates, the strength of the £, the level of real interest rates and the fall in inflation itself. So most commentators, and indeed the Treasury and Civil Service Select Committee, rather prefer our view that 'monetary conditions have been tight'.

There were many special factors at work last year, over and above the unwinding of years of distortion when the Supplementary Special Deposit Scheme was ended. In particular, the nature of the recession itself involved severe pressure on company finances. That is why it was particularly important to take account of all the various monetary aggregates, and of the level of real interest rates, in reaching decisions about Minimum Lending Rate. We have always recognised the need for wider judgment of this kind as, for example, in the Green Paper on monetary control published a little over a year ago.

The use of other indicators in the determination of short-term interest rates does not affect the fact that over the medium term there are great advantages in using for target purposes a broad aggregate like £M3, with its clear link with most aspects of macro-economic policy, especially public expenditure and taxation.

The Governor in his 1978 lecture expressed the view that 'in the present state of the art, we have chosen best in selecting £M3'.

Techniques of monetary control

Our approach to monetary control has been guided by three propositions. First, we have learnt that control cannot safely depend upon direct restriction applied to institutions. For with a financial system as well developed, and as closely integrated with world financial markets, as our own, control so achieved may well be control in name only. This is why we have dispensed with the corset.

Secondly, rather than depend upon controls of that kind we prefer to rely on instruments which have their effect on underlying monetary conditions – fiscal policy, funding and short-term interest rates. I shall say a little about fiscal policy in a moment. As for funding, we have already made two major improvements – the National Savings initiative and the introduction of an indexed gilt. We met our target for National Savings last year and are making a good start towards this year's objective of £3 billion. The indexed gilt can be seen as a major advance, which will significantly increase the range of options available for the conduct of debt sales. It emphasises our confidence that inflation will be reduced and will, when more indexed stock is issued, diminish uncertainty about future real interest rates.

The third proposition has been that we should follow an evolutionary approach. The extensive and interesting public debate which followed the Green Paper on Monetary Control confirmed that there were improvements to be made to the monetary system, and that control of the monetary base had some attractions. But to make such a step would be a major change with widespread implications for many parts of the financial system. Rather than move precipitately our approach has been to proceed step by step with all deliberate speed, making changes which are desirable in themselves and which will enable us to learn more about the way in which alternative methods of monetary control might operate.

Supporting policies

I have never believed that the setting of monetary targets can be enough by itself. There are other requirements. First of all, fiscal policy must be compatible with our monetary policy. Experience shows that it is virtually impossible to finance an excessive public sector deficit without adding to the money supply. Even were it possible, it could jeopardise success against inflation by adding to nominal incomes or precipitating a fall in the exchange rate. Excessive public borrowing could also, in some circumstances, increase the transitional costs of reducing inflation. The high interest rates which might be necessary to finance an excessive PSBR would bear most heavily on companies, leading to reductions in investment, and stockbuilding. If this more than offset the direct effect on aggregate demand of the PSBR itself, there would be higher unemployment in the short run as well as a weakening of growth prospects in the longer run. It is a measure of our determination to achieve a PSBR consistent with a lower monetary target that we were prepared to increase taxes to the extent that we did in the last Budget. The case for keeping taxes down in order to maintain incentives was in conflict with the government's anti-inflation objective. It was the fight against inflation that had to come first.

Monetary discipline must then be supported by fiscal discipline. That is a proposition that would be endorsed by virtually everyone who has experience of operating policy in finance ministries and central banks throughout the world. We indicated that we accept this constraint when we published in the Medium Term Financial Strategy an illustrative path for the public sector borrowing requirement, which we believe is consistent with the achievement of our targets for £M3. The path for the PSBR is not intended as a target in its own right. I repeat this because at times our approach to the PSBR has been characterised as much more rigid than in fact it is.

This leads me to digress briefly on the important and topical question of the treatment of investment by the nationalised industries. It has been suggested that, merely by waving a statistical wand, and decreeing that borrowing to finance investment for those industries should be excluded from the PSBR, then the existing restraints could be relaxed, if not abandoned. The truth is quite different. We have set targets for the money supply, and we do not intend to achieve them by some financial sleight of hand which distorts financial markets and raises the velocity of circulation. This means, in effect, that there is something rather like a cash limit applicable to the whole economy, not just the public sector. The monetary targets have implications for total nominal income and expenditure. These constraints are essential to the fight against inflation and that, rather than any target path for the PSBR, is the ultimate constraint on policy.

This does not mean that increased investment by nationalised industry can never be appropriate. What it does mean is that new projects must have demonstrably a better claim for a share in total spending than some other spending they will replace. Normally we would expect to find the offset elsewhere in the public sector. If not, it has to come from the private sector, whether in private investment or in consumer spending. There is, alas, nothing to be had without cost.

Pay

But it is not only government decisions which determine the side-effects of the anti-inflation policy – and the nature and extent of the adjustment costs. There is certainly room within the monetary targets for real growth in the economy. During this financial year we expect inflation to drop to 8 per cent, compared with a monetary target of 6–10 per cent and an upward trend in velocity of 1–2 per cent a year. But it is the response of individuals which will determine how this growth in money supply and the growth in money income which it permits will be divided between price inflation and a rise in real output. It is crucial that pay, prices and other variables should all adjust together, so as to achieve a satisfactory balance, within this 'national cash limit', between lower inflation on the one hand and more output and employment on the other.

Wages and salaries account for about two-thirds of the national income; they are the dominant share of business costs. If pay increases are too large, there is an inevitable risk that real activity will be squeezed by financial restraint: the result would be high unemployment and low, or even negative, growth. We have in any case been taking too much out of the economy in pay in recent years and leaving far too little for profits and investment. The real rate of return on capital employed in Britain in 1980 – excluding North Sea companies – was less than 3 per cent, a pitiful figure compared to the rate of return in countries like Japan. Moreover, since our pay rises have been much faster than those of our overseas competitors, further job losses have come through loss of competitiveness. Wage costs per unit of output almost quadrupled between 1970 and 1980 in the UK. In Japan and Germany they rose by only 70 per cent. Even recently, domestic labour costs have been a larger factor in our reduced competitiveness than the strength of sterling.

There is then no shortage of reasons for sustained moderation in pay bargaining. If increases in unemployment are to be avoided, then a progressive reduction in the rate of monetary growth does need to be accompanied by a more-or-less corresponding reduction in the rate of growth of average money incomes, including pay. It is this insight which, perhaps understandably, prompts people to call for an 'incomes policy'. That case has been accepted by each of the last three governments. As a member of the Heath government, I was closely involved in the administration of the policy. And, as with price controls, I came to learn that that kind of policy for incomes was not a sustainable answer to the problem. In a speech in 1976 I set out a list of objections to any kind of rigid incomes policy. I think they still hold good today. The first objection to the setting of wages targets (or 'wooden norms', as Lord Robbins described them) is that they seriously distort and could, over time, destroy the functioning of the labour market. Changes in relative wage rates are, as I said then, the lights that wink at each other across a market place in which hundreds of thousands of people change their jobs each month. The second major objection is a political one. If the state itself attempts to simulate the market place and to plan relativities throughout the economy, then important freedoms are diminished. The third objection is very practical. It has not proved possible, despite a series of ingenious attempts, to evolve a practical and durable method of making and enforcing these non-market judgments. The fourth objection to the establishment of an institutional incomes policy is the greatly increased leverage the trade unions (or their leaders) acquire over many matters that are properly the responsibility of the elected government. Under a variety of administrations the unions have exacted their own price for formal 'acceptance' of an incomes policy. They have secured major changes in policy, in the fields of taxation, prices, industrial relations law and other matters, often with harmful consequences. In the event, the risk of conflict between government and trade unions has, if anything, been increased.

None of this is to deny that government does have an important role in improving the processes of price and pay adjustment. It is certainly necessary to improve the functioning of the labour market so that the pay rates that emerge are not such as to price people out of jobs. The monopoly power of large trade unions is a major impediment. The closed shop, the law relating to picketing and other trade union privileges are all factors unbalancing the labour market and contributing to higher unemployment.

Since 1969, successive governments have sought by legislation and other means to tackle these problems. Last year's Employment Act was the latest move. It will be easier to make the further progress that is necessary if we can secure more widespread understanding of the crucial link between labour market rigidity – and indeed market rigidities of other kinds – and unemployment. For there are other distortions that have contributed to the rise in unemployment: the differential between rates of pay for skilled and unskilled workers, and between young people and adults. For example, in Germany apprentice wages by and large progress from about 30 per cent of adult rates to about 50 per cent during the apprenticeship. Here the range is usually much higher: in 1979 the figures for engineering were 42.5 per cent to 80 per cent and for the building industry 50 per cent to 90 per cent. The relation between benefit levels and rates of pay is another factor: this is why we are making a number of changes in relative benefit levels and in their tax treatment. And why we are seeking to reduce various other obstacles to labour mobility, in the housing market, for example.

Besides reducing labour market rigidities, we also have a responsibility to spread greater understanding of the implications of monetary and fiscal policies, and to influence inflation expectations. As I explained in a speech in 1975, government's intention to reduce the rate of monetary growth 'needs to be spelt out in a coherent stabilisation policy, intended to spread over three or four years'. This was the thinking that lay behind our publication of the Medium Term Financial Strategy. I was interested to see a recent study by the Hamburg Institute, which attributed Germany's success in containing inflation after the second oil shock to widespread belief in the determination of the authorities to stick to their monetary targets.

We have also attempted to spell out the consequences for employment of pay settlements not consistent with the monetary targets. There is now clear evidence of this realisation, particularly in the level of private sector pay settlements. People are learning – as they have in other countries – that the real value of their incomes cannot always be guaranteed. Past rises in the retail prices index are having less influence than the realities of the current situation. The task now is to maintain that process of education and perhaps above all to extend its impact within the public sector.

No one can be satisfied with the present system of wage determination in the public sector. The problem is an intractable one. My own ideas on this subject have changed more than once over the years. In 1974 many of us thought that we might be able to rely exclusively upon an independent agency to determine relativities in the public sector. By 1975 I was disposed to argue for indexation of public sector wages, to avoid friction at a time of high inflation. Six years on we can all see difficulties with each of those ideas.

But what I have said all along is that the government must have a policy for the pay of its own employees. In the last resort it is only government that can and must determine the resources that can be set aside for pay in the public service. We are now ready to embark once again upon the task of creating a workable and acceptable pay system for the civil service. We do not rule out the possibility of outside comparisons as one factor to be taken into account; but any system must ensure that pay rises take proper account of what the taxpayer can afford. The old comparability system failed to do this. Creating a new scheme will take some time. But the public sector must continue, along with the private sector, to play its full part in the necessary task of gearing down pay and prices and so improving the prospects for unemployment.

The same general need applies to the nationalised industries as well. The most obvious way of improving the level of nationalised industry investment, for example, is to change the balance between current and capital spending in the industries themselves. Part of the answer lies in seeking to strengthen the external disciplines on wages and other costs: by opening some industries to a measure of competition, by returning all or part of others to the private sector, by referring individual industries to the Monopolies and Mergers Commission, and by setting firm limits on external financing. The problem is magnified by the tendency of wages in this sector to move very closely together. Obviously we have not yet got the complete answer.

I have long believed that the chances of securing greater responsibility on the part of wage bargainers will be enhanced by as much openness as possible in the government's approach to economic management. The undue influence and disproportionate power of particular interest groups needs to be exposed by wider and more open consultation. It is only by making clear the nature of the national cash limit and the demands applied to it that we can discuss with sufficient effect the influence and role that each of the major participants can play. This is why we have tried within the framework of NEDC to promote wider discussion on these matters. We do this not with a view to striking a deal of any kind, but gradually to promote a wider ranging discussion where each party is helped to realise the claims that others have upon the economy. There is still a very long way to go. It may be that government itself has not yet been open enough. Trade unions too must continue to develop their willingness to join others in recognising the need for open and informed discussion of pay and competitiveness.

The NEDC then has opportunities of this kind to develop its role. So too do bodies such as the Treasury and Civil Service Select Committee, whose role is to provide a non-partisan commentary on government policy. Indeed it could be particularly instructive if the Committee now felt disposed to study the case for constructive reforms of the labour market and the case for pay moderation in the context of the need for improving competitiveness and controlling the costs of the public sector.

Removing other rigidities

But it is not only pay which needs to adjust more quickly if we are to minimise the costs of reducing inflation. The same need applies to prices. Thus the progress we have made on the supply side of the economy, which will have beneficial long-term effects, will also ease the process of transition. We have removed government controls – on prices as well as wages, dividends and the movement of currency across the exchanges – and we are taking other steps to strengthen the forces of competition, for example by widening the scope of the Monopolies and Mergers Commission. The combination of monetary deceleration and monopoly pricing could spell only loss of output and loss of employment. But if prices can adjust more freely to changed market conditions, this difficulty is greatly reduced.

Conclusion

Squeezing inflation out from an economy which has become accustomed to high rates over a period of years cannot be an easy or painless task. We have made a good start, but we still have a long way to go. It is not sufficient to apply anti-inflationary policies for a brief period. That would not permanently conquer inflation and it would condemn us to a continuation of our long economic decline. It will be particularly tempting to relax our vigilance as the economy begins to grow again, to fall back into bad old habits and throw away the hard-won gains. All my experience leads me to the conviction that we must resist this temptation. Proper monetary control must be maintained and the inflationary mentality must be eradicated – in government, and among individuals. When we have done that we will find that low inflation or even price stability need not be painful. Indeed I am convinced that the defeat of inflation will prove the key to the regeneration of our economy.

POSTSCRIPT: THE 364 ECONOMISTS – AFTER TWO DECADES

Some sentences stand out as the most fearful hostages to fortune. Yet others are graphic reminders of the critical battles which raged at the time. And some propositions, surprisingly, remain even today the subject of near-theological dispute.

Let me start with the critical battles of the day. The third Mais Lecture was delivered just two months after my most unpopular Budget (of March 1981). The 'fight against inflation', which had peaked at 22 per cent just a year before, was indeed of the highest importance. As in most other developed economies, monetary policy was playing an increasingly dominant role in that battle. Targets for progressive reduction in the rate of monetary growth had been set, as required, for the second and following years of my Medium Term Financial Strategy. Notwithstanding the depth of the recession we were experiencing, I had proposed substantial tax increases to reduce future public sector borrowing to levels consistent with the lower monetary targets.

All hell had broken loose. Cabinet colleagues were critical, backbenchers openly hostile. And the memorable 364 economists (including five of the six surviving former chief economic advisers to Her Majesty's government) had asserted, in a letter to *The Times*, that:

> There is no basis in economic theory or supporting evidence for the Government's present policies . . . There are alternative policies . . . The time has come to reject monetarist policies and consider urgently which alternative offers the best hope of sustained economic recovery.

Their timing could not have been more apt. The fall in national output came to an end in that very quarter. Over the next eight years, real GDP grew by an average of 3.2 per cent per annum. (In my Mansion House speech that autumn I was emboldened to joke that an economist is a man who knows 364 ways of making love – but who doesn't know any women.) By the end of my last year in the Treasury (June 1983) all the measured monetary aggregates were, for the first time ever, growing at rates within their target range and inflation was down to 5 per cent – lower than at any time since 1970.

The most important lesson which I draw from this experience is that our success in taming inflation (and in laying the foundations for sustainable growth) sprang directly from our determination to reject – in theory and in practice – the only specific advice of the mistaken 364, that 'the time has come to reject monetarist policies'. And in all my subsequent years of travel round the globe, I have been delighted (though not surprised) to find this lesson applied in virtually every economy.

In Peking's Great Hall of the People, for example, Paul Volcker and I (as members of a Japanese bank's advisory council) listened with pleasure when the Chairman of the National People's Congress, Qiao Shi, on being asked to outline his country's economic policy, opened with the words: 'We start from a prudently strict monetary policy.'

In Russia and Ukraine, again for example, it is axiomatic that inflation soars within months (yes: the equation is much simpler, and swifter, in such 'basic' economies) of any release of money by a hard-pressed central bank. And so on, from Chile to the Czech Republic, from Italy to India. I have found myself saluted in surprising places, as the man whose 1981 budget really did put monetary policy on the map!

Hence my astonishment, indeed dismay, at the gusto with which some monetary theologians are still seeking to determine which, if any, of those who managed economic policy in the 1980s now deserve to be categorised as 'genuine monetarists'. Leading this hunt, alas, is Professor Gordon Pepper, whose insights more than two decades ago were so influential in guiding Margaret Thatcher, Keith Joseph, myself and many others towards an understanding of the monetary imperative. In a forthcoming book with Michael Oliver,[1] Pepper distinguishes the 'genuine' sheep from the 'political' or 'pragmatic' goats. Some pioneers of monetary targeting – Denis Healey and Douglas Wass, for example – qualify (probably without much complaint from them) as self-confessed sceptics. Both Nigel Lawson and I, and the senior Treasury official most continuously involved, Peter Middleton, are all rated no more than 'political' monetarists. Terry Burns, Chief Economic Adviser throughout the period is, curiously, described simply as an 'international monetarist'. The only 'genuine' true believers are identified as Margaret Thatcher and Keith Joseph – perhaps significantly the two who were furthest from the coal-face of economic policy management.

It is only by studying the whole of the Pepper–Oliver text that one discovers why their 'genuine' believers turn out to be so few in number. For their central conclusion is that policy under Thatcher was no more than 'an exercise in political monetarism'. Why? Because, in their view, money could not and cannot be controlled by existing instruments. They conclude, re-affirming, one suspects, their long-revered premise, that 'the only remaining solution [is] monetary base control' (MBC).

Margaret Thatcher was attracted by that view, when Pepper (and one or two others) vigorously pressed the same case upon us at the time. We were then told that, by adopting MBC, we should be following not only the Swiss but also Paul Volcker's US example. Significantly, Pepper now acknowledges that this US 'monetary base' experiment (announced by Volcker in 1979) proved, on closer examination, to give no support to his case.

It may be thought, therefore, that I did justice to the case for MBC (which had been rejected throughout by those who would have to manage it, in the Bank of England), by publishing a Green Paper on the subject. And, after the ensuing public debate, telling my Mais Lecture audience that although the idea 'had some attractions', it would be 'a major change with widespread implications for many parts of the financial system'. Which is, I dare say, one solid reason why MBC has not been adopted as the foundation of monetary policy in any major economy.

In light of this analysis, when I find myself described – as I was (before Pepper), by the late Edmund Dell,[2] – as 'a naive monetarist', I am a shade more likely to shrink from the word 'monetarist' than I am from the word 'naive'. Naiveté, after all, is often not a million miles from common-sense! The very concept of 'believing in monetarism' – even of the 'ism' itself? – has a quasi-religious flavour, which few, if any, political or economic concepts deserve. 'A less naive Chancellor', concludes Dell, 'might have done a great deal less well . . . There is no evidence that a wiser Chancellor could have more sensitively modulated the severity of his action, if he was serious in his attack on inflation.'

On the basis of that generous, but very practical, assessment, I turn now to look for a moment at the way ahead, starting from the most outstanding of those 'hostages to fortune', which I mentioned in the first sentence of this note. For in my lecture I commended without qualification 'the lesson that, having moved to a system of monetary targets, you cannot have it both ways and also hold the exchange rate at a particular level'. Later experience very quickly reminded me that that was certainly too absolutist an assertion. I had indeed forgotten too that one of the secrets of worldwide economic success throughout the first (post-war) quarter century of my adult life was not only freedom from domestic inflation but also prolonged relative stability in the international value of our currency – thanks, of course, to Bretton Woods. As objectives for businessman and common citizen alike, international as well as domestic currency stability remains, as it has always been, highly desirable. No wonder, therefore, that the then Federal Reserve Chairman, Arthur Burns (Milton Friedman's tutor, no less), had within six years of the collapse of Bretton Woods concluded in favour of a return to what he expressly called a 'rule of law'[3] in the field of international financial affairs.

And within two years of that insight, the European Community had produced, as at least a regional response, the similarly 'fixed but adjustable' exchange rate mechanism of the European Monetary System. The incoming Thatcher government specifically committed itself to 'look for ways in which Britain can take her rightful place within' that system. And in the 1978 debate on the EMS itself, I had as Shadow Chancellor emphasised the need for international as well as national rules 'designed to eliminate inflation within national boundaries and to secure as far as possible stability between national currency units'.[4] During my time as Chancellor, however – still facing inflation well into the teens and having just myself ended forty years of exchange control – I endorsed the widespread view that the perception of sterling as an oil-linked – and thus very volatile – currency at that stage justified a cautious approach.

By 1985, however, the scene had changed substantially. The Governor of the Bank of England, the Chancellor, Nigel Lawson, and his predecessor, supported by all but one of our senior colleagues, were convinced that the time was indeed ripe for us to organise our accession to the exchange rate mechanism. The Prime Minister, alas, took the opposite view until five years too late, when she was persuaded, in 1990 to take the UK into the ERM, something we ended up doing for the wrong reasons, at the wrong time and, above all, at the wrong rate.

I remain convinced that if Britain had been an ERM participant, from 1985 onwards, in the design and management of the EU's monetary arrangements, Britain's own economic policy would have been less at risk, easier to manage and more successful. Moreover, I believe too that the wider EU approach towards economic and monetary union – the entire Delors project – would have been more broadly based, less automatistic and also more successful. Perhaps above all, Europe, Britain and the Conservative party would have been spared the gravely demoralising impact of Black Wednesday and all its consequences. After seven years in the System, the pound would have been much less exposed and Britain's Chancellor more streetwise and persuasive. More attention would in those circumstances have been paid to a reminder from the Chancellor that the ERM remained, like Bretton Woods, a 'fixed but adjustable' system. As the economic impact of German reunification became increasingly clear, revaluation of the Deutschmark could have been convincingly presented as not only acceptable but essential.

Remarkably, indeed almost perversely, the demise of the ERM was seized upon – for example, by George Soros – as strengthening the case for a single currency.

Samuel Brittan has made the same point: 'With the single currency and a single central bank [the] one way speculative option could not occur'.[5] This is, of course, only one of the economic advantages that can be delivered by a currency union. The rupee zone, for example, has been of enduring and enormous benefit to India's billion citizens. Inhabitants of the former Soviet Union have all mourned the loss of stability which prevailed throughout the old rouble zone. So too, former members of Britain's own sterling area – not least the two neighbours of Britain and Ireland.

I am not myself convinced of the other lesson which some seek to draw from history, that effective monetary union requires an unacceptable degree of political centralisation for its success. The euro does not lead to a European federation. 'Europe', as Professor David Currie has pointed out, 'is developing a new political form, based on cooperation between nation states where it is in their joint interests, where it is their mutual self-interest . . . buttressed by a framework of law . . . The euro both embodies this deeper cooperation and greatly expands the scope for it.'[6]

What about the 'loss of sovereignty' involved in losing so-called 'control' of our own exchange rate? I grieve much less than some others about this. Neither Margaret Thatcher nor I felt much in charge during the years when together we learnt that, in her words, 'you can't buck the market'. Over our first five years in office, the pound oscillated between US$2.40 and near parity. I thus find it easy to accept Willem Buiter's judgment that 'a national currency and independent national monetary policy are . . . a costly way of expressing preference for national sovereignty'.[7] Paul Volcker reinforces this argument, by pointing out that 'inward investors would prefer a market of three hundred million people with a predictable currency to a market of sixty million with a volatile one'.[8]

In that respect, the European economic environment changed fundamentally – and not least for Britain – when the single currency came into existence in January 1999. Staying outside emphatically does not offer Britain a continuation of the status quo ante. For insiders, the greatest benefit will be the elimination of exchange rate volatility. For Britain, too, joining the euro would mean that at least 80 per cent of all trade by British businesses – in Britain as well as throughout the euro-zone – will be carried out in one currency. Outside, however, the danger is that sterling will become a 'punchball currency', bouncing, as it is bound to do, between the larger dollar and euro blocs.

This is not the place to rehearse all the arguments for British membership of the single currency.[9] But it has given me the welcome opportunity to explain my long-standing belief that there is no inconsistency between my unqualified practical endorsement – not only during my time as Chancellor – of the central importance of monetary policy and my present strong support for the cause of a single currency over a wider than national economy.

Something like that kind of twin stability has been the goal of economic managers almost since the beginning of time.

Notes

Lord Howe of Aberavon, CH, QC, is former Chancellor of the Exchequer (1979–83), Foreign Secretary (1983–9) and Deputy Prime Minister (1989–90).

1 *Monetarism Under Thatcher – Lessons for the Future*, to be published by Edward Elgar in 2001.
2 In his excellently balanced book, *The Chancellors* (HarperCollins) London, 1996.
3 Address at Columbia University, April 1997.
4 This should lay to rest the oft-repeated but fanciful suggestion that my commitment to international monetary stability results only from my exposure, after 1983, to the 'corrupting' influence of the Foreign Office.
5 *Lessons for EMU from the History of Monetary Unions*, IEA, p. 43.
6 *Lessons for EMU*, IEA, op. cit. pp. 49–50.
7 *Financial Times*, 17 June, 1999.
8 LSE Magazine, June 1998, p. 42.
9 I have argued this more fully in, for example, 'Europe: single market or political union?', *Journal of Economic Affairs* (IEA) December 1999 and 'Say it Loud', *The Parliamentary Monitor*, Vol. 8, No. 9.

5 The instruments of monetary policy

The Rt Hon Robin Leigh-Pemberton (UK)

£31 E52
E43

It is a pleasure and privilege for me to have been invited to deliver this year's Mais Lecture. I am not, of course, the first Governor of the Bank of England to have been honoured in this way. My predecessor Lord Richardson, gave the inaugural lecture in a distinguished series as long ago as February 1978, and I should like, if I may, to take a quotation from his text as my point of departure this evening.

Policy objectives

Speaking against the background of high and variable inflation throughout the industrial world, and not least in this country, Lord Richardson described the essential aim of monetary policy in the following terms:

> Our first order of business must . . . be to restore confidence in the framework of the system. The crucial economic decisions, for example to undertake investment, involve an act of faith in the future. That faith has been undermined by uncertainty – uncertainty . . . about the future value of money, externally and internally.

Almost a decade later, maintaining confidence in the future value of money remains our first order of business. There is now, I believe, a much wider understanding that this is the limited, but vital, role which monetary policy can play in contributing to the more effective working of the economy. It is a necessary – though not in itself sufficient – foundation for the achievement of the more fundamental aims of economic policy – a strong and growing economy and higher employment and living standards.

The progress made against inflation has been substantial. From well over 20 per cent at times in the 1970s, the annual inflation rate, measured by the Retail Price Index, dropped decisively below 10 per cent in 1982 and has averaged less than 5 per cent over the last four years. Currently the underlying rate is around 4 per cent, but that is still above the inflation rate in most of our major competitors, and still sufficient to cause the value of money to halve in less than twenty years.

At the same time as inflation has been falling, output has recovered. Since 1981, after a severe recession – which was instrumental in breaking the inflationary psychology of the 1970s, however regrettable in many other respects – output has grown at an annual rate of almost 3 per cent. This is close to what would have been regarded, not very long ago, as the limit imposed by the growth of the economy's capacity, and the longest period of sustained expansion since the previous period of relatively low inflation in the 1960s.

Despite this progress towards achieving the ultimate objective of monetary policy, we have been less successful, at a more technical level, in achieving our *intermediate* aims. The policy framework for the past decade has been one of published targets for the growth of the money supply, based upon the expectation of a reasonably stable and predictable relationship between monetary growth and nominal income. In practice, for reasons which I explored at some length in a lecture at the University of Loughborough in October last year, and associated in part with the rapid change affecting our financial structure and our financial behaviour, this relationship, particularly as it applies to £M3 – our chosen measure of broad money – has proved less reliable than was initially hoped.

The simple, easily understood, rule which a £M3 target represented was no doubt always an oversimplification. Indeed this was acknowledged, as the policy framework evolved, through the addition of further targets and the progressive elaboration of some of the many other factors necessarily 'taken into account' in the real-world process of policy decision-making.

Initially, in the high-inflation environment of the time, that oversimplification served a useful purpose, adding credibility to the authorities' counter-inflationary resolve. Subsequently, frequent redefinition of the targetted aggregate and upward revision of the target range – often missed even so – resulted in public confusion rather than confidence, and it was for this reason that we have not set a broad money target for this year. But I would caution you against reading too much into this. In practice, little of substance has changed. The £M3 rule has never operated in a purely mechanical way: we have always been prepared to override its signals in the light of other, contrary, evidence on the state of monetary conditions. Equally, the absence of a £M3 target emphatically does not mean that the behaviour of broad money and credit is regarded as of any less importance than before. We continue trying to understand, and to explain publicly, the influences on broad money and their implications for policy. The reality, with or without any particular target, is that policy is directed pragmatically, on the basis of the evidence from a whole range of economic and financial indicators, towards its end objective; and the world is in my judgment too complex for it to be otherwise.

Given this reality, public confidence in policy is likely to depend upon the deeds of the authorities rather than on their words, and I am sure that the Chancellor of the Exchequer, Nigel Lawson, had this in mind when he spoke of the future rate of inflation as the judge and jury. After the experience of the 1970s it is hardly surprising that such confidence should have taken years to re-establish: but we are beginning to see it now, though we are continually conscious that it would quickly be destroyed if we were to depart from our intended counter-inflationary course.

Policy instruments

Let me then turn to the deeds of the monetary authorities, and their handling of the instruments of policy, which is the main substance of my lecture.

Outside commentators on monetary developments sometimes create the impression that those responsible for operating monetary policy sit in front of a battery of switches and levers, each one of which will produce a precise and certain response in some area of the financial markets or directly in some more distant part of the economy. I can assure you that there is only one switch in my room, and that is the light switch.

In practice we have only a very limited range of instruments though they can often be used tactically in different ways, and their effects can vary depending upon the particular circumstances prevailing at the time.

Controls

I leave to one side possibilities in the field of direct controls. I do this not for any doctrinal reason, but for the severely practical one that they are rarely effective in dealing with the source rather than the symptom of the problem. It is very tempting, and not at all difficult, to invent a control to suppress almost any financial development. Such developments are rarely a cause for concern on their own but as portending unfavourable consequences elsewhere. To stop such developments may do little to avert the unwelcome consequences even if it does disrupt the relationship on which the forecast was based. Money is the most fungible of all commodities and our experience over a long period is that the effect of direct controls is largely to divert financial flows, typically into less efficient channels, rather than to achieve any deeper purpose. These difficulties can only be greater now with the disappearance of traditional barriers between different financial functions and of distinctions between different financial activities, and with the merging of national markets into a global whole. Controls in one area would either be ineffective or spread rapidly as further and further controls were introduced to head off successive leakages from those already in place.

Fiscal policy

I leave on one side too the government's overall fiscal policy. There is no question that co-ordination of fiscal and monetary policy has an important role to play in the effectiveness of policy overall and we are fortunate that the arrangements in this country adequately provide for this. The nature of the close working relationship between the Treasury and the Bank ensures considerable consistency of purpose. In recent years the Medium Term Financial Strategy has formalised this consistency as it relates to the coherence of the financial consequence of fiscal policy with the government's monetary objectives. But at most points during the year the monetary policy operators have to take the fiscal stance, like so many other economic factors, as given.

The instruments we are left with then are the terms on which we provide liquidity to the banking system, government funding policy (or as some prefer long-term interest rates), and foreign exchange market intervention. As I shall explain, there are practical limits to the extent to which we can rely upon either funding policy or intervention, as well as limits to their effectiveness. To impose quantitative restrictions on the supply of liquidity to the banks would, as my predecessor pointed out in his Mais Lecture, inevitably risk unacceptable volatility in short-term interest rates. Thus, when you come right down to it, the only effective instrument of monetary policy is the short-term interest rate itself.

Interest rates

I embark upon this next part of my lecture with some trepidation. Generations of eminent economists have tried to identify the effects of interest rates on the economy, producing many valuable insights into a wide variety of different transmission mechanisms, but little overall, practical, consensus and little empirical support for their particular views. I say this without critical intent. As in other areas of economics, behaviour in response to interest rate changes is probably influenced at least as much by people's expectations about the future – in relation to prices as well as interest rates themselves, and I recall here again the passage from Lord Richardson's lecture with which I started – as by perceptions of the cost of money at any particular time. And expectations of course are notoriously difficult to observe, measure or model. Interest rates are almost invariably changed in response to an unanticipated development elsewhere in the system. This development will in itself also affect the financial and expenditure plans on which the interest rate change might be expected to impinge. Its impact can be isolated only if the other development is itself correctly identified. In some cases it will be a change of sentiment which inevitably eludes the statistician. In other cases it may eventually show up in the statistics but the variable delay between the changed perception which affects the financial markets and the events recorded in the statistics may well still confuse the econometric estimates. It is unsurprising therefore that opinions on the effects of interest rates should differ. But, as a central banker claiming to exercise influence over the economy primarily through our influence on interest rates, it is reasonable for you to expect views from me on at least some of the interest rate influences that strike me as potentially important.

One mechanism that might have been expected to operate is an influence running from interest rates – the cost of borrowing – to the demand for credit. In practice an important part of our monetary policy difficulties, running back for most of the post-war period has been the evident weakness of this influence. The growth of bank (and building society) lending to the private sector has for many years been well in excess of that of national income and has seemed impervious even to very large upward movements in nominal interest rates and even at times has reacted perversely.

In the 1960s and 1970s this could probably be explained by inflation, which meant that in real terms interest rates were in fact negative. More recently an important explanation has been the progressive elimination of direct controls which has resulted *inter alia* in much freer access to mortgage credit. The fact that during the period of controls inflation raised the value of houses while eroding the real value of the debt secured on it, meant that personal borrowers availed themselves of these new opportunities. Much of the recent growth of personal borrowing has been in this form, and it has been accompanied by a rapid increase in personal sector holdings of financial assets. To some extent, therefore, the personal sector's monetary behaviour during this period may reflect simply a redistribution of its portfolio of assets and liabilities without serious implications for future inflation.

In relation to companies' finances, the role of short-term interest rates may be to influence not so much the total level of their borrowing as their choice between borrowing from the banks and borrowing from the capital market. This choice has important monetary implications, and is a channel on which many foreign authorities rely. Uncertainty about inflation and nominal interest rate prospects made fixed-rate capital market intermediation unattractive to both borrowers and lenders in the 1970s, and companies ceased to issue bonds or debentures. This has changed in recent years and new sources of borrowing have opened up to many companies, including financial companies, as a result of financial innovation, providing new alternatives to bank finance. It seems possible that these developments will now make companies borrowing from the banking system more sensitive to short-term interest rates.

One might expect the demand for credit as a whole to be influenced primarily by the general level of interest rates. And this is likely to be true also of the demand for non-interest-bearing money. But neither of these effects has direct implication for the behaviour of the broader monetary aggregates. This will depend upon the range of factors determining the size of the banks' aggregate balance sheet. But, whichever side of the banks' balance sheet one looks at, it is clearly relative interest rates that matter. On the assets side, I have already mentioned the significance for companies' bank borrowing of its cost relative to the cost of capital market, or securitised, finance. Similarly, from the liabilities side, the size of the banks' balance sheet will depend upon the return to depositors on bank deposits relative to the return on competing, less liquid assets. In consequence the direct effect of a change in short-term interest rates on broader, interest-bearing, monetary aggregates is ambiguous.

Funding policy – a digression

It may be helpful if I were to digress briefly at this point and talk about funding policy. Given the uncertain response of both the demand for credit and the demand for money to movements in interest rates, funding policy came to play an increasingly important part in the pursuit of monetary targets in the early 1980s. Indeed we pursued a policy of 'overfunding' the public sector's borrowing need in order to neutralise some of the effect of high bank lending on the broad money aggregates. This can equally be seen as an attempt to control the growth of those aggregates by twisting the yield curve in the direction of increasing long rates relative to short rates, and so attracting funds out of the banks from monetary to non-monetary assets. In principle this could simultaneously have encouraged the switching of credit demand into the banking system but in practice for most of the period of overfunding the banks were far and away the dominant source of credit and there was little ground for hoping that modestly lower bond yields would persuade companies to look elsewhere for their funds.

Such operations might be considered part of the essence of the operation of monetary policy, and indeed it is. But by 1985 it had become clear that much of the faster growth of broad money relative to the growth of nominal income was due to changes in financial behaviour and the increasingly competitive and innovative financial system, with less disturbing implications for future inflation and nominal income growth. In these circumstances it would have been inappropriate to continue to pursue – whether through funding policy or interest rates – the original path for broad money growth which had been set on the basis of different assumptions about the relationship between money and income.

Moreover, overfunding increased the need for money market assistance; and by 1985 it had produced very large systemic shortages of cash in the money market, which we had to relieve by purchases of commercial bills. Some commentators saw these multiple transactions as producing only the form rather than the sub-stance of monetary control, while others suspected that they produced significant distortions in the short-term markets, possibly adding to the growth of bank lending. Whatever the justification for these concerns, they risked undermining the credibility of the policy stance as a whole and the decision was taken to stop overfunding. It was, of course, recognised that this decision would increase our dependence upon short-term interest rates as effectively the only instrument of policy. This in turn involved a change in the operational significance of the targets set at the time for non-interest-bearing narrow money (M0) and for largely interest-bearing broad money (£M3) because of their different responses to inter-est rate changes. In particular it had to be recognised that reliance on interest rates to bring £M3 back within its target range meant that it was unlikely that this could be achieved within the timespan of the target period.

Returning to my main theme, a further influence of a change in interest rates is likely to be its effect on wealth and incomes. For example, the value of many financial assets, such as government bonds and equities, will tend to fall as interest rates rise, and wealth-determined expenditures might then also fall. Similarly, economic agents that have net short-term or variable rate assets will enjoy higher income, which may lead them to spend more, while the effect on net debtors will be the reverse. There is no guarantee that these effects will balance each other. Households in total, for example, are net depositors with banks and building societies and are likely to benefit from higher cash receipts, as interest rates rise; but this is not true of each individual household nor of other sectors. Individuals with variable rate obligations will find their cash flows adversely affected, and their response to rising interest rates is likely to be sharper than that of its beneficiaries. Here too, therefore, the effect of interest rates is uncertain.

A more obvious effect of interest rates is on the exchange rate, though even this influence is not fully understood. At times the initial causality is reversed, running from the exchange rate to interest rates, perhaps as a result of some external development or shift in inflationary expectations. In these circumstances particularly, a rise in interest rates – if it is less than expected by financial markets or less than they suppose to be necessary to bring the situation under control – may have the effect of depressing the exchange rate. Similarly, it may take quite sizeable reductions in interest rates to prevent a currency from rising if confidence is running in its favour. But generally the likely direction of interest rate influences on the exchange rate are reasonably clear: a more serious problem is that on occasion this effect may be an unwelcome consequence of interest rate action which is otherwise desirable on domestic grounds.

I suppose that many commentators might regard the experience of 1980–81 as a classic example of this kind of dilemma. This you will recall was a period of exceptional strength for sterling, partly as a consequence of North Sea oil – and despite the ending of exchange controls – but partly too as a result of the tight monetary policy which we were pursuing. My own view in that instance is that the combined financial pressure from interest rates and the exchange rate was necessary to break the inflationary psychology and I doubt whether we would have reached our present relatively favourable position without it.

But our more recent situation certainly provides a good example. The fall in the oil price last year required an accompanying fall in the exchange rate if we were to avoid an unsustainable balance of payments problem; it also provided an unusual opportunity in that lower oil prices were an offset to the inflationary effects of the depreciation Since then, the situation has changed. The domestic economy is buoyant in substantial part because of the competitive gains to the non-oil sectors from last year's depreciation, the demand for credit and broad money growth are both somewhat rapid and asset prices – for example equities and house prices – are also advancing strongly. Despite some more reassuring evidence, for example from the behaviour of M0 and more direct indications of the rate of inflation over the next year or so, these are grounds for not wanting at present to see interest rates fall too far or too quickly. But equally we do not wish to see the exchange rate rise because of the damage this would inflict on industrial confidence at a critical juncture – especially when we cannot be sure whether the present shift of sentiment in sterling's favour is relatively short-term speculation or something more lasting.

Inevitably one is left wondering whether perhaps an explicit exchange rate objective would be helpful in such circumstances. It is possible that it would if the markets were convinced that the conflicting pressures were likely to be short-lived and the exchange rate target capable of being adhered to. But it is important to recognise that in other circumstances the essential dilemma would remain unchanged. The major EMS countries, for example, have domestic monetary objectives as well as their exchange rate targets, and they take both seriously enough to be presented with serious dilemmas from time to time.

Intervention – a further digression

As it is we have, as you will be aware, tried to help square the circle by sizeable exchange market intervention. This has certainly given us some added room for manoeuvre on interest rates. But, like funding policy, intervention too has practical limits especially for one country acting alone. Concerted intervention by several countries, whether designed to bring about an agreed realignment or to stabilise one or more currencies, can be more potent. In either case, intervention to restrain upward pressure on the exchange rate has the immediate consequence of adding to domestic liquidity and producing a bulge in broad money growth. These effects can, over time, be sterilised through additional funding, but this would not be without consequences for government bond yields; and there could come a point at which intervention intensified the inflow of foreign exchange both through this effect on yields and by obstructing the movement in the exchange rate itself and preventing it from equilibrating opposing views among market participants. Intervention therefore cannot be an adequate solution to a *sustained* conflict between domestic and external objectives, though it can help to make the situation more manageable for a time, and avoid unnecessary internal or external adjustments where the inflows subsequently reverse. Given the present-day scale of capital flows through the foreign exchange markets, the scale of intervention may need to be very large indeed if it is to be at all effective.

The mechanisms that I have identified – and my list is certainly not intended to be exhaustive – will, each individually, affect economic behaviour and the development of nominal income, their precise effects depending upon the surrounding circumstances at the time. But the important point is that they do not operate in isolation but simultaneously and in combination. Though, at any particular time, one or other individual effect may be comparatively weak or ill-determined, what matters from the standpoint of the impact of monetary policy is their aggregate effect, which may be greater than the sum of the parts. And it is broad assessments of the likely aggregate effects – rather than detailed, partial analysis – that seem to me in practice likely to determine the responses of both the financial markets and the wider economy.

So far I have confined myself largely to the effects of interest rates on financial flows and asset prices, and have alluded only in passing to possible implications for real expenditure. This had enabled me to place little emphasis on the distinction between nominal and real interest rates. With given inflation expectations a rise in nominal rates implies that real rates are also higher – and in many cases higher nominal rates will lead to a downward revision of inflation expectations. Higher real interest rates mean that resources today become more expensive relative to resources at future dates. Thus more future consumption can be bought by giving up a given amount of consumption, or leisure, today, and more machines could be bought in future for each machine not put in place today. This change in relative prices should in principle have the direct effect of discouraging current consumption and investment expenditures and encouraging their planned deferral. In practice this would be a difficult relationship to exploit for policy purposes. First, the evidence suggests that the intertemporal substitution effect is relatively weak compared to cash flow and other effects of interest rate changes. Secondly, inflation expectations and thus real interest rates, are very difficult to measure, and while there is a presumption that raising nominal interest rates raises real ones, possibly more than point for point, it would be quite wrong to assume that real interest rates were higher in one period than another merely because nominal ones were.

As a result, our discussions about interest rate policy, though grounded in economic analysis, will often be concerned too with the likely overall impact on financial and business confidence in the given situation, and with the tactical implementation of interest rate decisions to try to achieve the required effect. I should like therefore to conclude with a few remarks about how, in an operational sense, we seek to exert our influence on interest rates.

The operation of interest rate policy

There is a popular perception that the monetary authorities dictate the general level of interest rates, and it is of course true that we are able to exert a very considerable influence on it. But the extent of our influence should not be exaggerated. The financial markets are themselves an immensely powerful influence which we can never afford to ignore. At times, if market sentiment is uncertain and if the authorities are relatively confident in their view of the appropriate policy stance, the Bank's lead may be readily followed. But at other times, if we sought to impose a level of rates against strong market opposition, we are liable to be forced to change our stance. This could result from pressures at other points on the money market yield curve beyond the point at which we were ourselves operating, or in the foreign exchange or gilt-edged or equity markets, any or all of which could have effects on the wider economy that were inconsistent with our policy aims at the time. We need always therefore to try to work with the grain of the markets to achieve the required effects.

This is true whatever the particular technical arrangements for exerting official influence on interest rates that are in place. Some people have read into the changes in those arrangements that have occurred over the years – from Bank Rate to Minimum Lending Rate to our present somewhat more flexible method of operation through the rate at which we purchase eligible commercial bills from the discount houses – much greater significance than is justified. While it is the case that the particular technical arrangements can provide for a greater or lesser *degree* of market or official influence, and that the relative influence exerted by the market and the Bank can change with circumstances, both influences are always present.

Operating within this constraint, the Bank can vary its tactics flexibly in order to try to achieve different effects on sentiment. Often our aim will be to slow the momentum of an interest rate movement sought by the markets rather than obstruct it altogether. In that case we need to think ahead to the possibility of further moves, and there are major tactical decisions to be made as to whether a move made sooner rather than later, or a larger rather than a smaller move, will produce the best eventual outcome from a policy perspective. In some circumstances, as for example last autumn, delaying a move can result in a smaller eventual move than the markets were suggesting; in others, such as the 0.5 per cent reduction made ahead of the Budget this year, the judgment was that, had we delayed further, until the facts of the Budget were known to the markets – which would normally have been desirable – the pressure would have intensified for an overall larger reduction than the eventual 1 per cent that seemed prudent to us at the time on policy grounds.

In seeking to influence the size and timing of interest rate changes we can operate with a higher profile – through publicised 2.30 pm lending to the market, for example, which is the equivalent of the earlier MLR announcement; or we can operate more discreetly through varying the scale of assistance in relation to the market's needs or the terms on which we lend privately to the discount houses. When there is an interest rate change we can either follow a move in base rates initiated by the clearing banks or we can choose to anticipate a move that they might make on the basis of the rates prevailing in the interbank market.

Depending on market perceptions of the stance of policy, and the strength of prevailing pressures, these different tactics can have different effects on sentiment in the financial markets, and that in turn, as interpreted by the media can have different effects on the perceptions and behaviour of the wider economy.

Conclusion

Chancellor, I have deliberately set out in this lecture to explain some of the limitations that apply to the operation of monetary policy, because I believe that this central part of the Bank of England's function will be better understood if there is a clearer perception of what we can and what we cannot hope to achieve. I am frequently asked why we do not take some particular action, for example, to raise or lower interest rates, to have this or that impact on some other particular aspect of the economy, such as the exchange rate or the growth of consumer borrowing which my questioner sees as self-evidently desirable. I hope to have explained to you that the process of monetary management is rarely as simple as that; our ability to achieve selective effects is circumscribed and we need to be conscious of the *overall* effects of what we do.

The reality is the following:

- The instruments of monetary policy are limited, indeed in essence we are dependent upon a single instrument – the short-term interest rate.
- Our understanding of the precise effects of interest rates on the economy is limited, though I have no doubt of the direction of those effects in the round, and no doubt that they are powerful.
- Our ability to determine interest rates is limited, though, here too, I have no doubt that it is a powerful influence.

But we have a clear understanding of the aim of monetary policy. This aim, too, is limited – though I would argue, crucially important. Monetary policy cannot, of itself, deliver a strong economy or full employment or greater industrial efficiency. It can lay an essential foundation for the achievement of those aims by resolutely pursuing the stabilisation of the value of money. That, I can assure you, remains our central banking purpose.

6 Monetary policy in Britain and Europe

Eddie George

I was delighted to have been invited to deliver the sixteenth Mais Lecture – until some two or three months ago when you asked me to suggest a title! I confess that, at that stage, I had not really thought about what I should talk about – so I offered you the portmanteau title of 'Monetary policy in Britain and Europe', hoping, like Mr Micawber, that something would turn up – either here or on the Continent – to give some topicality to what I might say. Well happily, Vice Chancellor, it has. On 6 May, just four days after taking office, the Chancellor of the Exchequer announced some radical changes to the monetary policy framework in this country – including changes to the role and constitution of the Bank of England. I should like to discuss some of those changes this evening against the background of the monetary policy framework being developed in Europe, in preparation for the introduction of the euro, including the role of the future European System of Central Banks (ESCB) . But I should like to discuss them in the context of the approach to economic management more generally in Europe and this country and perhaps I might start with that.

Overall economic management

Sweeping generalisations are of course always dangerous. But from my particular vantage point at least, there has, over the past decade or more, been a clear change of emphasis – across Europe but much more widely internationally – *away* from short-term, macro-economic, demand management as the means of promoting the agreed end-objectives of economic policy, of growth of output and employment, and of rising living standards, and *towards* the need for macro-economic stability in the medium and longer term. Where before the implicit assumption appeared to be that the supply-side of the economy would respond relatively flexibly to increasing demand, there is now the perception that over-ambitious short-term demand management, which attempts to push capacity to its limits or even beyond, can generate instability and uncertainty, damaging capacity growth in the longer term by distorting economic decision-making in relation to investment, for example, or in relation to resource allocation.

The result is a broad consensus – across countries but also across a wide part of the political spectrum within countries – on the need for macro-economic policy to be directed towards stability and sustainability in the medium and longer term. This consensus is reflected in the Maastricht Treaty – through the famous convergence criteria. It is reflected, too, in the arrangements for the conduct of macro-economic policy now being put in place for the introduction of the single European currency – including the monetary preparations for the European Central Bank (ECB), and the agreement on the fiscal Stability and Growth Pact recently confirmed by the European Council in Amsterdam.

But alongside this collective commitment to macro-economic stability, there is a growing recognition that stability, on its own, is not enough. While it may be a *necessary* condition for achieving sustainable growth of output and employment, and rising living standards – the truly good things in life – and while stability may indeed be the most that macro-economic policy can contribute in the longer term to those agreed end-objectives, it is not in itself a *sufficient* condition for achieving them. So attention everywhere is now focussing increasingly on the structural characteristics of our economies which essentially determine their underlying, supply-side, rate of capacity growth.

The issue is starkly illustrated by the fact that despite very substantial progress towards macro-economic stability within the European Union as a whole in recent years – including real progress towards effective price stability (with measured inflation now below 2 per cent) and strenuous efforts everywhere to cut back public sector deficits as required by the Maastricht convergence criteria – output has stagnated, growing at an average annual rate of only 1 per cent or so over the past five or six years, and unemployment has risen inexorably, to around 11 per cent across the Union as a whole. And while it is true that activity may now be beginning to recover, the pick-up is very largely driven by external demand – with the domestic economy still depressingly weak.

Against this background, the need for greater supply-side flexibility within Europe is increasingly widely acknowledged. And there are elements of common approach to bringing it about. These were reflected, for example, in the Resolution on Growth and Employment adopted at the European Summit in Amsterdam a week ago, which talks of the need to improve European competitiveness – with special attention to be given 'to labour and product market efficiency, technological innovation and the potential for small and medium-sized enterprises to create jobs'. It talks, too, of improving 'training and education systems, including life-long learning, work incentives in the tax and benefit systems and reducing non-wage labour costs, in order to increase employability'. But these policy approaches are not well-defined across Europe, and it is probably at this stage stretching a point to speak of even a 'broad' consensus on specific approaches in this area. Even where particular needs for change have been identified nationally, recent experience in some countries suggests that there can be formidable resistance to bringing it about.

The new government in this country is clearly joined in the European consensus on the need for macro-economic stability; and it too emphasises the importance of supply-side flexibility, indeed its thinking in supply-side issues 'clearly influenced the Amsterdam Resolution which I have just mentioned. To quote a recent article by the Chancellor:

> The Labour government is committed to monetary stability so that businesses and families can plan for the future; to fiscal stability; and (on the supply side) to higher levels of investment in both people and business; to a modernisation of our welfare state, and not least, to free trade and a constructive engagement in Europe.

This country's approach overall to economic management is, therefore, wholly consistent with that of our European partners; and we start from a somewhat more comfortable position, in which our own recent progress towards greater macro-economic stability has in fact been accompanied by somewhat stronger growth of activity – averaging over 2.5 per cent over the past five years – and by a sustained *fall* in unemployment to around 7.25 per cent on a comparable ILO basis.

Monetary management

Within this overall economic policy context, there is a particular commitment, throughout the European Union, to monetary stability; and I should like now to consider some of the very recent changes to our own monetary policy framework against that background.

Objective

I begin with the *objective* of monetary policy which, both here and on the Continent, is allocated specific responsibility for achieving and maintaining price stability.

The Maastricht Treaty states that 'The primary objective of the ESCB shall be to maintain price stability. Without prejudice to the objective of price stability, the ESCB shall support the general economic policies of the Community.'

In his statement to the House of Commons on 20 May, the Chancellor said: 'The Bank (of England)'s monetary policy objective will be to deliver price stability, and, without prejudice to this objective, to support the government's economic policy, including its objectives for growth and employment.'

At this level, our respective missions are effectively identical. But it is important to understand that price stability is not simply an end in itself, but a means to the end of *sustainable* growth. What in fact we are, in principle, trying to do in maintaining price stability is to keep the growth of monetary demand more or less continuously broadly in line with the underlying capacity growth in the economy – in effect using price stability as an indicator of stability in the economy as a whole. And although we cannot hope to achieve that in practice with any great precision, we can reasonably aspire to help to moderate the economic cycle rather than aggravate it, as so often in the past.

The Maastricht Treaty makes no provision for any further definition of the ECB's primary objective. It is left for the ECB's Governing Council to determine how to interpret 'price stability' in any particular circumstance. Indeed the ECB will need to decide whether it has a specific target for inflation at all, or whether, operationally, it adopts an intermediate monetary target, or elements of both.

In the case of the United Kingdom it is the Chancellor who determines the precise inflation target, which he has subsequently set at 2.5 per cent for the Retail Price Index excluding mortgage interest payments, and the Chancellor reserves the right, in extreme economic circumstances, to override the Bank of England's operational independence in seeking to achieve the government's target.

In practice, in either case, the degree of latitude that these arrangements apparently provide is likely to be limited by the need to maintain the credibility of the commitment to price stability, with financial markets and with the public at large. But in the United Kingdom at least, where public support for monetary stability is more recently established than it is, for example, in Germany, the elected government's public and explicit commitment to low inflation may provide reassurance, and help to secure greater acceptance of the policy.

In any event the Bank's remit under the new arrangements is unmistakably clear. We are charged with delivering the government's inflation target. Operationally that means that we are to aim consistently to achieve 2.5 per cent on RPIX as a *mid*-point, so that, with a balanced distribution of risks, there should be an even chance of outturns – at the end of our two-year forecasting horizon – either above or below 2.5 per cent. The measure of our success will be how close we in fact come to 2.5 per cent, not on any particular date, but on average over time.

Transparency and accountability

The clear separation of responsibility for setting the inflation target (the political decision) from responsibility for achieving it (the technical decision) also helps to ensure that the government and the Bank are separately accountable for their respective roles in the monetary policy process. And in this area of accountability, too, there are considerable differences between the arrangements that will apply to the ECB and to ourselves.

In the case of the ECB, the Treaty requires that it

> shall address an annual report on the activities of the ESCB, and on the monetary policy of both the previous and current year, to the European Parliament, the Council and the Commission, and also to the European Council. The President of the ECB shall present this report to the Council and to the European Parliament, which may hold a general debate on that basis.

In addition the ECB President and the members of its Executive Board may be invited, or volunteer, to appear before the competent Committees of the European Parliament.

In the case of the Bank of England:

1   The minutes of the Monetary Policy Committee's (MPC) meetings to deter-
     mine interest rates will be published, identifying how each member voted,
     with an explanation of why the individuals who voted against were opposed
     to the majority decision.
2   The MPC's performance will be reviewed regularly by a reformed Court of
     Directors, and the Bank's Annual Report will be debated in the House of
     Commons.
3   The Bank will continue to publish its quarterly Inflation Report, reviewing
     both the outturn and the prospect for inflation in relation to the target; and
     the Treasury Select Committee will take evidence from the MPC on the
     Inflation Report.
4   And, as Chairman of the MPC, the Governor is required to write an open
     letter to the Chancellor if inflation strays by more than 1 per cent either side
     of the 2.5 per cent target. The letter would refer as appropriate to the Infla-
     tion Report, and explain why inflation was adrift, how long the divergence
     was expected to last, and the action taken to bring it back on course.

Taken as a whole, these arrangements provide for greater transparency of, and
greater accountability for, the technical monetary process than anywhere else in
the world.

Now I do not suppose, quite honestly, that anyone would particularly enjoy this
degree of public scrutiny. But it will certainly help to concentrate the minds of the
MPC members, and it is, I believe, a necessary feature of our new arrangements.

The technical implementation of monetary policy – even with a very clearly
defined objective – is not at all easy at the best of times. We have in practice a
single instrument – the short-term interest rate – the precise effects of which on
the economy are by no means perfectly understood, including by ourselves. We do
know that it can take up to a couple of years or more to have its full effects. So we
have to rely substantially on uncertain forecasts, that are subject to unforeseeable
shocks. Policy judgments in these circumstances are necessarily an art rather than
an exact science, no matter how much we apply science to informing those judgments. And the judgments themselves need to be constantly reviewed and
frequently revised as relevant new information becomes available.

Transparency in these circumstances can only encourage a better informed
public debate and a more sophisticated public understanding of the issues. That
in turn can only help to strengthen confidence in the process – unless of course
we make a frightful hash of it! I shall be surprised – and somewhat disappointed –
if the ECB Governing Council does not go to considerable lengths to explain its
policies to the public at large, for similar reasons, even if it is not actually required
to do so by statute.

The decision-making framework

Reflecting its multinational character the policy-making body of the ECB, the Governing Council, will comprise the Governors of the participating country central banks plus the six members of the Executive Board. Our own MPC will comprise four 'outside' members directly appointed by the Chancellor, together with five Bank executives – the Governor, two Deputy Governors, and two Executive Directors. The common characteristic is that in each case the decision-makers will be professional experts rather than representatives of particular interests. Any doubts that this would in fact be the case in relation to the outside appointments to the MPC were certainly immediately dispelled when the names were announced: together with our inside appointees, they are, as a team, as well qualified professionally for the task we have been set as I can imagine anywhere in the world – and we certainly need all the help we can get.

The processes of the Committee are inevitably still evolving. It will, as you would expect, be supported by the whole, considerable, range of the Bank's monetary, economic, statistical and market expertise, supplemented by intelligence from the Bank's network of regional agencies with further front-line input both from the non-executive members of Court and from our wide range of industrial, commercial and financial contacts.

The Committee will be closely involved in the preparation of the quarterly *Inflation Report*, contributing to both the analysis and the forecasts. And, of course, it will meet regularly on pre-announced dates each month – the dates determined by the monthly cycle of statistical information – to take its decisions on monetary policy. These monthly meetings are spread over three days: a whole-day* meeting to receive briefings from the Bank staff on the latest developments; an afternoon meeting to identify and discuss the important underlying issues, and any tactical considerations there may be; and a final morning meeting to decide upon any necessary policy action. The Committee will need also to provide for emergency meetings in the event of a crisis, but if we are successful in our task of achieving permanent, long-term, stability I would hope that that will prove to be a very rare occurrence.

Implementation of policy

Compared with the complexity of the decision-making process in relation to interest rates, implementation of those decisions is relatively straightforward.

In the case of the ECB, the short-term interest rate will basically be contained within a corridor, bounded, at the top, by an overnight lending facility to the commercial banks, and, at the bottom, by an overnight deposit facility in which the banks can place surplus funds. Within the corridor the market interest rate will be steered by means of open market repurchase operations. The ECB may also require commercial banks to hold with the system minimum cash reserves; and it

---

* The briefing meeting was reduced to a half-day from September 2000.

will offer a limited amount of longer term credit to commercial banks at market rates; neither of these features appear to us to be necessary for monetary policy purposes, but they represent an element of continuity from the arrangements which currently apply in some prospective member countries.

In our own case the arrangements are even simpler. The decision on interest rates will be announced at noon following the final, morning, meeting of the MPC, and the chosen interest rate will be applied in our daily money market operations – mostly these days through repurchase operations in gilt-edged securities. Limited facilities for late lending to the remaining discount houses and the settlement banks are available to ensure the smooth functioning of the payments system at the end of the day.

Looking at the monetary policy arrangements, planned for Europe and as they now are in this country, as a whole, it is clear that while there are significant differences of detail – such that our own arrangements would certainly require considerable further modification to make them compatible with membership of the ESCB – the essential similarities are much greater than the differences. Crucially the primary monetary policy objective of price stability is the same, and the responsibility for achieving that objective is in each case entrusted to a broadly based group of technical experts not subject to political influence. That does not of course guarantee that we will, here or in Europe, succeed in achieving permanently greater stability but, perhaps presumptuously, I do think it gives us every chance of doing so.

Concluding remarks

Mr Chairman, what I have tried to do this evening is to draw attention to what I see as a very striking coincidence of basic approach to economic – and in particular monetary – management within Europe but also between Continental Europe and this country. We are clearly, it seems to me, on parallel tracks as far as our commitment to macro-economic, both fiscal and monetary, stability is concerned, though we may be travelling at different speeds when it comes to supply-side flexibility.

That coincidence of basic approach is a prerequisite for sustainable economic convergence within Europe – without it I do not see how monetary union could be on the agenda. But the question that is often then put to me is, if in fact we are on parallel tracks – in terms of our basic approach – why then do we not get on the same train and commit ourselves to joining monetary union. So let me conclude with just a few remarks on that subject.

The potential attraction of travelling together with our European partners is very clear. There would, other things equal, be real economic advantages in exchange rate *certainty* across the single market area, which can only be realised through the single currency. The same *certainty* cannot be achieved by the countries of Europe independently pursuing macro-economic discipline, although that should over time help to minimise the degree of intra-European exchange rate volatility.

But there are real risks.

We are not all starting from the same station. Domestic demand in this country, for example, is currently growing at a rate which we cannot sustain for very long without the emergence of inflationary pressures. In the major countries of Continental Europe, on the other hand, domestic demand remains, as I say, relatively subdued. The possibility of such cyclical divergences will not simply disappear on 1 January 1999 and they would seriously complicate the operation of a single monetary policy. So too would a variety of possible internal or external shocks which affected euro member countries in different ways or to different degrees.

But more fundamentally – and I can't keep up the railway analogy – I am frankly nervous at the prospect of introducing the euro at a time of very high and very different rates of unemployment across Europe. It is not that I think unemployment can be addressed directly by more expansionary macro-economic polices – that ought to be clear from my earlier remarks. I share the view that unemployment needs to be addressed fundamentally through supply-side policies – though it may be that the problem is currently being aggravated in the short term by the heroic attempts being made to meet the fiscal criteria according to the Maastricht timetable in a context of cyclical weakness. The problem is that we cannot be confident how individual countries may respond to this situation. My concern is that the persistence of these wholly unacceptable levels of unemployment across Europe, and the very real difficulty of implementing appropriate supply-side reforms, could begin to undermine public support for macro-economic stability in some countries – even though significant relaxation on this front would provide at best only short-term relief. In that case, economic convergence, if it were achieved, could prove difficult to sustain. There are perhaps some suggestions that this may be beginning to happen; and it may be for this reason that the foreign exchange markets are implying that they expect relative euro weakness – to our own considerable embarrassment as a result of the corresponding strength of sterling's exchange rate. I have no doubt that, if the euro goes ahead, the ECB would in fact seek determinedly to exercise its statutory responsibility for maintaining price stability within the euro area. But its job would be enormously more difficult if this came to be seen, at least in some countries, within the euro area – however mistakenly – as an obstacle to the end-objectives of economic policy, including particularly increasing employment.

My conclusion, Mr Chairman, from all this is that whether or not the euro proceeds on the present timetable, and whether or not the UK is a part of that, the really important thing for European prosperity is that the present broad policy consensus holds together. But if we are to be able to hold on to macro-economic stability – as we must, then we have to find answers to the urgent problem of European unemployment. That involves addressing the problems of supply-side flexibility as an immediate priority. And that, Vice Chancellor, is the message that the new government has recently carried to Europe.

7 Financial and monetary integration

Benefits, opportunities and pitfalls

Professor Dr Dr h.c. Hans Tietmeyer

E31 E52 F36 F33

First of all, I wish to thank you very much for your kind invitation.

I am pleased to have the opportunity to give this year's Mais Lecture and to share with you some of my thoughts. It is a great honour for me to be invited to continue the sequence of outstanding personalities who have established and maintained the tradition and reputation of the Mais Lecture with their talks.

At the same time, I am happy to be here in London once again. For every visitor, London is a wonderful city full of culture and history.

For a central banker, London is, in addition, a large and efficient financial centre. Its strong points include, not least, the academic infrastructure in economics and business. The City University Business School is making an important contribution to that.

I should of course like to add I come from a financial centre on the continent which likewise has some strong points. And experience shows competition is always stimulating for both sides.

Thus, the two financial and monetary centres, London and Frankfurt, go some way towards symbolising tonight's topic, 'Financial and Monetary Integration: Benefits, Opportunities and Pitfalls'.

I

I should like to begin with the hypothetical question: What will historians of the future regard as the most important, forward-looking features of the close of the twentieth century?

Perhaps they will point to the following three features:

Firstly, following the outcome of the competition between the political systems, the competition of the economic systems between a market economy and a centrally planned economy likewise seems to have come to an end.

At any rate, the state socialist model as a competitor of the free market economy has foundered

- not only because it was dissolved in and together with the Soviet Union and its former sphere of influence;

- what is more, it is no longer a serious reference model for the development of emerging economies; not even for China.

Secondly, economic historians may, later on, perhaps see the present time as a period of dramatic technical and economic upheaval – of 'creative destruction' in Schumpeter's phrase.

In particular, basic innovation in microelectronics is being reflected

- in lots of procedural innovations which are now more and more reaching application status;
- and in many product innovations becoming increasingly marketable.

And thirdly, we contemporaries are speaking more and more of an era of progressive economic integration, at both a regional and a global level. Globalisation is the keyword in today's discussion.

These three features are of course interlinked.

- The victory of the market economy system and the decline in transportation and communication costs are fuelling global integration.
- Global competition, in turn, is fostering the search for new applications of the technical possibilities.
- And especially in a dynamic period with large adjustment requirements in almost all sectors of the economy, a centrally planned economy is especially inferior to a market economy.

All three features have a common thrust. They work in the direction of overcoming national frontiers and administrative barriers.

The old dream of internationalism therefore holds out the promise of coming true.

But the more this open, increasingly barrierless world becomes reality, the more evident it grows that this is not a perfect or simple world. On the contrary:

- In the wake of the former east-west conflict, conflicts within countries or in individual regions have not become less common. Indeed, some conflicts which had previously been obscured have only now come to light.
- And the technological changes and economic globalisation are not only a source of greater prosperity. They at the same time pose huge challenges. The developed industrial countries are particularly feeling the need for reform in their labour markets and social security systems. This is especially true of countries in continental Europe.

II

Progressive economic integration is, of course, not a new phenomenon.

But there are many indications that this process has accelerated and intensified in the last ten years, both quantitatively and qualitatively.

Economic integration is a comprehensive process.

It is increasingly affecting the real economy. The international interdependence of national economies is increasing.

A new quality is emerging. For the growing interdependence is no longer based solely or primarily on trade in finished products or commodities.

Especially, the process of developing and producing goods is being increasingly split up internationally. This is possible

- because national frontiers have become increasingly permeable and communications have become more intensive;
- because transportation and communication costs have fallen sharply;
- and because, in particular, the emerging economies have likewise become more integrated in the world economy; this, above all, markedly facilitates direct investment there.

The front runners of such integration are of course the global financial markets. They are able to take the best advantage of the disappearance of transaction barriers and the new technological options.

In a world of increasing real economic interdependence, and with global financial markets, the question of monetary integration is also becoming more urgent.

The calculability and appropriateness of monetary relationships is becoming more important.

- Globalisation therefore increases the overall pressure to pursue a stability-oriented monetary policy everywhere. If a country, especially a bigger one, drops out, this may lead, in an integrated world economy, to serious damage due to volatile financial market prices.
- And this is why many countries are switching over to monetary co-operation, or even to pegging their exchange rates.

One part of Europe is now going a radical step further.

Eleven EU countries will enter into monetary union on a durable basis at the end of this year. That union will then pursue a single supranational monetary policy decided by a supranational and politically independent central bank.

A number of countries will closely watch the outcome of this experiment, which may change Europe considerably.

This is true in particular of those countries of the European Union which do not wish to join the monetary union as yet. Accession candidates in central and eastern Europe, too, will of course watch developments with keen interest.

But countries in other parts of the world as well will focus their attention on the euro area. This is because some countries in South America or Asia are beginning at least to contemplate the option of a monetary union. Even if they still have a long way to go.

III

What is it that prompts sovereign states to follow this basic trend towards economic integration, even if of course it does not always lead as far as is planned for Euroland?

Essentially, three more or less major benefits may be derived from any form of economic integration:

Firstly, more integration leads to more competition. Competitive pressure enhances efficiency.

Secondly, integration changes market structures.

Markets become larger.

- Enterprises are able to exploit economies of scale.
- National economies can specialise to a greater extent.
- Resources are fed into a larger pool from which they can be allocated more efficiently.

And market breadth increases. The consumer can choose from a wider range of products offered.

Thirdly, integration reduces information and transaction costs. This applies in particular to monetary integration, too.

But what is invariably true is also true of economic integration: there is no such thing as a free lunch.

First of all, it is helpful to distinguish between market integration and policy integration.

- Market integration mainly implies dismantling barriers and obstacles. Then national markets can grow together.
- Policy integration goes further. It also implies that countries co-ordinate or even harmonise the general direction of movement in individual sectors of national policy, or individual parameters.

The countries which join an integration process must clearly appreciate three potential problem areas:

First problem area: market integration going beyond national borders poses increased domestic challenges.

- For instance, integration in the international division of labour accelerates structural change and calls for more internal flexibility, especially on the labour market.
- And liberalising capital movements places demands on the domestic financial

sector, which must be able to handle international capital flows that may rapidly change direction.

Second problem area: to be really efficient, market integration with the elimination of barriers may require a minimum of policy integration.

- This applies, for example, to some protection provisions for products and in the production process.
- Different tax systems may of course likewise distort cross-border goods and financial flows.
- And if capital markets are globalised, different approaches to monetary policy may contribute to volatility. Such volatility may have a strong impact on financial and real investment.

But, and this is the *third problem area*: policy integration is itself a two-edged sword.

It may make markets more efficient. But it can also contribute to curbing policy competition.

That may involve risks:

- An excessive tendency towards centralisation may arise which does not take sufficient account of diverging conditions.
- The delineation of responsibilities may become blurred if mixed responsibilities arise with undue bureaucracy.
- In the worst-case scenario, efficient policy solutions may no longer be implemented. Policy innovation is blocked.

Countries must be able to come to terms with these three risks and problem areas in their efforts to co-ordinate or integrate their policies, if they are to secure the benefits of integration. Striking the right balance here is not always easy.

IV

The financial markets are something like the flywheels of globalisation.

Free capital movements and efficient financial markets greatly facilitate direct investment. They provide the basis for transactions and for the safety of payment flows, which are the financial equivalent of real integration.

The global financial markets promote and strengthen market structures.

They also make it possible for investment in emerging economies to be funded privately, rather than officially, today on a much greater scale than previously.

Capital is allocated today, more than it used to be, in accordance with economic, rather than political, criteria.

Conversely, the integration of the emerging economies into the global financial markets provides new investment outlets for savings.

This must also be seen against the backdrop of the ageing populations in most industrialised countries. They, in particular, must accumulate and invest capital today so as to be able to maintain their relative standard of living in the future, too.

And the global capital markets have assumed a role which is bearing fruit in the disciplining of national policies.

They offer opportunities, but also pose a risk, to countries which fail to follow the economic constraints. Nowadays they are an effective part of the checks and balances.

These important benefits of the international capital markets are sometimes wrongly disregarded in the ongoing debate.

But the financial crises being encountered by some east Asian countries have, of course, highlighted the risks, too.

A number of emerging economies have become swiftly integrated in the global financial markets. Not all of those countries have adjusted their internal structures at the same pace and as thoroughly. That makes them vulnerable.

Two weaknesses, in particular, may become their Achilles' heel:

- a domestic financial sector which is unable to handle large capital flows in a sufficiently sound manner, and
- an overly rigid exchange rate pegging to one or more other currencies.

Exchange rate pegging can in some cases and for some length of time produce positive effects. An overly rigid exchange rate peg, however, can have problematic consequences:

- It may jeopardise the competitiveness of an economy, and especially exports.
- It may fetter domestic interest rate policy. It thereby makes it more difficult to fight inflation in periods of heavy capital inflows.
- And it may tempt residents to borrow in foreign currencies at relatively favourable nominal interest rates.

These consequences may make a country vulnerable, as we have seen already in the Mexican case in 1994–5.

In addition, some risk factors are inherent in the market.

- The international financial markets mostly have a tendency towards short termism. A major part of international lendings and borrowings is at fairly short term.
- And they quite often tend to follow a self-reinforcing herd instinct in periods both of euphoria and of scepticism.

Both factors, any domestic weaknesses and the properties of the international financial markets, may cause a potential for a reversal in sentiment for a currency to build up.

Mostly triggered by some special economic or political change or other, the exchange rate of a currency may go down very fast, in many cases to an overly low point. An 'undershooting' of the appropriate relationship occurs.

Such a slump in the value of a currency can hit the economy of the country concerned with a massive force, especially if that country is heavily indebted in a foreign currency.

What is to be done?

Two points in particular are important:

Firstly, the functioning of the financial markets must be maintained or strengthened.

- On the one hand, to this end the markets need more, better and more up-to-date information on the level, maturity and denomination pattern of the debts of potential risk countries. Sufficient transparency is of particular significance for the functioning of the financial markets.
- On the other hand, the IMF must not encourage moral-hazard attitudes on the part of investors and recipient countries by bailing out private investors. Losses caused by misjudgments and enforced adjustment in the event of wrong behaviour are as much an integral part of a functioning market as are profit opportunities.
- And crises should not invariably lead to a rollback on the part of private investors. Private funding of investment is in principle superior to public funding. Ways must be found to safeguard the long-term interests of private investors. Though there is probably no panacea, various approaches are being considered, and rightly so.
- The IMF above all has to act as a catalyst maintaining or restoring countries' access to private capital. A policy of bailing out private investors is heading in the wrong direction.

Secondly, it is important for countries to eliminate their domestic weaknesses or prevent them from arising in the first place. This includes:

- Being careful about overly rigid exchange rate pegs.
- Strengthening domestic supervision of the financial system.
- And above all: strengthening domestic competitive structures in the goods markets and in the financial sector.

V

Cynics might now say Europe should make sparing use of the advice: 'Be careful with exchange rate pegs.' After all, eleven European countries are actually on the road towards monetary union. And hitherto they have also largely linked their mutual exchange rates, though not always without any problems in the past.

Monetary union does in fact represent a maximum of policy integration in the monetary field.

- Monetary policy is not merely co-ordinated, but unified.
- And that will be for good, because in practice this step cannot be reversed.

There were of course also some other options.

With the European Monetary System, Europe's approach has for a long time been that of an exchange rate arrangement with fixed but adjustable parities; at times there have been some considerable difficulties, but in the end the system has proved largely successful. That goes in particular also for the period after the widening of the fluctuation margins.

Nevertheless, this approach falls short of full monetary integration and the strategy of a single currency.

At the time, your country above all proposed another, less ambitious solution than full monetary union; I am referring to the adoption of a parallel currency, to be used as a common currency.

That would probably have triggered a currency competition. Depending on its design, that solution could, however, also have adversely affected the scope for monetary action of the central banks of the existing hard currency countries and thus jeopardised their anti-inflation policy.

A parallel currency would presumably have got stuck. It might perhaps have been able to crowd out weaker currencies. But whether also a currency of the D-Mark's standing would at least be doubtful. This is true, at any rate, of the specific form of monetary policy activities discussed at the time.

Be that as it may, in the Maastricht Treaty a more far-reaching solution was adopted.

A large majority in the EU opted not merely for a common currency. It also wanted a single currency.

There are sound economic reasons in favour of a single currency; incidentally, also sound political reasons, at least, if a more thorough-going political integration is being sought.

Above all, the single currency makes it possible fully to exploit the economic benefits of integration.

- Competition will be given maximum encouragement in the single market by the complete transparency of prices.
- Factor allocation will no longer be impaired by domestic exchange rate uncertainty.
- Exchange-rate-related information and transaction costs will be minimised by a single currency.
- The euro financial markets will have an optimum depth and breadth.

But what applies to economic integration in general also applies to monetary integration in particular: these benefits will not come automatically and not without corresponding challenges.

How can monetary union secure the benefits? What risks are looming?

Monetary union is faced with three major challenges:

86810131

212

45 of228)

- Firstly, the aforementioned benefits for the goods and financial markets will materialise only if the euro remains lastingly stable. Only then will the euro lead to full price transparency, reduce costs and become an attractive investment currency.
- Secondly, monetary union must not trigger or exacerbate economic tensions. Broadly speaking, an essential requirement that must be met is: one size fits all.
- And, thirdly, monetary union must not give rise to political tensions between the participating states.

These challenges arise against the backdrop of the specific conditions presented by monetary union. The euro will be legal tender in an area which consists of largely sovereign national states whose policies – other than monetary policy – will largely remain their responsibility.

That may lead to a dilemma

- between the requirements of a supranational currency, and
- the political pattern in Europe, which will continue to be determined by the national states and their policies.

The euro needs a high degree of flexibility in the economies of the participating countries.

But there is no European economic and structural policy which can ordain such necessary flexibility from above. And even if there were a responsibility at the European level for doing so, the possibility could not be ruled out that, ultimately, the result would be more rigidity, rather than more flexibility.

At the same time, there is no regional revenue equalisation scheme, comparable to the systems operated in a national state. A social and transfer union cannot and must not make up for any lack of flexibility and competitiveness. For the upshot would probably be not only less flexibility, but possibly also more political disagreement.

At the same time, however, the euro needs discipline on the part of national fiscal policy, at least as far as fiscal deficits are concerned.

Otherwise there is a risk of conflicts, because large debts in some countries will attract the savings of the euro area as a whole, and contribute to higher interest rates for everyone.

- Fiscal policy, however, will largely remain a national responsibility.
- That is why it is so important that the Growth and Stability Pact should prove to be effective in future.

How can the euro function against this background?

The 'classical' answer of the Werner Group in the early 1970s (of which I was a member at the time) was: Europe must set up political union parallel to the monetary union.

Thus, supranational political structures were supposed to ensure that Europe met the requirements of a supranational currency.

Maastricht adopted a different approach.

It left the rift between supranational money and national policy structures. To that extent, it has sometimes been dubbed 'a construct with a limp'.

If, however, there is no supranational political authority to meet the requirements of a supranational currency, then the participating countries must do so on their own initiative, of their own accord or in their own interest.

The Maastricht Treaty therefore also set important rules for the fiscal discipline of member countries. And compliance with those rules is likewise jointly monitored.

However, what ultimately will be crucial for the functioning of the Stability Pact will, above all, be the countries' ability and willingness to abide by those rules on a sustained basis.

A monetary union, under the Maastricht Treaty, therefore needs a large measure of common 'stability culture' in all participating countries.

And another point, the euro can function as a depoliticised currency only in this specific form.

The ultimate monetary target, i.e. monetary stability, must not be subordinated on a discretionary basis to other goals. And monetary policy must be conducted by a politically independent central bank.

That may be considered in some quarters to be an overly German postulate. But in my view this is implied not only by the requirements of a lastingly stable currency, but also by the logic of a monetary union comprising several countries.

For if *one* country subordinates its *own* currency to political objectives other than stability, that may have unpleasant consequences for other countries, given globalised financial markets. But still, one could live with that.

If, however, *eleven* countries try subordinating their *common* currency to their respective primary political objectives, things will really get pretty chaotic in the union.

That way, the euro would gain the confidence neither of the citizens nor of the financial markets. The upshot would, rather, be all too likely to be permanent political conflict.

The euro must not come under the influence of the *domestic* interests of individual countries. Monetary policy must be geared to the situation in the euro area as a whole, taking responsibility for maintaining stability of the common currency.

Some of the incidents in Brussels during the first weekend in May may in this context have been a timely warning, and a lesson to be learned by all.

VI

There can be no doubt that monetary union implies the irreversible loss of the sovereignty of the participating countries in the monetary sphere. Some loss of identity and of the symbolism of a nation state will of course also be associated

---

with giving up the national currencies. In Germany, this also means the loss of a symbol of economic reconstruction after the war.

Monetary union thus reinforces an overall trend towards global economic integration, especially also as a consequence of the global financial markets: the nation state forfeits some of its freedom to shape events.

In some countries and some quarters there are also fears

- about the immediate forfeiture of sovereign rights, as in the case of the currency,
- and also about an uncontrolled dynamic integration process which will – automatically, as it were – relegate the nation state into the background.

Here in the UK (but not only here) there seems to be some concern about an uncontrolled *political* integration drive in Europe: the fear of a 'superstate of Europe'.

Even if this fear is manifest to some extent in continental Europe, too, there is, at the same time, rather, more concern about an uncontrolled *economic* integration drive caused by increased competition. In Germany, there is, in addition, concern that the stability of the euro might not match that of the D-Mark.

At all events, the common underlying question is similar:

- If European integration and/or globalisation reduces the economic and social management capacity of the nation state,
- and if the citizens' democratic 'say' in events remains tied to the institutions of the nation state,

does it follow that a democracy problem is emerging?

This question is of course much too sophisticated to be answered in a few sentences. I only wish to note two points.

Firstly, regarding the fear of a superstate of Europe.

It is without doubt important that monetary union must become a success. This means that in the distant future, too, it should not generate crisis situations which then – of necessity – will give rise to tendencies towards overly strong centralisation which actually no one wants.

The lasting functionality and stability of monetary union is a prerequisite for political subsidiarity in Europe.

Just as stable money is and will remain an essential prerequisite for internal subsidiarity in society.

Even with further political ties, that by no means is bound to lead to a superstate of Europe.

And secondly, the extent to which cross-border integration and globalisation are seen as a democracy problem depends, not least, on one's understanding of democracy.

It is correct that open frontiers make reallocation more difficult. Anyone who regards reallocating income and wealth as the essence of democracy must indeed consider integration and globalisation to be a threat.

If, however, democracy is seen rather as a control mechanism against undesirable political developments, then the international financial markets will be regarded, rather, as a supplement and less as a threat to democracy.

Thus, the financial markets may often penalise an undisciplined fiscal policy quickly and massively. The burden arising from a long-term unsound policy therefore becomes evident much more quickly.

Democracy in the sense of control can then function better.

VII

The global financial markets are certain to test the euro, the political and economic conditions in the euro area and the stability orientation of the European Central Bank as well. Basically, they are already doing so today, even though the euro and the European Central Bank do not exist yet.

It would be an illusion to believe that the global financial markets look critically only at the emerging countries.

The vital asset of a central bank is credibility.

The decisions taken in Brussels to fill the vacancies on the Executive Board of the ECB essentially enhanced that credibility, if anything.

Actual independence from the influence of political bodies is essential for the future credibility of the European Central Bank.

In my view, independence does not at all conflict with the requirements of democracy as long as the European Central Bank abides by its mandate.

Of course, adequate transparency of its decisions in the sense of explaining them to the general public and stating the reasons for them, are important. Accountability in this sense vis-à-vis the European political bodies, and especially vis-à-vis the European Parliament, is useful and right.

However, accountability must not undermine the largely unpolitical character of the euro or its supranationality. Accountability vis-à-vis the national parliaments would not, in my view, be consistent with the euro's supranationality.

From the very outset, it will therefore be essential for the European Central Bank to gain and retain the necessary confidence of the markets.

Credibility normally develops gradually, on account of one's own track record.

To that extent, it seems to be a privilege to be able to inherit credibility from the national central banks. In this context, the Bundesbank, as the guardian of the D-Mark (the long-standing anchor currency of the EMS) naturally plays an important part.

In various respects the D-Mark and the Bundesbank have acted as the model for the euro and the ECB.

Seen from a historic perspective, however – and in conclusion I should like to come back to that point – here are some far more impressive models.

As far as longevity and historical consistency are concerned, I hope that the euro and the European Central Bank will also try to emulate the pound sterling and the Bank of England. This is true, at least, if one disregards some periods in the Old Lady's history which were not quite so successful.

Viewed over the longer term, anyway, the UK has had more success with its currency than Germany, which saw two hyper-inflations and the collapse of its currency in the first half of this century.

But – if I am rightly informed – in this country, too, the question of whether your currency may one day disappear and be replaced by the euro is no longer completely unthinkable.

But that is of course your decision; specifically – if I have got it right – the decision of your government, Parliament and the British people.

POSTSCRIPT

Since the beginning of 1999, eleven of the fifteen EU member states have had a common monetary policy and a common currency, the euro. Although the bank-notes and coins of the national currencies will not be superseded until early 2002, in economic terms the national currencies have only been components of the common currency since 1999, with absolutely fixed conversion rates relative to one another and to the euro.

Experience of monetary union to date has largely been in line with what I said in my 1998 Mais Lecture. The euro has already demonstrated some of the benefits, opportunities and pitfalls I mentioned then.

The disappearance of exchange risk within the monetary union has substantially reduced the erstwhile hedging costs, has fostered competition on many markets in the euro area, and has promoted structural changes in many economic and political fields. On the one hand, this has improved the outlook for growth and employment but, on the other (as expected), it has also engendered a considerable need for adjustment in the economic and political sphere.

With respect to internal monetary stability, the euro has so far, on the whole, fully met the standard set in the past by the stablest member currencies, despite the divergent cyclical situations of the participating nations. That owes a great deal to the unambiguous stability-oriented monetary policy pursued by the European Central Bank.

Externally, however, in relation to other major currencies (the dollar, the yen and the pound sterling), the exchange rate of the euro has been surprisingly weak in its first two years. This has presumably been mainly because of the still unresolved structural economic and political problems in a number of member states, and the insufficiently clarified outlook for further economic and political integration in Europe

Monetary union will undoubtedly present many opportunities in future, too, as well as fresh challenges for the countries concerned. But a conclusive verdict on the lasting success of monetary union on the basis of the Maastricht Treaty will only be possible in the longer run.

Part II

8   The British experiment

The Rt Hon Nigel Lawson MP

(US, UK) F31 E31 E52 E62

I am deeply honoured to have been invited to deliver this year's Mais Lecture. As a City institution, the Mais Lecture is still in its infancy; but it is an unusually precocious infant, having already fully realised the hopes of those who fathered it.

Continuity of policy

I am not, of course, the first Chancellor of the Exchequer to have been thus honoured. My distinguished predecessor, Geoffrey Howe, was the author of the 1981 Mais Lecture.

'I have chosen as my title "The Fight Against Inflation"', he began, speaking at a time when inflation in this country was still in double figures. He went on to explain:

> This is not because inflation is the only aspect of the economy on which government should have a policy, or indeed because the conquest of inflation is our only goal. The ultimate goal must be to restore the British economy to growth and prosperity: defeating inflation is one crucial condition for that. The other is by improving the performance of the economy, by making it more flexible and adaptable in its response to technological change and developments in market conditions. Both tasks are vital. But while the conquest of inflation may not be a *sufficient* condition for sustainable economic growth, it is, we believe, a *necessary* condition.

Re-reading this explanation, it is hard not to be struck by three things.

The first is that, during the intervening years, the policy approach embraced there has been unequivocally vindicated by events. Inflation has been reduced to 5 per cent – the lowest level since the 1960s – and we are now embarking on the fourth year of a sustained economic recovery which has already seen the nation's output surpass the pre-recession peak.

The second is that, not surprisingly, given the vindication of events, the approach to economic policy set out by Geoffrey Howe in the 1981 Mais Lecture remains an accurate description of the policy we are pursuing today.

But third, and rather more surprisingly, given the continuity of policy and its undoubted achievements, there exists in many quarters a curious confusion about the thrust of government policy at the present time.

Has the emphasis of policy changed from the defeat of inflation to the promotion of growth and employment? And even if it hasn't, given the present low level of inflation and high level of unemployment, isn't it high time it did? It is important to dispel that confusion, for it rests upon a fundamental fallacy.

It is of course true that this government has attached, and continues to attach, greater importance to the conquest of inflation than did most if not all of its postwar predecessors. But the idea that this and this alone is what distinguishes us is to misunderstand the fundamental nature of the new approach to economic policy that was inaugurated in 1979, and has been pursued ever since.

Every government is concerned about inflation, just as every government is concerned about prosperity and unemployment. The question is, what is the cause of inflation and its cure, and what is the cause of unemployment and *its* cure.

The roles of macro and micro policy

The conventional post-war wisdom was that unemployment was a consequence of inadequate economic growth, and economic growth was to be secured by *macro*-economic policy – the fiscal stimulus of an enlarged Budget deficit, with monetary policy (to the extent that it could be said to exist at all) on the whole passively following fiscal policy.

Inflation, by contrast, was increasingly seen as a matter to be dealt with by *micro*-economic policy – the panoply of controls and subsidies associated with the era of incomes policy. The conclusion on which the present government's economic policy is based is that there is indeed a proper distinction between the objectives of macro-economic and micro-economic policy, and a need to be concerned with both of them. But the proper role of each is precisely the opposite of that assigned to it by the conventional post-war wisdom. It is the conquest of inflation, and not the pursuit of growth and employment, which is or should be the objective of macro-economic policy. And it is the creation of conditions conducive to growth and employment, and not the suppression of price rises, which is or should be the objective of micro-economic policy.

Needless to say, this fundamentally important role reversal implies a major change in the nature of the macro and micro policies themselves. Instead of monetary policy simply accommodating increased Budget deficits (except when periodic sterling crises brought the process to a temporary halt), fiscal policy has to be in harmony with declining monetary growth. And instead of micro-economic policy consisting of increasingly numerous forms of intervention and interference with market forces, its role is now seen as removing controls and allowing markets to work better.

But at this stage the most important point to emphasise is that this government is pursuing simultaneously both a macro and a micro policy, that the one complements the other, that the macro policy is unequivocally directed at the continuing reduction in inflation, with the ultimate objective of stable prices, and that the micro policy is equally wholeheartedly designed to make the economy work better and thus generate more jobs. Thus the whole argument as to whether the emphasis of policy has or ought to have switched from the defeat of inflation to the promotion of growth and employment can be seen to rest on a simple fallacy.

The United States conundrum

The recent performance of the US economy, however, has greatly added to popular confusion over the role and capability of macro and micro policy. Like ourselves, the United States has been pursuing a rigorously anti-inflationary monetary policy. Unlike us, she has pursued a lax fiscal policy leading to a greatly increased budget deficit. Yet while the United States has enjoyed the same success as we have in getting inflation down, she has a very much better record than ours over employment.

This has led a number of observers to conclude that it is the American budget deficit that is the *cause* of her markedly better employment performance. Not so. There is indeed an important lesson to be learned from the US experience, but it is not that.

For one thing, the American option, which rests on the unique position of the dollar as the world's reserve currency, is not open to any other country. Indeed, how long it is open to the United States, as her consequential current account balance of payments deficit climbs into the stratosphere, is a question that has yet to be answered – and in the meantime the high level of nominal and real US interest rates imposes uncomfortable strains on the debtor nations and, largely through them, on the world's banks.

But the key point in this context is that the superior US employment record goes back well before the relatively recent increase in her budget deficit. Over the past fifteen years, the average annual level of unemployment in Western Europe has declined only once – in 1973. Over the same period in the United States, unemployment has declined in almost as many years as it has increased.

Over the past ten years, the total number of people in work in Western Europe has fallen. In the United States over the same period, the number of people in work has risen by over fifteen million.

This sharp contrast has not been the product of macro policy. It has been almost entirely due to the more efficient, competitive, innovative and adaptive labour and goods markets in the United States.

Over the past ten years, the workers of Western Europe have seen their real earnings rise by around an eighth; over the same period, their American counterparts have been prepared to accept a small reduction in real earnings. Relatively free markets, the spirit of enterprise, and workers who prefer to price themselves into jobs rather than out of them, are a powerful engine of employment. There is indeed an important lesson to be learned from the American experience, but it has nothing to do with the deficit.

The medium-term framework

I have identified one major and fundamental innovation of policy as the dedication of *macro*-economic policy to the conquest of inflation, and *micro*-economic policy to the conquest of unemployment. Another has been the setting of policy firmly within a medium-term framework – and sticking to it.

I well remember the mood of 1979, shortly after we had been elected for the first time, when the argument among the commentators was whether the U-turn would come in a year's time – or in six months. So far as I can recall, the 'smart' money was on six months.

Things have changed since then; and a major element in securing that change has been the Medium Term Financial Strategy, the cornerstone of the government's macro-economic policy. Not the least of the virtues of the MTFS has been the discipline it has imposed on government itself.

But a medium-term approach has also been a vital part of conditioning expectations so that the private sector could see the degree of adjustment necessary and the overall approach that the government would take – in other words the 'rules of the game'.

In a market economy the private sector is bound to take into account its expectations of the behaviour of the government when deciding its own behaviour. This goes for companies and employees alike. When macro-economic policy was directed to maintaining (or attempting to maintain) desired levels of real demand and was prepared to accommodate whatever inflationary pressure arose along the way, this was soon appreciated by those involved in decisions about output, prices and pay.

Now that the approach to policy has changed it has been essential to set out clearly and for some years ahead the framework the government would pursue. It has been an explicit aspect of policy that it would *not* accommodate inflationary pressure. In effect, the MTFS has set out a nominal framework designed gradually to reduce the growth of money GDP and improve the division of that growth between real output growth and inflation. It was clear that unless and until the private sector believed that the government meant what it said, inflation would be slow to come down and the transitional impact on output prolonged. An explicit medium-term approach has been a necessary part of earning that credibility.

Of course statements of intent are not enough. Credibility has to be earned, and when the private sector attempted to test the determination of government in the early stages with wage and price pressure during 1979 and 1980 it was essential to maintain the framework of policy, come what may. That credibility now exists, and serves to buttress the medium-term strategy as a clear guide to the intentions of government.

Monetary policy

Although changes in particular targets and assumptions have been made, the essential point is that the policy recognises the fact – and it is a fact – that inflation is above all a monetary phenomenon, in anything other than the short run.

You cannot have sustained inflation unless governments pursue financial policies that accommodate higher inflation. One of our central aims has been to maintain monetary conditions that are consistent with steadily reducing inflation. And intermediate targets have an essential part to play.

It is not enough for the government simply to say that it is going to reduce inflation. That could just as well have meant further controls, offering at best temporary success. It was vital to demonstrate the government's long-term commitment to appropriate monetary policies.

I do not pretend that operating monetary targets has been easy at a time of rapid financial innovation – here as in the United States. Monetary developments have required, and will continue to require, intelligent interpretation and the exercise of appropriate discretion. But intermediate targets will continue to play a vital part in the government's macro-economic strategy.

. . . And its evolution

Largely for reasons of continuity and simplicity, monetary policy was framed initially in terms of sterling M3, although it was explicitly recognised from the start that other aggregates contained useful information and would have to be monitored.

In the early stages of the MTFS the meaning of the sterling M3 figures was severely distorted by the ending of foreign exchange controls and the abolition – which might usefully have occurred rather sooner – of the corset. These changes were important and necessary in their own right on micro-economic policy grounds, but they undoubtedly made it more difficult to interpret developments during the summer of 1980.

It was clearly important to assess the performance of £M3 in the light of the behaviour of other measures of money, and of other indicators of financial conditions, such as asset prices and the exchange rate. In particular, the narrow monetary aggregates – notably M0 – were growing very slowly at the time.

We reached the view that monetary conditions were, in fact, sufficiently restrictive to bring inflation down. With the benefit of hindsight, that was the right assessment. The difficulties with £M3 continued, to a lesser extent, during the next financial year 1981–2. In 1982, the targets for £M3 were re-set to take account of the structural changes that had affected the financial system; and the new targets were met in both the following years.

The role of other measures of money was made explicit both in 1982 and again in this year's Budget, when targets were set for both narrow and broad monetary aggregates. I have made it clear that both targets have *equal* weight in guiding policy decisions – a point which I suspect has not yet been fully grasped by market commentators.

And we continue to pay attention to other relevant indicators of financial conditions, such as the exchange rate. Over the period as a whole, by maintaining appropriate monetary conditions, and exercising judgment in the assessment of these conditions, the rate of growth of money GDP has been brought down from about 15 per cent in 1978–9 to about 8 per cent last year. This is broadly the pattern that was envisaged when the MTFS was first launched. Monetary policy has led neither to overkill nor to the accommodation of inflation.

Inflation and unemployment

It is, incidentally, sometimes argued that the reduction of inflation has been brought about not by the government's monetary policy but by three million unemployed. The implication is that high unemployment has reduced wage demands which in turn has reduced inflation. This view derives from the widespread error of seeing inflation in terms of a simple cost-plus framework.

In fact, a look at the pattern of wage and price increases makes it clear that wages did *not* lead the disinflationary process. If anything they followed. The reduction of inflation originated in the goods market – as evidenced by the initial decline of profit margins—and only gradually permeated through to wage settlements.

So far from high unemployment being the cause of lower earnings and thus lower inflation, it was the failure of wages to adjust at a time of falling inflation that was responsible for much of the increased unemployment, from which we continue to suffer.

Fiscal policy

The other crucial dimension of the MTFS has been the approach to fiscal policy and the Budget judgment. Successive versions of the MTFS have set out a framework within which monetary growth could be brought down without – in the words of the original 1980 MTFS – 'excessive reliance on interest rates'. Each version of the MTFS has included projections of a path for the PSBR which is considered to be consistent with the monetary objectives at acceptable interest rate levels. The full consequences of having an excessive PSBR may take some time to come through.

While the outstanding stock of government debt relative to income would tend to grow at a faster rate than was consistent with the existing structure of interest rates, there is a seductive argument that quite large changes in the PSBR only influence the total outstanding stock of debt slowly and that a period of high borrowing may therefore not be too disruptive. In fact, however, the long-term consequences would tend to be foreseen by the financial markets, and the effects on interest rates brought forward as a result of changes in expectations.

Even more important, in practice, the markets might not believe that the government was prepared to allow real interest rates to rise to the extent necessary to persuade people to accept a higher stock of government debt. They might instead expect increased monetisation of the deficit, with the result that inflationary expectations and nominal interest rates would tend to rise.

Budget deficits and interest rates

Thus even relatively small changes in the PSBR path from that perceived to be consistent over a period of years with existing trends in wealth and portfolio shares could have major effects on interest rates, particularly long rates, if they are expected to be other than temporary.

There has been a lot of ink spilled recently as some have tried to argue there is no relation between Budget deficits and interest rates. It is true that a simple-minded historical statistical comparison of interest rates and Budget deficits proves little. But this is because much of the variation in deficits has been cyclical – with high deficits at times of recession – and so has much of the short-term variation of interest rates. Over the cycle low interest rates and high deficits often go together in recessions – and vice versa in upturns. But that is most unlikely to be the pattern for successive years of structurally high deficits – then the tendency for high interest rates is likely to be dominant. Developments in the relative behaviour of interest rates in the US and UK provide some evidence of the impact of a sustainable period of different deficit profiles.

In 1975–6 at the time of peak borrowing by the previous government UK long-term interest rates were 6 per cent higher than equivalent US rates. In 1979 the gap was still 4 per cent. Now the position has changed. For the first time since the end of the last war UK long-term interest rates are lower than US rates. And the gap has gradually widened so that now it is around 2 per cent.

The road to recovery

Despite some initial difficulties, partly associated with the onset of the recession, the strategy of reducing the PSBR as a percentage of GDP has been successfully implemented.

The crucial decisions were taken in Geoffrey Howe's 1981 Budget; substantial increases in tax revenue brought the deficit back onto a downward path. It was a very unpopular set of measures, not least among the economics industry.

We now know that the bottom of the cycle occurred very shortly afterwards. I do not want to push the suggestion of causality too far. There had been signs in the forward indicators before the budget that the bottom of the cycle was imminent and indeed that was the message in the Treasury forecast published the previous December. But there is no evidence that the Budget of 1981 'deepened the recession' as 364 economists confidently predicted at the time. Rather, it was a significant turning point both in terms of the public's acceptance of the determination of government policy, and in economic performance.

It is sometimes suggested that the turnround was simply the natural stockbuilding cycle that was dampened by the Budget action. I would simply observe that there was not much being said at the time about stockbuilding cycles or imminent recovery – except by Treasury ministers themselves. In my speech to the IFS in March 1981 I answered the hypothetical question more common then than now – 'but where is the growth going to come from?' in these terms:

> The most obvious answer is that, just as the recession had as three important components a massive wave of destocking, a sharp increase in the savings ratio, and the world recession, so the recovery is likely to be assisted by a slowing down in the rate of destocking, as inventories approach the desired level, by a fall in the savings ratio, as inflation and inflationary expectations fall, and by some upturn in the world economy.

Exchange rate policy

A further frequent source of misunderstanding has concerned the government's exchange rate policy. Intervention has been restricted to occasions when there was a risk of disorderly markets. Otherwise it is not clear that intervention serves much purpose unless it is unsterilised – in other words, it is allowed to affect monetary policy generally.

In this case it needs to be seen in the light of other aspects of monetary policy. Exchange rate movements *can* be a useful guide to the tightness or looseness of monetary conditions, but this is by no means always the case. It is important to ask why the exchange rate has been moving. If it is a reflection of policies overseas the case for taking it into account is rather weaker than when it appears to reflect domestic monetary conditions. Much current discussion of the exchange rate is in any case vitiated by the emphasis commonly laid upon the various measures of competitiveness, which gives the impression that a rise in the exchange rate and a rise in domestic costs relative to other countries come to much the same thing.

I doubt if this is ever the case; but, certainly, given a policy of controlling the money supply with the intention of controlling total nominal spending their effects are quite different. Exchange rate appreciation may have adverse affects upon net exports but there is a beneficial impact on domestic spending from lower inflation. The effects on GDP are therefore ambiguous. With an increase in domestic prices and costs, however, this is not the case. Net exports suffer but so does domestic spending as the higher costs and prices bump up against the monetary target. (For precisely similar reasons, incidentally, exchange rate depreciation is simply a sub-optimal way of bringing about lower real wages.)

The plain fact is that the recession of 1980–81 owed much more to the unwarranted cost increases in 1979–80 than to the rise in the exchange rate. Implicitly many critics argue that exchange rate policy should have been operated to accommodate that wage pressure. But that would have flown directly in the face of the declared strategy to bring down inflation. A refusal to accommodate that wage pressure was an essential part of changing the implicit belief of the private sector that government would accommodate whatever action it chose to take.

On to stable prices

That phase is now over. The government's commitment to the further reduction of inflation is well understood. Inflation has fallen further and faster than any of our critics thought possible when we first put the strategy in place. But from now on progress is bound to be slower. Double-digit inflation was, in essence, an aberration of the 1970s; fortunately, thanks to the policies embarked on in 1979, it never persisted long enough to become embedded in expectations or a part of our economic bloodstream. But low levels of inflation *have* been the norm – as indeed they are throughout the industrialised world. Stable prices are a blessed condition, but one that we in this country have not experienced other than very fleetingly for fifty years.

To achieve stable prices thus implies fighting and changing the culture and the psychology of two generations. That cannot be achieved overnight. But let there be no doubt that that is our goal.

The enterprise culture

In the field of micro-economic policy, too, what we are seeking to do is to change a psychology, to change a business culture. The abolition of pay controls, price controls, dividend controls, foreign exchange controls, bank lending controls, hire purchase controls, industrial building controls – all these have been beneficial in themselves, but will bring even greater benefit to the nation as part of the process of rediscovering the enterprise culture. A process that will be carried further by progressive reductions in the burden of taxation – provided we maintain, as we must, the downward trend of public expenditure as a proportion of GDP. And one that will be further promoted by the onward march of privatisation and the breaking up of monopolies and restrictive practices – not least in the City of London.

In this context, moreover, the labour market is clearly of vital importance; and the labour legislation already enacted, and that currently before Parliament, present a long overdue start in a key area of the national economy. On almost all of these fronts we are opposed, inevitably, by vested interests of one kind or another. On almost all of them it will take time for the changes to have their full effect. But the climate *is* changing: of that there can be no doubt. And my Budget this year was an attempt to assist that change.

The importance of profitability

At the heart of the enterprise culture must lie a commitment to profitability, which, over the years, the Corporation tax changes embodied in this year's Finance Bill should serve to reinforce. But already one of the most encouraging aspects of the present recovery is the sharp recovery that is occurring in company profits. Gross trading profits of all industrial and commercial companies, net of stock appreciation, rose by around two-fifths between 1981 and 1983 as a whole; and will be significantly up again this year.

The CBI have forecast that the net real rate of return before interest and tax at current replacement cost may exceed 8 per cent this year for non-North Sea industrial and commercial companies. This compares with 4 per cent in 1981 and will be the highest rate of return since 1973. Even that, however, is well below the returns of 10–12 per cent that were the norm during the 1960s. The trend is in the right direction, but it still has further to go.

The prospect for jobs

It is the rediscovery of the enterprise culture, operating within the framework of markets progressively liberated from rigidities and distortions, that will provide the only answer to the curse of unemployment, and the only true generator of new jobs. So far, although the numbers in work are now rising, unemployment has yet to fall. But that is no reason to accept the dismal thesis that in the technological world of today, rising unemployment is inevitable. It isn't – as the American experience so clearly shows.

Moreover, it is important to recognise that, in the UK, a very significant part of the increase in unemployment over the past five years is simply the emergence into the open of the unsustainable disguised unemployment of the second half of the 1970s, when overmanning – in manufacturing in particular – was rife. In 1979 the level of productivity in UK manufacturing was well below that of the rest of Europe, let alone the United States. The potential for a rapid and substantial catching up was clearly there. That potential is now being realised, with an average growth of manufacturing productivity of around 6 per cent a year for the past three years, and little sign of slackening. In the short term this represents a very painful adjustment. But in the longer term it will mean not only higher living standards, but higher levels of employment, too.

Conclusion

In conclusion, I owe you an explanation of the title I have chosen: The British Experiment. That experiment, if experiment it is – and I borrow the term from those who have been less than enthusiastic about it – consists of seeking, within an explicit medium-term context, to provide increasing freedom for markets to work within a framework of firm monetary and fiscal discipline. It stands in contrast to the post-war trend towards ever more *ad hoc* interference with free markets within a context of increasing financial *in*discipline.

That was the road that led to stagnation, unemployment – and above all accelerating inflation. *That*, in truth, was the experiment that failed. But many of those who embarked on it did so not because they believed in it. They did so because they had reached the conclusion that political and electoral pressures in a democracy gave them no option.

The true British Experiment is a political experiment. It is the demonstration that trade union power *can* be curbed within a free society and that inflation *can* be eradicated within a democracy. And the growing success of that demonstration is of the most fundamental importance to us all.

9 The economic framework for New Labour

The Rt Hon Tony Blair MP

Introduction and overview

It is an honour to be invited to deliver this year's Mais Lecture – a series which has already made its mark in our national economic life.

Tonight, I want to set out the economic framework of a new Labour government. I can summarise my argument as follows:

1   The traditional distinction between measures which focus on economic management and measures designed to improve the underlying performance of business is false. Macro and micro policy are indivisible.
2   Low inflation is not simply a goal in itself. It is the essential prerequisite both of ensuring that business can invest and that supply-side measures can work to raise the capacity of the economy to grow.
3   Those measures require a new partnership between government and industry that is not the *laissez-faire* of the new right or a return to the old-style corporatism of the old left, but the determination of a set of specific objectives necessary for long-term economic strength.
4   Raising the standards of education and skills is an economic as well as social imperative.
5   Tackling long-term unemployment is essential to reducing spending on welfare dependency, is right in itself, and is entirely compatible with the above economic goals.
6   Tax and spending questions cannot ultimately be divorced from the state of the economy, and the only route to maintain a reasonable tax burden is through economic strength.

I can already hear Conservatives claiming that they agree with these objectives. But on the record of sixteen years, this cannot be sustained. We have had two severe recessions, industrial policy has often been neglected, education and skills undervalued, and long-term unemployment ignored. It remains to be seen whether in this economic cycle their mistakes are avoided or repeated. Short termism was and is still the hallmark of economic policy, whether under Mrs Thatcher or John Major.

However, I believe it is possible to establish a new economic consensus around the principles I have just outlined. I don't care in the least that there will be areas of agreement between left and right, though the differences are also fundamental.

I am an unashamed long termist. Though the actions of a Labour government will be immediate, they will be aimed at the long term. If this country is to grow in strength in what is an increasingly competitive global market, it must learn the lessons of the past and move beyond its battles.

I shall also argue that post-war economics has suffered from two forms of short termism: the belief, up to the 1970s, that performance of British industry could be regulated primarily through demand management; and, from the late 1970s onwards, the insistence that monetarism would take care of inflation and the real economy would look after itself. The first was normally associated with the left, and the second with the right, though in reality governments of both left and right shared some of the conventional wisdom.

The new world market, which today is industrially and financially transformed, demands a new economics. What I outline tonight is a new economic framework:

- to deliver low and stable inflation which allows business to invest
- to rebuild Britain's long-term industrial strength
- to raise dramatically the education and knowledge base of our workforce
- and to tackle the evil of long-term unemployment

Economic theory and its relevance to policy makers have featured in several Mais Lectures. In 1984, Nigel Lawson, then Chancellor of the Exchequer, sought to combine theory and practice in a lecture entitled the 'British Experiment', in which he set out the guiding principles that had governed economic policy since 1979.

It remains one of the clearest outlines of the economic ideas that have dominated Conservative economic policy. Although much has changed since the 1980s, many of the main themes of the Lawson lecture continue to guide policy today.

Tonight, I want to examine the philosophy that has lain behind economic policy since 1979. I will say where the Labour approach agrees with the Conservatives, and where we strongly disagree. I will also outline a coherent framework for a new consensus between economists and politicians which I believe is the best way forward for Britain in the late 1990s.

My main conclusions are these:

- First, the 1984 Mais Lecture was right to argue that inflation is an evil which must be controlled. But, if anything, it underestimated the importance of a permanent and credible macro-economic framework to control inflation. For temporary fluctuations in inflation – short-term failings of macro-economic policy – can have permanent damaging effects on the ability of the economy to sustain high levels of output and jobs.
- Second, deregulation of labour, product and financial markets is not enough

to deliver medium-term supply-side improvements. The government has a responsibility not only to control the volatile behaviour of the private sector through macro-economic policy. It must also promote partnerships with the private sector to improve economic performance.

- Third, a lower level of overall taxation is preferable to a higher level. But the 1980s have shown that, whatever the government intends, high taxation can be imposed on the economy as the penalty for economic failure. An improved supply-side performance is the key to the durable control of inflation and the burden of taxation. The British experiment of the 1980s has bequeathed to the economy low levels of investment, high levels of social security spending on unemployment and high levels of taxation. We must break free of this spiral.

Since Lawson left the stage, up until the last election successive Chancellors have continued to be dominated by short-term considerations. Since the election the government has had to deal with the consequences and put the public finances on a more even keel. The present Chancellor claims that this time it will be different, but leaving aside the most recent differences with the Bank on inflation, there are few who doubt that taxes will be cut ahead of the election, irrespective of their economic justification.

Looking back over the period since the war, no one economic 'school' has ever had all the answers. Most have at different times provided useful insights into economic and financial problems, but have failed to anticipate change, and to adjust to it. This is a defect, I would argue, which applies to the post 1979 economic philosophy, just as much as it did to the earlier 'Keynesian' consensus. Once more, it is time for change, a post-monetarist framework.

Lawson's argument

I shall start with a reminder of what Lord Lawson said eleven years ago. Lawson argued that the focus and content of economic policy which had prevailed in the post-war period needed to be turned upside down.

What was the consensus in that period?

It was that macro-economic policy, in the form of demand management was the key to stimulating growth and maintaining full employment. Meanwhile, micro-economic policy – above all various measures of wage control – was the key to low inflation.

Lawson asserted the exact opposite. He said that macro-economic policy should be responsible for controlling inflation, and should have no role in stimulating growth or creating jobs. The other side of the coin was that micro-economic policy should be concerned with promoting economic growth and jobs, but should have no role in controlling inflation.

Furthermore, Lawson argued that, within both the micro and macro areas, the key instruments of policy should change. The crucial macro instrument was not budgetary policy – the variation of taxation and public spending to prevent

recessions – but monetary policy. Interest rates should be set to achieve low inflation, and that was an end to the macro-economic responsibility of the Chancellor.
Elsewhere, the private sector could be left to look after itself.

This belief in market forces governed the supply side too. According to
Lawson, the government should accept no responsibility to help the market
function successfully through intervention. Instead, it should cease interfering
with market processes wherever practicable.

Deregulation and privatisation were the only instruments through which this
was to be achieved. Once government was off the back of the private sector, the
private sector would ensure that rapid growth and full employment were
achieved.

And Lawson made one final point. The reduced role for government was to be
reflected in a gradual reduction in the share of tax and public spending in GDP.
Lower marginal tax rates would further increase the private sector's incentive to
make the economy succeed.

This analysis in fact represented a return to the nineteenth century when
economists asserted that real (output) and nominal (money) variables in the economy could be determined entirely independently of each other. According to
them, there was only one level of growth and employment which the economy
could sustain over the medium term. They went as far as to call these the 'natural'
levels of output and employment.

They said that the government should look after inflation, while growth and
employment should be left to look after themselves.

I strongly dispute this thinking. It probably had no place in nineteenth-century
economics, and certainly has no place near the dawn of the twenty-first-century.
Yet its appeal for many people stemmed from the failures of an earlier period of
economic management now usually known as the post-war Keynesian consensus.
It is to this that I now turn.

Policy up to 1976

There is no doubt that some of those in the vanguard of the 'British Experiment'
were too dismissive of the record of most post-war governments.

It is too easy to forget the scale of economic and social problems that confronted Britain in the wake of the war, and the neglect of the pre-war years. Of
course mistakes were made by the 1945 Labour government but the world's finest
welfare state was built, and the huge task of taking the economy off a wartime
footing was accomplished. Economic reconstruction would have gone even
further but for the continued need to ration scarce resources, and to re-arm for the
fight against communist aggression in Korea.

Conservative and Labour governments in the 1950s and 1960s committed
errors too. They had an exaggerated belief in demand management, and showed
too little concern for the gradual build-up in inflationary pressure which took
place from one cycle to the next.

Yet they provided this country with an unprecedented period of prosperity and full employment, with GDP growth averaging almost 3 per cent. Many historians now label this the golden age of British economic performance.

Admittedly, it seemed no golden age at the time. Growth was lower than that of many countries in Europe, but this was to be expected. The post-war period was one in which reconstruction enabled other countries to 'catch up' with the economic and technological leadership of the United States. The potential benefits of 'catch up' to Britain were less than to the devastated economies of continental Europe.

However, there is also no doubt that there were deeper seated reasons for the deterioration in the underlying performance of the British economy compared with most of our major competitors.

One of the most important reasons was the polarised hostility between management and unions. There was fault on both sides, but the atmosphere of trench warfare which so often existed on what was then called 'the shop floor' was unacceptable in a modern economy. Industrial action was frequent, unpredictable and crippling to industrial efficiency.

This contributed to another cause of our relative failure – a lack of high quality investment.

Whichever way we look at the evidence, two things are clear.

First, the UK has invested too little in plant and equipment in the post-war era, and the quality of that investment has often been poor.

Second, Britain has neglected the impact on economic growth of investment in human capital, particularly training, an area where the UK has had a poor record since the war and one that is of rising importance. Indeed, the increasing globalisation of the world economy means that the required level of education and skills are now being set by international standards, and we continue to be left behind.

So, we must encourage long-term investment. But if companies are to invest they must have a relatively stable macro-economic framework in which to plan.

I do not need to remind anyone that in the last twenty-five years, the UK has been one of the most volatile of all the major economies. Since 1970 the British economy has suffered more recession years than other major developed economies, and the average UK inflation since 1970 has exceeded all major economies except Italy.

Even in the most successful years of the post-war period, governments frequently failed to provide the stable macro-economic background that companies need.

In the immediate post-war period governments sought to fine tune the economy to eliminate short-term fluctuations. However, it proved very difficult to gauge the appropriate timing of policy changes so that governments exacerbated the next boom instead of preventing the current slump. Moreover, in trying to reduce cycles in economic activity, government policies accommodated real shocks to the supply side of the economy – wage shocks, or oil shocks, for example. The consequence of this was inflation.

The story of the breakdown of the Keynesian consensus in the mid 1970s is familiar to us all. By 1976, inflation had run out of control, and Britain's external balance of payments situation was unsustainable. The Callaghan government faced a crucial decision, perhaps the most crucial in all of our post-war economic crises, on which direction to take.

One possibility was for the UK to go down the path of protection, withdrawing from the world's trading system, and seeking to return to a kind of wartime command economy. Fortunately, this path was swiftly rejected. Instead, macro-economic policy took an entirely new turn.

The British experiment

In his Labour Party conference speech in 1976, Jim Callaghan sounded the death knell of the post-war Keynesian consensus, when he openly admitted that the UK could no longer expect to borrow and spend its way out of recession. 'I tell you in all candour', he said 'that option no longer exists.'

From 1976 to 1979, the Labour government had a tight budgetary regime, and introduced monetary targets into the UK for the first time, not it should be recalled at the instigation of the IMF, but through Denis Healy's own initiative. The beginnings of the 'British Experiment' were beginning to emerge, but it was not until Mrs Thatcher and Sir Geoffrey Howe arrived on the scene in 1979, with Nigel Lawson in a junior role at the Treasury, that the real years of the British experiment really started.

It was then that the whole panoply of new measures started to develop, all of them based on the intellectual underpinning outlined in the 1984 Mais Lecture.

Accordingly, the aims of macro-economic policy became more medium term, and policy objectives were all confined to monetarist objectives. These included money supply targets, the rate of growth of money GDP, the exchange rate or inflation itself.

But if attempts to manage demand failed in an earlier period, the UK's experience exposed serious flaws in this approach too.

Three reasons stand out.

First, though the ultimate objectives have stayed broadly the same, the framework for policy has been extremely inconsistent, with one regime after another failing to meet stated objectives. Since 1979, there have been at least four major lurches in the framework of monetary policy:

- **Monetarism**, the primacy of the domestic money supply or M3, from 1979 to 1983.
- **'Lawsonomics'**, the mix of monetary and exchange rate targets, from 1983 to 1989.
- **The ERM**, a fully blown exchange rate regime, from 1990 to 1992.
- **Domestic inflation targets**, from 1992 to the present.

Second, the political influence on short-term monetary decisions in the 1980s, exacerbated by the effect of interest rates on the housing market, meant that policy makers resisted raising interest rates until there was overwhelming evidence of inflationary pressure, and then tightened too much. That is the real nature of the debate between the government and the Bank of England.

The third problem which undermined the effectiveness of monetary policy during the 1980s was the failure to use monetary and fiscal policy in a co-ordinated fashion. In the late 1980s, fiscal policy was being relaxed, with tax cutting budgets in 1988, 1989 and 1990 at a time when interest rates were being kept high to curb inflationary pressure. That meant interest rates had to be pushed that much higher to slow down the economy and curb inflationary pressure.

The new monetary framework introduced after the exit from the ERM is still too politicised. If the public finances improve more quickly than the Treasury anticipates, there is little doubt that the Chancellor will cut taxes even if the improvement is solely due to faster than expected demand, thus repeating one of the crucial policy errors of the late 1980s. Even if they do not improve, we can assume that taxes will be cut, regardless of the economic circumstances.

Looking back at the entire period of the British experiment, it is far from clear that the overall performance of the UK economy has been any better than it was under the Keynesian consensus.

- Unemployment has more than doubled since 1979, and there seems little or no prospect of it returning even to 1970s levels, still less to 1950s or 1960s levels, under present policy.
- Inflation has come down, but little more than it has elsewhere in the world.
- The huge proceeds of North Sea oil somehow seem to have been squandered, without any significant improvement in domestic investment.
- Tax as a share of GDP has not been reduced.
- The growth in GDP – the ultimate judge and jury – has been under 2 per cent, around 1 per cent less than was achieved in the Keynesian years.

Where the British experiment was right

One of the main problems with 1980s-style monetarism was that it thought there was nothing positive to learn from the successes of the Keynesian era. It threw the baby out with the bathwater. I do not want to make the same mistake in the late 1990s.

Macro-economic policy must be directed to keeping inflation low and as stable as possible. The idea that inflation can be stabilised at around 5–10 per cent, with permanent benefits to growth, is pure and dangerous fantasy. It would soon accelerate and output will have to be cut to bring it under control.

And it is undoubtedly true that improvements in the supply side are vital to increasing the underlying growth rate of the economy. This explains Labour's emphasis on investment in education, training and infrastructure.

There was undoubtedly a need to change the climate of industrial relations. For example, the key elements of the 1980s legislation affecting trade unions will be retained. Indeed, if Labour's initiatives in the 1960s had been fully implemented, the 1970s might well have turned out differently in a number of ways.

Lawson was also right to stress the need to focus on the medium term. The post-war years are littered with short-term economic decisions which, taken for initially quite sensible and pragmatic reasons, have resulted cumulatively in a protracted period of decline

Where the British experiment was wrong

However, despite these areas of agreement, something went very badly wrong with the 'British Experiment'. It was put forward as laying the foundations for enhanced economic performance, but in key respects it did not.

The root cause for this failure lies with mistakes in macro-economic policy. A number of mistakes can be identified.

First, the design of the macro-economic framework itself, the MTFS.

As I explained earlier, the policy regime changed whenever it seemed convenient. Sterling M3 came and went. Monetary aggregates were 'monitored' rather than targeted. The exchange rate came into greater prominence. And so on.

The result was that an excessive amount of reliance came to be placed in the judgment of the Chancellor. The medium-term framework was increasingly defined in virtually any way the Chancellor chose. Herbert Morrison once defined socialism as 'anything a Labour government does!' The MTFS came to be anything that the Tories chose it to be.

In the end too much flexibility became a liability and the MTFS lost its credibility with the markets.

The second failure of macro-economic policy was the reluctance to recognise that the government has to respond to excessive imbalances in the economy even if they are produced by the private sector. The 1984 mantra was 'public sector bad, private sector good'.

Because of this, the government remained far too relaxed as trade and the current account deficits ballooned through the late 1980s. Because they reflected deficits of the private sector Lawson took the view that they would adjust reasonably smoothly. In the end such a casual approach came to grief.

The trade gap had to be financed by foreigners being ready to acquire sterling denominated assets in the UK They would only do this if they believed the returns would be attractive. This would only be the case if economic growth was strong and as long as inflation remained low so that currency depreciation was a low risk.

But if growth stalled or if inflation threatened to accelerate, a large trade deficit became a problem. The number of foreigners willing to hold UK assets and lend to UK citizens dried up. Interest rates had to be raised to extreme levels to prevent an outright collapse in the pound. The result was recession – a recession caused by the volatile behaviour of the private sector, and the government's dogmatic refusal to worry about it until far too late.

Most fundamental of all, there was a complete failure to appreciate the inter-connection between macro-economic and micro-economic policy. Since the two were deemed to be separated – again for reasons of dogma and doctrine – the government failed to see that changes in micro-economic policy may need to be offset by shifts in macro-economic policy.

Furthermore, this interconnection means that macro-economic failure which allows inflation to get out of control can have long-term consequences for the real economy. And here I come to a key point. The classical split between inflation on the one hand, and output or employment on the other hand, turned out to be entirely false.

The failure of macro-economic policy had permanent effects on the supply side of the economy through the reduction in investment, the withering of the capital stock and the rise in numbers of long-term jobless. This reduced productive capacity, raised the sustainable level of unemployment, and reduced the trend growth rate of the economy.

Furthermore, the volatility of the economy is reflected in capital markets. In the past five years the gilt market has been more volatile than any other major bond market, putting up the cost of capital. And after every recession, businesses need more and more convincing that recovery is this time 'for real'. This is why businesses have been so slow to invest in the current recovery, with the result that capacity constraints have again reappeared with unemployment still far too high.

A recession of some sort was almost inevitable after 1988 if inflation was to be reduced to an acceptable level, but the impact of such a recession goes beyond the immediate loss of output and employment. It has permanent debilitating effects on the economy's ability to sustain high levels of growth and employment.

In contrast to monetarist theory, a failure of policy that affects nominal economic variables will have a disastrous medium-term impact on real ones too.

Unless the government learn the lessons of the 1980s they will repeat its mistakes.

Lessons from the post-war era

So what lessons should we draw from the eventual failure of post-war Keynesian economics and the more recent setbacks for the British experiment?

First, the control of inflation through a tough macro-economic policy framework is even more important than the Tories have said. Of course, the control of inflation is vital in its own right. But what is even more crucial is that, in practice, the 'classical' split between inflation and output cannot be maintained. Temporary failures over inflation have permanent adverse effects on the real economy – on output and jobs. The only way this can be avoided is to put in place a tough, credible and transparent macro-economic framework which will stand the test of time. This a Labour government would do.

Second, while the Tories correctly observed that both macro- and micro-economic policy measures were necessary to achieve economic success, they have failed to appreciate the extent to which failure in the former could swamp improvements in the latter. They are also wrong to see these instruments as separate or separable – they are in fact complementary. The one should support the other; the one should compensate for the failings of the other.

Third, the Tories have placed far too much faith in the benign and self-correcting nature of private sector behaviour once deregulation had taken place. In fact, total reliance on the private sector is just as wrong as over-reliance on the public sector. Deregulation alone cannot cure the ills of our economy. The public sector must accept its responsibility to act in partnership with the private sector to transform the supply side of the economy. This is a responsibility which Labour will gladly accept.

Fourth, we have learned and relearned that co-operative attitude between workers and management at the workplace is vital. The union excesses of the 1970s were wrong, but it would be just as wrong to replace them with an attitude of worker subservience to an almighty management. The successful companies are based on partnership and co-operation, not class war or old-style management domination.

Fifth, unemployment is not just a social problem, but an economic problem as well. The Tories' indifference to the climb in long-term unemployment in the 1980s and 1990s is indefensible. We must make a clear commitment to get long-term unemployment down.

Finally, we have learned that the ability to improve public services, or to cut taxation, is derived from, and cannot be divorced from, economic success. A low-tax economy is only possible if we first have a high-success economy.

New Labour – the macro framework

The first priority for a high-success economy is a tough and coherent macroeconomic framework for policy.

We must recognise that the UK is situated in the middle of an active global market for capital – a market which is less subject to regulation today than it has been for several decades. Since it is inconceivable that the UK would want to withdraw unilaterally from this global marketplace, we must instead adjust our policies to its existence.

Global capital markets have advantages as well as perils for a British government. They provide access to overseas and domestic savings; but capital flows, which nowadays are far more important than trade flows in determining the value of the currency, can swiftly move against policies which fail to win investors' confidence.

An expansionary fiscal or monetary policy that is at odds with other economies in Europe will not be sustainable for very long. To that extent the room for manoeuvre of any government in Britain is already heavily circumscribed

There is little point in trying to eliminate all the fluctuations of the economic cycle, but getting the overall framework for fiscal and monetary policy right is the biggest single thing that will encourage business to invest. This in turn will enable a Labour government to mount a sustained attack on the country's economic and social problems.

If we get this right, it becomes possible to improve in imaginative ways the supply side. Equally, failure will undermine other policies to improve industrial performance.

The macro framework has two elements – the monetary framework, and the fiscal framework, including the level of tax and spending in the economy.

The monetary framework

As the Shadow Chancellor said last week, a Labour government will have an explicit target for low and stable inflation.

Controlling inflation is not only an objective in itself. It is an essential pre-requisite of sustainable economic growth on a scale sufficient to attain the social and political aims of the Labour Party, including high durable levels of employment and rising living standards.

To help achieve low and reasonably stable levels of inflation a Labour government will introduce a number of changes affecting the relationship between the Treasury and the Bank of England.

The monthly meeting between the Chancellor and the Governor of the Bank of England and the subsequent publication of the minutes have been a sensible innovation.

However, reform needs to be taken further as the existing arrangements do have some drawbacks. I will mention only two.

First, its effective working is peculiarly dependent on the personalities involved. To be fair, whatever other difficulties there may have been, so far this one does not seem to have been a problem. But it could become one and potentially it adds an unnecessary element of instability into the making of monetary policy.

Secondly, the overall effect of the recent innovation is probably to have increased the power of the Bank relative to the Treasury, though this is not entirely clear cut. Unfortunately, however, there has been no increase in the accountability of the Bank to the democratic process, and insufficient increase in the transparency of its operations.

How are we to move forward?

Germany's economic record and the potential role of the Bundesbank demands attention. Of course Germany's prosperity since the end of the war is based on much more than the independence of the Bundesbank, but confidence in the overall stability of monetary policy has certainly been a factor.

However, it is not always possible or desirable to transpose institutions unchanged from one country to another. The institutions themselves will to some extent reflect different cultures and traditions. For example, there is no doubt that, for historical reasons, the role of the central bank in Germany has a much greater political resonance with the electorate than is conceivable in Britain. This is reflected in the Bundesbank's position within the constitution and differences must be heeded in any relationship between the Bank of England and the government in Britain.

Three main points should be noted from Germany's experience.

First, although the Bundesbank's inflation record has been good, it has in practice shown a much greater degree of operational pragmatism – a willingness to deviate from monetary targets, for example, – than its rhetoric or reputation might imply. One reason for this, of course, is its own track record. The lesson from this is that credibility can enhance the room for policy manoeuvre.

Second, the operations of the Bundesbank allow it to move interest rates in small steps. This is less disruptive to business than the larger hikes that have characterised moves in Britain.

Third, although the constitution of the Bundesbank formally guarantees its independence from the political process, this is not absolute. In the aftermath of German unification, even the Bundesbank became concerned about whether its freedom of manoeuvre could be guaranteed. In a democracy political acceptance for monetary decisions ultimately has to be retained.

We have to design an institutional arrangement that fits Britain, and it may use the best practice from a number of other countries.

Our objective is clear. This is to reform the Bank of England so that it can carry out its increasingly important functions in an open and more accountable manner. Gordon Brown spelt out a series of reforms last week. We will then watch the track record of the Bank before deciding what, if any, further steps should be taken towards greater operational responsibility for the Bank in interest rate policy.

Fiscal policy, and the level of taxation and spending

Last week, the Shadow Chancellor stated our fiscal framework. This emphasised that the ratio of public debt to GDP would be stabilised at a prudent level, and that the 'golden rule' of public finance would be observed by a Labour government. This means that public borrowing will be used only to finance investment, not public consumption. Even then it must be prudently undertaken.

Tonight, I want to comment on the implications of this framework for the level of taxation and government expenditure in the economy.

Macro- and micro-economic policy affect each other and this has important implications for taxation and spending, and illustrates the sterile nature of the debate on these issues in recent years.

For example, proper control of public spending is needed for macro-economic reasons, but if this results in disproportionate cuts in capital spending it will have a damaging impact on the supply side of the economy.

Likewise the supply side performance of the economy may be improved by reductions in marginal rates of income tax, but if badly handled this can lead to uncontrolled booms, as it did in the late 1980s.

In any case, the changes that have occurred in Britain and the world economy mean that the debate over taxation and spending have to recognise a much narrower range of options than before.

The growing integration of the world economy – in which capital, and to a lesser extent labour, moves freely – means that it is not possible for Britain to sustain budget deficits or a tax regime that are wildly out of line with the other major industrial countries. One of the requirements of our tax structure is to attract enterprise into the UK from overseas.

I want to make one thing clear. In government, controlling public spending is a long and gruelling slog. But, the alternative is far worse, as we have seen from the past, when excessive spending in the short term has had to be retrenched with painful long-term consequences for business and the public services.

The long haul also applies to taxation. No one wants a return to penal taxation and, of course, the objective of any government is to lower rather than to increase the tax burden on ordinary families. But lower taxes depend on a successful economic policy.

The debate on this subject needs to become more realistic on both sides. The Right often promises to cut both taxes and spending irrespective of circumstance. The old Left was perceived as believing that higher taxation and spending are a good thing in themselves.

Neither side is right, as the recent experience of both Labour and Conservative governments has shown. The first planned a large increase in public spending, but in the end was forced to retrench with large cuts in spending.

The second promised to cut taxes, but has been forced to impose the biggest tax increases in peace-time history as the rest of its economic strategy hit the rocks.

Neither government wanted to reverse course. Both were forced to do so because economic policies as a whole failed to deliver an acceptable performance from the real economy.

An economic strategy that puts investment and economic growth at the centre of the agenda cannot ignore the implications of these objectives for the taxation of companies, savings and individual incomes.

But the real point is that decisions on taxation and spending are dependent on the overall performance of the economy. And the type of spending is just as important as its overall quantity.

Economic success over the medium term will enable a Labour government to reduce the amount of spending that simply mops up the consequences of economic failure – rescue spending – and raise the proportion that is available for renewal spending, especially on investment, education and training.

This is the opposite of what has happened under the Conservatives. In the three years since the last election public spending has averaged about 44 per cent of GDP. This year, it may fall a little, to reach roughly the same proportion of GDP as it did in 1979.

But since 1979 spending on renewal areas has fallen from 13.5 per cent of GDP to just over 10 per cent, a difference of about £20bn. Meanwhile, economic failure has meant that rescue spending, on unemployment and social security, has risen from 8.5 per cent of GDP to nearly 12 per cent. This reorientation of the type of spending within the total has been much more important than changes in the total itself.

New Labour – micro-economic strategy to build long-term strength

So, as I have emphasised, to increase the underlying growth rate of the economy has to recognise the importance of both macro- and micro-economic policy and the connection between the two.

In the area of micro-economic policy, it is important to distinguish those areas which are best carried out by government, which by the private sector and those where a partnership between the two is the best way of raising the performance and capacity of business.

When I spoke to the British Chambers of Commerce earlier this month I set out our plans to build Britain's long-term economic strength by co-operating with industry and commerce. We seek co-operation in seven key areas:

- unlock human potential through education and training
- develop modern infrastructure
- harness and spread new technology
- encourage investment and longer term thinking
- tackle long-term unemployment
- open up world markets for British business
- encourage small- and medium-sized firms.

Tonight I want to focus on three particular aspects of micro-economic policy – the flexibility of labour markets (which received particular attention in the Mais Lecture in 1984); the treatment of long-term unemployment; and investing for the longer term.

Flexibility and employment

The 'British experiment' attached huge importance to the need to deregulate labour markets in the UK, which were contrasted unfavourably with those in America.

While we clearly cannot ignore the recent employment record of the US, we should be wary of drawing simplistic conclusions. The benefits of deregulated labour markets have not been unqualified and increased flexibility has not been won without costs.

The cost and price of labour are important, but 'flexibility' is not just about cutting costs. The best of our international competitors do worry about costs, but they also do much, much more than that. They accept, along with the government, responsibility to nurture and improve the skills of their workforce.

Britain cannot take the 'cheap labour' route. We will never be as cheap as the low wage economies and in any case most of our competition is still with other advanced industrial countries. Short-term savings may lead to longer term costs. Deregulation may even accelerate de-skilling.

For example, if deregulation leads to a large increase in part-time or contract labour, with little commitment between firms and employees, companies may well be less able or willing to finance training or apprenticeships to the same extent that they would if there was a longer term relationship with their workforce. I do not believe there is any conflict at all between sensible minimum standards at work, including on pay, and a successful labour market. Indeed, I think the one complements the other.

Labour market flexibility should involve a new partnership between companies and workers that goes well beyond that of the buyer and seller of a commodity. Flexibility within businesses is as important as flexibility in the labour market external to the firm.

The key ingredient here will be to ensure that we create a fully educated labour force conversant with the skills necessary to implement the new technology. An educated worker is a confident worker – and a confident worker is more likely to show the flexibility needed for success. This form of flexibility is increasingly important in a period of rapid technological change.

A central fault of the Tories, in this and other areas, has been that they think that deregulation is enough. It is not. We are developing plans – such as the University of Industry, the broadening of the scope of A levels, and the improvements proposed in vocational training – to ensure that the British labour force no longer falls behind the skill levels available to business overseas.

Long-term unemployment

Long-term unemployment is an economic as well as a social problem, for the economy as a whole and for the individual.

Between 1979 and 1986 the long-term unemployed rose to just under 1.5 million. This has devastating long-term effects. The longer people are out of work the less likely they are to return to a job via the normal workings of the labour market. As the number of long-term unemployed becomes entrenched, it raises the overall unemployment rate which is compatible with low and stable inflation. An economic upturn is not enough to cut long-term unemployment significantly and this will be reflected in proportion of public spending taken up with what we have called 'rescue spending' – on the costs of economic failure.

In our Budget submission last November we proposed eight initiatives to tackle the combination of demotivation, lack of skills and opportunities. These included:

- reform of the benefits system, so that welfare payments are used to support work not unemployment
- reform of the labour market, including a tax rebate, for employers taking on the long-term unemployed
- and reform of child care and training opportunities, to support single parents to enter the labour market

Indifference to long-term unemployment is economically and socially unacceptable. If not tackled, it will remain a drag anchor on our economy and its costs will squeeze out much needed investment.

Long termism in finance and industry

Much of the UK's relatively poor economic performance can be put down to a lack of high quality investment over many years. It is much harder to identify the causes.

It is sometimes argued that the causes of low investment are the cost and terms of finance associated with the financial structure in Anglo-Saxon economies which is compared unfavourably with Germany and Japan, for example.

The strengths of Germany are said to be the close relationships between the banks and the company sector, in which the former take long-term equity holdings and are thought to be active participants in developing long-term strategies for companies. Japan's success is put down to the 'seamless web' between government, banks and industry. Both are preferred to the Anglo-Saxon structure in which institutional shareholders are thought to focus on short-term performance of companies reflected in stockmarket prices.

This may sound compelling but, in fact, the relationship between finance and industry reflects a number of different historical and cultural factors that cannot be transposed with success. Furthermore, there are a number of problems with this oversimplified view of our difficulties.

First, the Anglo-Saxon structure has not stopped the US economy being dynamic and strong.

Second, the decline in the UK's industrial performance predates the development of powerful institutional shareholders, and there are plenty of examples of once cash-rich companies with household names failing because of the lack of a successful strategy within the companies themselves.

Third, the actual relationship elsewhere is sometimes more complicated than it appears. For example, there is some evidence that German firms which have supervisory boards – seen as a means of encouraging longer term decisions – make less use of bank finance – seen by some as the key to Germany's industrial success – than those which do not.

Fourth, in continental Europe the trend may well be away from bank finance and towards a more Anglo-Saxon model. This partly reflects the need to develop financial structures able to cater for the demands for pensions from an ageing population. To this extent well developed financial institutions give the UK a head start in dealing with some common problems.

Having said all that, a long-term perspective does seem to be lacking in the UK financial sector. We are examining ways in which changes in the tax regime, or in take-over regulations which might sensibly be modified to encourage a long-term mentality in industry and the City. We have already undertaken to examine the CBI proposals for the reform of capital gains taxation.

But it is a mistake to believe that short-termism stems only from the City. The behaviour of the companies themselves needs to be monitored as well. Often, it is the management which initiates the expansion of a company by mergers and acquisitions rather than through natural growth. Of course they then need to get institutional backing, but the initiative starts from within the company itself.

So the UK may be suffering as much from unaccountable management as from an excessive City preoccupation with short-term profits.

I do not want to paint the picture too starkly, but it is important to develop a more fruitful relationship between the providers and recipients of finance. These issues are being actively considered in several quarters, and provided the implications of any changes are fully thought out and considered, I believe a Labour government would in some respects be knocking at an open door.

I hope that a step-by-step approach will be adopted. Legislation might ultimately be needed in some areas, such as the information provided in company accounts, but initial progress might be made without it. For example, although it would be wrong to exaggerate the significance of non-executive directors, at the moment many are too close in a personal sense to their chairman or chief executives. We will be discussing with the major financial institutions ways of increasing the effectiveness of non-executive directors as watchdogs for shareholders.

This is only one example, and its immediate impact might not be dramatic, but it is illustrative of a wider approach that over time could bring a longer term perspective for investment decisions.

Conclusion

There is no point in arguing that everything about the British economy is awful or that the government has done everything wrong. And I have not done that tonight.

There is some good news, but the latest recovery has nevertheless exposed once again the persistent nature of some fundamental weaknesses, for example the re-emergence of capacity constraints and of inflationary pressures while unemployment remains far too high.

At present, any pick-up in inflation looks likely to be modest compared with the 1980s and I hope the Chancellor is right when he says that interest rates are near the peak.

Most decisions to move interest rates involve fine judgment. But small mistakes on monetary policy can become cumulative and over a period of months or years, inflation creeps back into the system. The risk of that happening is all the greater if decisions are reached for short-term political reasons.

That has been the UK's experience.

It is the structure within which policy decisions are made, rather than the merits of any particular decision, that holds the key to curbing inflation, and improving the supply side of the economy, on a permanent basis.

When Nigel Lawson delivered his Mais Lecture in 1984, the 'British experiment' was at a relatively early stage. Since then, the full implications of the experiment have become apparent, as have its weakness.

As in the 1970s, we now need to recognise that a new approach is needed. I have outlined the key planks of the economic approach of new Labour.

First, our recognition that the theoretical split identified by nineteenth-century economists and which provided the intellectual underpinning of the 'British Experiment' breaks down in practice, largely because of the interconnection between the macro and micro economy. Failure to control inflation affects the real economy and vice versa. Short-term mistakes have long-term consequences.

Second, our belief that a macro-economic framework to keep inflation low and stable is even more important was said in the 1980s. Far from being an alternative to Labour's long-term investment strategy, controlling inflation is an essential part of it.

Third, our acceptance that too much reliance has been placed on deregulation alone to improve the supply side of the economy. There is an active role for government – particularly in, though not confined to, the improvement of human capital. In a world in which education, training and skills will increasingly be tested by global standards, any country which falls behind may be faced with huge social as well as economic consequences.

Fourth, our belief that much of the current debate on taxation and spending is parochial and sterile. The boundaries for changes in both are much reduced, and both are dependent on the performance of the economy, not on a priori assumptions about the desirability of particular levels of either. The key questions therefore become not how much to spend but what to spend it on, and how to improve the performance of the economy. That is what really matters to us all.

I came into politics because I believe passionately that a fair society and a more efficient one go hand in hand. By providing long-term economic strength and by raising the education and opportunities of all our citizens, we can achieve the stronger and more cohesive society I want to see. Social aims without economic means are empty wishes. By uniting the two we can build a better future for all our people.

It is to this that our new economic approach will be applied.

POSTSCRIPT

In 1995 I put the economic policies of the post-1979 Conservative governments into wider post-war perspective. I examined the strengths and weaknesses of the 'British Experiment' outlined by Nigel Lawson in 1984. I said that it would be wrong to argue that the then government had done nothing but make mistakes or that everything about the British economy was awful, but I did draw attention to failings that needed to be put right. These included the politicisation of monetary policy and the too limited perspective on improving supply-side performance. I outlined the approach that a Labour government would adopt if elected in the pending election.

Essentially, the failings of the previous government's policy were these:

- instability in economic management
- too many people on benefit who should have been in work not just for social but for economic reasons; and
- insufficient investment in the economy's future; particularly education, skills, science, technology and transport.

Our task in government has been to preserve those things that the previous government got right, e.g. a more flexible labour market, or an open economy, but to remedy the failings. We inherited an economy at an advanced stage of a cyclical upturn that began in late 1992. Unemployment was falling, inflation had dipped to 2.5 per cent for the first time in twenty-eight months but the economy was growing at an unsustainable rate and without action by the incoming government, inflation was heading for 4 per cent.

The Chancellor (for the first and last time) raised interest rates and gave the Bank of England operational independence. The markets endorsed the decision with a step-reduction in long-term interest rates that have since converged with those in Germany. This, of course, helps reduce the cost of capital for business.

From time to time the decisions of the Monetary Policy Committee (MPC) have inevitably been criticised by commentators. But no one seriously argues today that the new policy framework has not been a success. The point I would stress is the same one I made five years ago. 'It is the structure within which policy decisions are made, rather than the merits of any particular decision, that holds the key to curbing inflation and improving the supply side of the economy on a permanent basis.'

Rises in short-term interest rates are not good news for mortgage holders or business, but postponing necessary rises only means higher and more painful increases later. There is little doubt that the previous government put-off raising short-term interest rates for political reasons and this made the task more difficult for the newly formed MPC in 1997–8. Since then it has been able to act in a pre-emptive fashion and the framework for setting interest rates is one of the reasons that the UK economy has adjusted with relatively modest fluctuations in output compared with the previous twenty years or so. Long-term interest rates are the lowest for thirty years and short-term interest rates have averaged less than half the levels seen in the late 1980s and early 1990s.

Fiscal policy is the other pillar to the macro-economic policy framework that I outlined in 1995.

At the first opportunity the incoming government tightened fiscal policy. This was not a return to short-term fiscal fine-tuning that in the past has usually ended up reinforcing the economic cycle rather than dampening it. The fiscal tightening took place to put the public finances on a sustainable path for the medium and longer term. This was necessary because the previous government had left the public finances in poor shape, with borrowing still high despite over five years of economic expansion and a steeply rising burden of public debt. Adjusting for the economic cycle, fiscal policy has been tightened by more than 4 per cent of GDP since 1996–7.

I emphasised the importance of a soundly based macro-economic platform in 1995 as 'the biggest single thing that will encourage business to invest. This in turn will enable a Labour government to mount a sustained attack on the country's economic and social problems.'

From this platform of macro-economic stability the government has put in place measures to improve the supply side of the economy and reform the welfare state.

Properly functioning labour and product markets are essential to raising the level of productivity and living standards. As I made clear in 1995, the cost and price of labour is important but 'flexibility' is not just about cutting costs. It involves creating an educated and trained workforce that is adaptable.

Nor in a modern economy is 'flexibility' incompatible with minimum standards. We have implemented a minimum wage while at the same time increasing the incentive to work as part of a focussed policy to get the long-term unemployed back to work. The launch of the New Deal has proved a success and it is now being extended to wider groups who have been excluded from labour market participation. The Working Families Tax Credit is designed to make work pay while beginning to remedy a particular problem of child poverty.

In the Mais Lecture I said that I believed that an efficient and economically successful society and a fairer and more cohesive one were part of the same whole. Neither can be sustained indefinitely without the other.

It is because of the decisions that were made in the first couple of years after the election that we were subsequently able to plan for an increase in public expenditure to address some deep-seated problems in education and health in particular, but in other areas too.

The wider supply-side agenda I outlined in 1995 requires an effective competition policy as well as high quality infrastructure of transport, science, technology and communications.

But public spending can only be sustained if the economy can support it. We have completed two spending reviews that set out plans for three years ahead. Substantial sums of money are involved, but the plans are based on cautious economic assumptions and tough fiscal rules.

When I gave the Mais Lecture in 1995, Labour was in Opposition, untried in government for eighteen years. We did our best to reassure the electorate before the election and have established our competence since. In the nature of things, governments and economies periodically hit rough weather. But we have put in place an economic framework that should help us ride out any storms and take advantage of more favourable times. Measures to improve the supply side of an economy and reform the welfare state inevitably take time to bear fruit. We have made a good start. I outlined the route in 1995 and there is still much to be done, but our sights are unashamedly set on the long term.

10 The conditions for full employment

The Rt Hon Gordon Brown MP

IUK)

£24 I38
£52 £62

Introduction

My first words from the Treasury, as I became Chancellor and announced the independence of the Bank of England, were to reaffirm, for this Government, our commitment to the goal first set out in 1944 of high and stable levels of growth and employment.

Now in this Mais Lecture – which has been, from time to time, a platform for politicians of all parties to reflect, to analyse and – as is the case with us politicians – often to get things wrong, I will seek to detail the conditions in our times under which the high ideals and public purpose contained in this economic goal of 1944 can be achieved.

Full employment – defined as in 1944 as 'high and stable levels of employment' – was a reality for the twenty years after the Second World War. But rising unemployment in the 1970s was followed in the 1980s by unemployment rising to above three million, beyond its peak in the 1930s. As recently as 1997, 20 per cent of working age households – one in five – had no one in work.

Some believe that full employment can be restored only by a return to macro-economic fine tuning. Others believe that in the new more open economy governments cannot hope to meet the 1944 objectives. I reject both the dogma of insisting on old ways and the defeatism of abandoning the objectives.

So since 1997 the new Government has been putting in place a new framework to deliver the objectives of high and stable levels of growth and employment. And as I said in New York last month there are four conditions which must all be met – and met together – if we are to deliver in our generation those objectives of 1944:

- first: stability – a pro-active monetary policy and prudent fiscal policy to deliver the necessary platform of stability;
- second: employability – a strengthening of the programme to move the unemployed from welfare to work;
- third: productivity – a commitment to high quality long-term investment in science and innovation, new technology and skills;
- fourth: responsibility – avoiding short termism in pay and wage bargaining

across the private and public sectors, and building a shared sense of national purpose.

I will show that these conditions – requirements for stability, employability, productivity and responsibility – are and have always been the necessary conditions for full employment.

The first condition, stability, is needed to ensure a sustainable high demand for labour. The second, employability, promotes a sustainable high supply of labour. The third, raising productivity, provides a sustainable basis for rising living standards. And the fourth, responsibility in bargaining, ensures a sustainable basis for combining full employment with low inflation.

And I will show that the failure to meet these conditions led to persistently high unemployment in Britain in recent decades. And I will demonstrate how by putting these conditions in place we are restoring the goal of full employment for the next century.

The 1944 White Paper

If we start with that famous 1944 White Paper, we see that the government of the time was clear that if full employment was to be sustained all these conditions – stability, employability, productivity and responsibility – had to be in place.

While the 1944 White Paper asserted the need for active macro-economic policy – to balance supply and demand, it also recognised there was no long-run gain by trading lower unemployment for higher inflation. Indeed, the 1944 White Paper included an explicit requirement for stability. And I quote: 'action taken by the government to maintain expenditure will be fruitless unless wages and prices are kept reasonably stable. This is of vital importance to any employment policy.'

As important for future generations, was the White Paper's recognition that macro-economic action was a necessary but not sufficient condition for full employment and that policies for stability had to be accompanied by policies for employability, productivity and responsibility, not least in pay.

The 1944 White Paper stated that 'it would be a disaster if the intention of the government to maintain total expenditure were interpreted as exonerating the citizen from the duty of fending for himself and resulted in a weakening of personal enterprise'. It required that 'every individual must exercise to the full his own initiative in adapting himself to changing circumstances. The government . . . will also seek to prevent mobility of labour being impeded' and said 'workers must be ready and able to move freely between one occupation and another'.

And the 1944 vision was explicit about responsibility in pay, saying 'if we are to operate with success a policy for maintaining a high and stable level of employment, it will be essential that employers and workers should exercise moderation in wages matters'.

So while that White Paper is remembered for its commitment to pro-active monetary and fiscal policy, it should also be remembered for its emphasis on employability, productivity and responsibility not least in pay. And the evidence suggests that it was the accumulating failure – cycle by cycle – to meet not just one but all four of these conditions together that led to the rise of unemployment from the late 1960s onwards.

First the post-war years. The 1945 government was resolved that Britain never would return to the unemployment of the 1930s. Indeed over the first two decades it seemed that it was possible to sustain both low inflation and low unemployment, a period many have called a golden age for the British economy.

But we all now accept that a more detailed historical examination reveals that successive governments left unaddressed underlying long-term weaknesses. Once price and capital controls were dismantled, these weaknesses began to be revealed in low productivity and recurrent balance of payments difficulties.

Governments repeatedly attempted to address these problems – through policies to enhance employability, productivity and responsibility. Indeed, the theme of the 1960s was a productivity revolution to be achieved through national planning, of the 1970s a social contract which would responsibly resolve distributional conflicts, of the 1980s deregulation which would 'set the economy free'.

Supply side action to improve productivity, included the NEDC, the national plan, regional plans, the IRC, and later the NEB – all attempts to harness new technology to the productivity challenge and secure high growth. Supply side action to enhance employability on the labour market ranged from selective employment taxes to trade union reforms.

But the swift succession of improvisations to control pay – which ranged from guiding lights and pay pauses, to latterly 'severe restraint' and the social contract – showed just how elusive was the shared purpose necessary for pay responsibility to work.

In their desire to maintain the 1944 objectives, even as supply side action failed, governments resorted to attempting to control the economic cycle through doses of reflation.

And every time the economy grew from the 1950s onwards, a familiar pattern of events unfolded – a pattern we characterise as the British disease of stop go – rising consumption unsupported by sufficient investment, growing bottlenecks and balance of payments problems as the sterling fixed exchange rate link came under pressure – and then monetary and fiscal retrenchment as growth in the economy had to be reined back.

Unemployment around 300,000 in the mid 1950s rose to over half a million in the late 1960s and 1 million by the late 1970s, and with hindsight we can conclude that at no time in this period was Britain meeting all the conditions judged in 1944 to be necessary for full employment.

- despite the promise of stability, no credible institutional arrangements were put in place to deliver that stability;
- despite talk of rights and responsibilities in the labour market no serious reform of the Welfare State was instituted, even though – from the late 1960s onwards – growing global competition and new technologies were transforming our labour markets;

- despite repeated expressions of concern about our productivity gap, no long-term strategy for tackling it ever succeeded;
- while pay restraint was a central issue for most of the period, the initiatives that were introduced to ensure pay responsibility were invariably short term and were not underpinned by a broadly based consensus that resolved the difficult issues.

Each time governments sought to restore the shared, long-term purpose of 1945, they found it more – not less – difficult and attempts to do so descended into a mixture of exhortation – like the 'I'm backing Britain campaign' – and a British version of corporatism – vested interests cooking up compromises in smoke-filled rooms in London, far removed from the workplaces where such agreements would have to be sustained. The national consensus – which Mr Wilson sought around his national plan, Mr Heath sought around low inflation, Mr Callaghan sought around the social contract – broke down in a series of divisive conflicts – state versus market, capital versus labour, public versus private.

And the more governments failed on pay, productivity and industrial relations, the more they fell back on short-term 'fine tuning' in a doomed attempt to square the circle and deliver higher living standards and jobs despite sluggish productivity growth: problems massively compounded by the collapse of the Bretton Woods system of fixed exchange rates and the 1973 oil shock.

So the golden age gave way to the era of boom and bust. With each successive cycle, a clear pattern developed. Unsustainable growth, leading to stagnation, and cycle by cycle to ever higher levels of inflation and unemployment. Inflation rising from 3 per cent in the late 1950s to 9 per cent in the early 1970s and more than 20 per cent by 1975. Unemployment, ratcheted up every cycle and doubling over the period.

What began in 1944 as a comprehensive long-term strategy for growth and employment built on a commitment to stability, employability, productivity and responsibility had by the 1970s descended into short termism and rising unemployment. Quite simply, governments could not deliver growth and employment through a macro policy designed to exploit a supposed short-term trade off between higher inflation and lower unemployment.

A crude version of the 1944 policy – using macro policy to expand demand and micro policy to control inflation – simply could not work. And it was this insight that the 1979 government seized upon with what they termed a medium-term financial strategy to return Britain to economic stability. But they went further than simply arguing that 'fine tuning' was the problem. For them the very idea that dynamic economies required active governments was the problem.

As they stated, their policies reflected a neo liberal view of the state:

- first, the application of rigid monetary targets to control inflation – choosing in succession £M3, M1, then M0, then when they failed, shadowing the Deutschmark, then the Exchange Rate Mechanism as the chosen instrument for monetary control;

- second, a belief in deregulation as the key to employability – in the absence of an active labour market policy or an active, reformed Welfare State;
- third, as the route to higher productivity, again deregulation alone in capital and product markets – a philosophy of 'the best government as the least government';
- fourth, the rejection of consensus.

The clearest intellectual statement of the new position was Nigel Lawson's Mais Lecture in 1984. Its central thesis was that the proper role of macro-economic and micro-economic policy 'is precisely the opposite of that assigned to it by the conventional post-war wisdom'.

The conquest of inflation, not the pursuit of unemployment, should be the objective of macro-economic policy. The creation of conditions conducive to growth and employment, not the suppression of price rises, should be the objective of micro-economic policy.

On one point, arguing against a crude version of the 1944 policy – using macro policy to expand demand and micro policy to control inflation – he drew the right lesson from the failures of previous decades.

But far from tackling the boom-bust cycle endemic to the British economy, the early 1980s and 1990s saw two of the deepest recessions since 1945. And even at the peak of growth in 1988, unemployment was still over two million. Before it rose again to three million in 1993.

As the late 1980s boom showed the government eventually relapsed into the very short termism it had come into government to reverse. Just as the fine tuners had in the 1970s given way to the monetarists, so now monetarism lapsed into fine tuning.

By the mid 1990s, the British economy was set to repeat the familiar cycle of stop go that had been seen over the past twenty years. By 1997 there were strong inflationary pressures in the system. Consumer spending was growing at an unsustainable rate and inflation was set to rise sharply above target; there was a large structural deficit on the public finances. Public Sector Net Borrowing stood at £28 billion.

The new economic framework

So against a background of mounting uncertainty and then instability in the global economy, we set about establishing a new economic framework to achieve the four conditions for high and stable levels of growth and employment – to promote new policies for stability, employability, productivity and responsibility.

We started by recognising we had to achieve these 1944 objectives in a radically different context – integrated global capital markets, greater international competition, and a premium on skills and innovation as the key to competitive advantage.

A platform of stability

The first condition is a platform of economic stability built around explicit objectives for low and stable inflation and sound public finances – in our case an
inflation target and a golden rule – along with a commitment to openness and
transparency.

The new post-monetarist economics is built upon four propositions:

- because there is no long term trade off between inflation and unemployment,
  demand management alone cannot deliver high and stable levels of
  employment;
- in an open economy rigid monetary rules that assume a fixed relationship
  between money and inflation do not produce reliable targets for policy;
- the discretion necessary for effective economic policy is possible only within a
  framework that commands market credibility and public trust;
- that credibility depends upon clearly defined long-term policy objectives,
  maximum openness and transparency, and clear and accountable divisions of
  responsibility.

Let me review each proposition one by one. A few decades ago many economists
believed that tolerating higher inflation would allow higher long-term growth and
employment. Indeed, for a time after 1945, it did – as I have said – appear
possible to 'fine-tune' in this way – to trade a little more inflation for a little less
unemployment – exploiting what economists call the Phillips curve.

But the immediate post-war period presented a very special case – an economy
recovering from war that was experiencing rapid growth within a rigid system of
price and capital controls. We now know that even at this time 'fine tuning'
merely suppressed inflationary pressures by causing balance of payments deficits.

And by the 1960s and 1970s, when governments tried to lower unemployment
by stimulating demand, they faced not only balance of payments crises but
stagflation as both inflation and unemployment rose together.

Milton Friedman argued in his 1968 American Economic Association Presi-
dential Lecture that the long-term effect of trying to buy less unemployment with
more inflation is simply to ratchet up both.

And here in Britain conclusive evidence for this proposition came in the 1980s
experience of high inflation and high unemployment occurring together. So,
because there is no long-term trade off between inflation and unemployment,
demand management alone cannot deliver high and stable levels of employment.
Friedman was right in this part of his diagnosis: we have to reject short termist
dashes for growth. But the experience of these years also points to the solution.
My conclusion is that because there is no long-term trade off between inflation
and unemployment delivering full employment requires a focus on not just one
but on all the levers of economic policy.

The second proposition in the new post-monetarist economics is that applying
rigid monetary targets in a world of open and liberalised financial markets cannot

secure stability. Here experience shows that while Friedman's diagnosis was right his prescription was wrong. Fixed intermediate monetary targets assume a stable demand for money and therefore a predictable relationship between money and inflation. But since the 1970s, global capital flows, financial deregulation and changing technology have brought such volatility in the demand for money that across the world fixed monetary regimes have proved unworkable.

So why, even as monetary targets failed, did the British government persist in pursuing them? Why even as they failed was their answer more of the same? The answer is that they felt the only way to be credible was by meeting fixed monetary rules. And when one target failed they chose not to question the idea of inter- mediate targeting but to find a new variable to target, hence the bewildering succession of monetary targets from £M3 to M0, then shadowing the Deutsch- mark, then the Exchange Rate Mechanism as the chosen instrument for monetary control.

As with fine tuning, the rigid application of fixed monetary targets was based on the experience of sheltered national economies and on apparently stable and predictable relationships which have broken down in modern liberalised global markets.

And yet the more they failed, the more policy makers felt they had to tie their hands, first by adding even more monetary targets and then by switching to exchange rate targets. But having staked their anti-inflationary credentials on following these rules, the government – and the economy – paid a heavy price. The price was recession, unemployment and increasing public mistrust in the capacity of British institutions to deliver the goals they set.

What conclusion can be drawn from all this?

Governments are in theory free to run the economy as they see fit. They have, in theory, unfettered discretion. And it is not only the fact that they have this unfet- tered discretion but the suspicion they might abuse it that leads to market distrust and thus to higher long-term interest rates. That is why governments have sought to limit their discretion through rules. The monetarist error was to tie policy to flawed intermediate policy rules governing the relationship between money demand and inflation. But the alternative should not be a return to discretion without rules, to a crude version of 'fine tuning'. The answer is not no rules, but the right rules. The post-monetarist path to stability requires the discipline of a long-term institutional framework. So my second proposition – that in a world of open capital markets fixed monetary targets buy neither credibility nor stability – leads directly to my third.

The third proposition is that in this open economy the discretion necessary for effective economic policy is possible only within a framework that commands market credibility and public trust.

Let me explain what I mean when I talk of the new monetary discipline: in the new open economy subject to instantaneous and massive flows of capital the penalties for failure are ever more heavy and the rewards for success are even greater. Governments which lack credibility – which are pursuing policies which are not seen to be sustainable – are punished not only more swiftly than in the past but more severely and at a greater cost to their future credibility. The British experience of the 1990s is a case in point. It shows that once targets are breached it is hard to rebuild credibility by setting new targets. Credibility, once lost, is hard to regain. The economy then pays the price in higher long-term interest rates and slower growth.

On the other hand governments which pursue, and are judged by the markets to be pursuing, sound monetary and fiscal policies, can attract inflows of investment capital more quickly, in greater volume and at a lower cost than even ten years ago. The gain is even greater than that. If governments are judged to be pursuing sound, long-term policies, then they will also be trusted to do what is essential – to respond flexibly to the unexpected economic events, that inevitably arise in an increasingly integrated but more volatile global economy.

So, in the era of global capital markets, it is only within a credible framework that governments will command the trust they need to exercise the flexibility they require. This leads to my fourth proposition – a credible framework means working within clearly defined long-term policy objectives, maximum openness and transparency, and clear and accountable divisions of responsibility.

It is essential that governments set objectives that are clearly defined and against which their performance can be judged. That is why we have introduced clear fiscal rules, defined explicitly for the economic cycle. That is why, also, we have a clearly defined inflation target. Let me say why it is so important that our inflation target is a symmetrical target. Just as there is no gain in attempting to trade higher inflation for higher employment, so there is no advantage in aiming for ever lower inflation if it is at the expense of growth and jobs.

If the target was not symmetric – for example, if in the UK case it was 2.5 per cent or less rather than 2.5 per cent – policy makers might have an incentive to reduce inflation well below target at the cost of output and jobs. Instead a symmetrical target means that deviations below target are treated in the same way as deviations above the target.

But to be credible, the monetary and fiscal framework must also be open, transparent and accountable. The greater the degree of secrecy the greater the suspicion that the truth is being obscured and the books cooked.

But the greater the degree of transparency – the more information that is published on why decisions are made and the more the safeguards against the manipulation of information – the less likely is it that investors will be suspicious of the government's intentions. That openness needs to be underpinned by accountability and responsibility.

So public trust can be built only on a foundation of credible institutions, clear objectives, and a proper institutional framework. The flaw in the previous government's economic policy was not just the failure of monetary targets. It was that the 'medium-term financial strategy' had no credible foundation – it was neither consistent in objectives, nor transparent in its operation, nor underpinned by credible institutional reforms.

Failure led, after 1992, to some reform. The inflation target was an important step forward. But it was ambiguously defined and it was not underpinned by anything other than an improvised and still highly personalised institutional framework. Minutes of meetings between the Bank of England and the Chancellor were published, but they could not allay the suspicion that policy was being manipulated for political ends. In fact despite the then government's commitment to an inflation target of 2.5 per cent or less, financial market expectations of inflation ten years ahead were not 2.5 per cent or less but 4.3 per cent in April 1997, and never below 4 per cent for the whole period. Long-term interest rates remained 1.7 per cent higher in Britain than in Germany.

This has changed significantly in the last two years, long-term inflation expectations have fallen from 4.3 per cent to 2.4 per cent, a figure consistent with the Government's inflation target; the differential between British and German long-term interest rates has fallen from 1.7 per cent, to just 0.2 percentage points.

I believe the explanation for this improvement lies in the immediate and decisive steps that our new Government took in May 1997 – to set clear monetary and fiscal objectives, to put in place orderly procedures including a new division of responsibility between the Treasury and an independent central bank, and to insist on the maximum openness and transparency.

Contrary to Nigel Lawson's distinction between the roles of macro-economic and micro-economic policy as set out in his 1984 lecture, we recognise that the role of a macro-economic policy is not simply to bear down on inflation but by creating a platform of stability to promote growth and employment; and that an active supply-side policy is necessary not only to improve productivity and employment, but to make it possible to sustain low inflation alongside high and stable levels of growth and employment. In other words, macro-economic and micro-economic policy are both essential – working together – to growth and employment.

In short we have sought to learn the lessons of the post-war years and build a new platform of stability. Making the Bank of England independent was and is only one of the institutional reforms that form our new post-monetarist approach to economic policy.

First, clear long-term policy objectives:

- a pre-announced and symmetrical inflation target;
- and strict fiscal rules to ensure sustainable public finances.

Second, well understood procedural rules:

- a clear remit for the Monetary Policy Committee of the Bank of England to meet the inflation target set by government supported by the open letter system and the Code for Fiscal Stability;
- and effective co-ordination between fiscal and monetary policy – including the presence of the Treasury representative at the Monetary Policy Committee meetings.

Third, openness and transparency to keep markets properly informed, ensuring that institutions, objectives and the means of achieving the objectives are seen to be credible:

- publication of the minutes and votes of Monetary Policy Committee meetings;
- and transparency in fiscal policy including the independent auditing of key fiscal assumptions.

It is the same search for stability in an open economy that has led to European Monetary Union.

And at the global level, the same lessons are being learned. In Washington last month, the IMF agreed a new framework of codes and standards, new economic disciplines for openness and transparency to be accepted and implemented by all countries which participate in the international financial system. These codes and standards – including fiscal, financial and monetary policy – will require that countries set out clear long-term objectives, put in place proper procedures, and promote the openness and transparency necessary to keep markets informed.

With the reforms we have already made in Britain, I believe that we have now – for the first time in this generation – a sound and credible platform for long-term stability for the British economy. We will not make the old mistake of relaxing our fiscal discipline the moment the economy starts to grow. The same tough grip will continue.

The Monetary Policy Committee will be and must continue to be vigilant and forward-looking in its decisions, as we build a culture of low inflation that delivers stability and steady growth.

We will not repeat the mistake of the late 1980s. Those who today are arguing that economic stability comes by opposing necessary changes in interest rates and by avoiding the tough decisions necessary to meet the inflation target would risk returning to the boom and bust of the past. We can achieve high and stable levels of employment and meet our inflation target. Indeed we will not achieve and sustain full employment for the long term by failing to meet our inflation target.

This credible platform of stability, built from the solid foundations I have just described, allows people to plan and invest for the long term. This is our first condition for full employment.

Welfare to work

The second condition for full employment is an active labour market policy matching rights and responsibilities. The idea of a fixed natural rate of unemployment consistent with stable inflation was discredited by the evidence of the 1980s. For even when the economy was growing at an unsustainable pace – above 5 per cent in 1988 – in all regions of the country there were high levels of vacancies including vacancies for the unskilled alongside high unemployment.

How did this happen? Part of the explanation was the 'scarring' effect on skills and employability inflicted by the deep and long recession of the 1980s. Partly also the mismatch between the skills and expectations of redundant manufacturing workers – and the new jobs in service industries. Partly the failure to reform the Welfare State especially its unemployment and poverty traps which, for many, meant work did not pay.

So there was a rise in what, in the 1980s, economists termed 'the non accelerating inflation rate of unemployment' or the NAIRU. Whether measured by the relationship between wage inflation and unemployment as Phillips stressed in the 1950s – or vacancies and unemployment as Beveridge had highlighted in the 1940s – Britain had clearly seen a dramatic structural deterioration in its labour market. The same level of wage pressure or vacancies existed alongside much higher levels of unemployment than in the past.

So the new Government has taken a decisively different approach to employment policy over the past two years aimed at reducing the NAIRU. All our reforms are designed for the modern dynamic labour market, now being transformed by the new information technologies. We recognise that people will have to change jobs more often, that skills are at a premium and that reform was needed in the 1980s to create more flexibility.

The New Deal which offers opportunities to work but demands obligations to do so is the first comprehensive approach to long-term unemployment. Designed to re-engage the unemployed with the labour market, it addresses both the scarring effect of unemployment and the mismatch between jobs and skills. The Working Families Tax Credit and associated reforms that integrate tax and benefit are, for the first time, making work pay more than benefits, and our educational reforms including lifelong learning, the university for industry, individual learning accounts and our computers for all initiative will tackle skill deficiencies.

The last two years have brought record levels of employment and sharp falls in youth and long-term unemployment – early signs that our policies are having an impact. But with still 1.2 million claimant unemployed and others excluded from the labour market – even at a time when there are around one million vacancies spread throughout all areas of the country – there is much more to do. The Working Families Tax Credit is now being extended to new employment credits for the disabled and for those over 50. And as the New Deal extends its scope from the under-25s to the long-term unemployed opportunities to work and obligations to work will be extended together.

The more our welfare to work reforms allow the long-term unemployed to re-enter the active labour market, the more it will be possible to reduce unemployment without increasing inflationary pressures. And the more our tax and benefit reforms remove unnecessary barriers to work, and the more our structural reforms promote the skills for work, the more it is possible to envisage long-term increases in employment, without the fuelling of inflationary pressures.

Productivity

Next our third condition: only with rising productivity can we meet people's long-term expectations for rising standards of living without causing inflation or unemployment. It is important to be clear about the relationship between productivity, employment and living standards.

Low productivity can exist side by side with low unemployment if people accept that living standards are not going to rise – as happened to the United States in the 1980s. But rising productivity can exist side by side with high unemployment if we pay ourselves more than the economy can afford. If people demand short-term rewards which cannot be justified by economy-wide productivity growth, the result is first inflation and then the loss of jobs. That has been the historic British problem – repeated bouts of wage inflation unmatched by productivity growth leading in the end to higher unemployment.

Indeed, between 1950 and 1996 productivity growth in Britain was only 2.6 per cent a year compared to 3.7 per cent and 3.9 per cent in France and Germany. But if we can now achieve rising productivity, bridging the gap with our competitors, high levels of employment and rising living standards can go together.

Britain cannot assume that the new information technologies will automatically bring the higher productivity growth now seen in the United States. So we must work through a new agenda that involves a shared national effort to raise our game. Policies to encourage higher productivity will be the theme of the Government's Pre-Budget Report on 9 November.

While thirty years ago governments responded to the productivity challenge with top-down plans, and grant aid primarily for physical investment, today the productivity agenda is more complex and more challenging. So we are developing new and radical policies for the modernisation of capital and product markets, the encouragement of innovation and an enterprise culture open to all, as well as the building of a modern skills base.

Responsibility in pay-setting

I come now to our fourth and final condition for full employment – responsibility, not least in pay, and by responsibility I mean, as I have stressed throughout this lecture, a willingness to put the long term above the short term, a willingness to build a shared common purpose. To succeed we must all be long termists now.

The reality of the more complex and flexible labour markets of Britain today is that pay decisions are dictated not by the few in smoke-filled rooms but made by millions of employees and employers across the country. And the more that we are all persuaded to take a long-term view of what the economy can afford, the more jobs we will create, the more we can keep inflation under control so interest rates can be as low as possible.

The Bank of England have to meet an inflation target of 2.5 per cent. The target has to be met. Unacceptably high wage rises will not therefore lead to higher inflation but higher interest rates. It is in no one's interest if today's pay rise threatens to become tomorrow's mortgage rise.

The worst form of short termism would be to pay ourselves more today at the cost of higher interest rates tomorrow, fewer jobs the next year and lower living standards in the years to come. So wage responsibility – to rescue a useful phrase from a woeful context – is a price worth paying to achieve jobs now and prosperity in the long term. It is moderation for a purpose.

But responsibility means not just responsibility in pay but building a shared commitment to achieve all the conditions necessary for full employment – in other words to work together as a country to promote stability, employability and higher productivity too.

It is undeniable that the shared economic purpose of 1945 broke down in fifty years of endless and sterile divisions between capital and labour, between state and market and between public and private sectors, denying Britain the national direction it needed. Britain and the British people can now move beyond these outdated conflicts.

Building a consensus around the need for stability, employability, productivity and responsibility we can define anew a shared economic purpose for our country. The conditions for full employment can be met. And the surest way is that the whole country is determined to meet them.

Part III

11 Benefits and costs

Securing the future of social security

The Rt Hon Peter Lilley MP

H55
H50
IUKI

Introduction

You have asked me to speak about the impact of social security on the economy. I am happy to do so. But we must never lose sight of the fact that the most important thing about the social security system is not its economic consequences but its social purpose. The system exists to serve people in need. Indeed in Beveridge's terms it is the sword which slays the evil Giant of Want.[1] The system may need reshaping to cope with a world which has changed radically since Beveridge. But the system has been outstandingly successful in providing an income in those periods of life when people cannot earn or face extra costs – because of sickness, disability, unemployment, caring for relatives or old age.

Nor must we equate social security with state provision. Around £500 billion invested in private pension schemes *alone* is a measure of the enormous scale of private sector provision already. One of Beveridge's key principles was the partnership between state and individual, and the importance of fostering self provision. In his report he declared 'The State in organising security should not stifle incentive, opportunity, responsibility; in establishing a national minimum, it should leave room and encouragement for voluntary action by each individual to provide more than that minimum for himself and his family.'

Beveridge also recognised that it was crucial that any system be affordable. 'The insured persons', he wrote 'should not feel that income for idleness, however caused, can come from a bottomless purse.' So it is not a sin against the spirit of Beveridge to discuss the financial, let alone the economic, consequences of the benefit system. Indeed I believe the links between social security and economic policies are immensely important, reciprocal and too often ignored. It is unforgivable to forget the social purpose of social security. But it is a dangerous mistake to put social security and economic policy in two distinct boxes.

Best social policy is vibrant economy

In fact a vibrant economy – generating jobs, opportunities, skills and the means to save for future needs – can do far more to achieve the objectives of social security policy than could any feasible enhancements of our welfare system. On the other hand, social security has a profound impact on the economy. It influences the size of the active labour force, the effort devoted to work, the level of savings and investment, the burden of tax and public borrowing, the scope for public spending on other programmes and attitudes towards risk and enterprise which are of immeasurable importance. We cannot eliminate the pressures on our social security system just by stimulating the economy. Nor can we solve our economic problems just by curtailing social security programmes. However, we can and should look much more closely at the links between social security and economic performance. Above all any reform of social security should seek to maximise social well-being whilst minimising its negative economic impact.

Economic consequences of state social security

If anyone doubts whether the scale and scope of state provision of social security has any impact on economic performance, they only have to contrast the extremes of the old Eastern European command economies with the fast-growing free-market economies around the Pacific rim. In the People's Republics, the state generally monopolised the provision of social security to provide a generous level of support relative to national income and to protect people from the impact of economic change. People who were in effect redundant and unemployed usually remained on their firm's payroll until they voluntarily moved elsewhere or retired. The net effect was a massive level of unemployment (albeit concealed); a labour force lacking motivation, mobility or self reliance; and a low level of voluntary saving and provision for retirement or temporary loss of income. The economies stagnated, stalled and eventually collapsed. The very attempt to provide over-ambitious universal protection resulted in a meagre level of benefits through the failure of the economy to grow. And the attempt to insulate individuals entirely from the impact of economic change within the system exposed them all to the collapse of the system itself. Of course lack of competition and private ownership were also part of the problem.

Sweden has a highly competitive free enterprise industry and labour market, yet has still found its exceptionally generous social security system a crippling burden. Public spending on social protection, excluding health, was over a quarter of GDP in 1990[2] – more than twice the UK level. Few doubt that this was the drag anchor that made Sweden one of the slowest growing economies in Western Europe over the last two decades. Finally, last year, faced with financial collapse, all parties agreed to a programme of wholesale reform. The Lindbeck report[3] commissioned by the Swedish government represents one of the most radical proposals for scaling down state involvement in social security yet seen.

At the other end of the spectrum are many of the countries of the Pacific rim. There the role of the state in the provision of social security is less developed. There is far greater reliance on private and family provision both for life-cycle needs (such as childhood, sickness, retirement) and for economic risks (such as unemployment and redundancy). This seems to be associated with very low unemployment, high mobility and motivation, very high propensity to save and invest – and dynamic growth. But it also presumably involves suffering for those who fall through the net of family or private provision, about which we rarely read, but which I and most of our compatriots would find unacceptable. There is no more question of this country moving to a Pacific-style social security system than of our adopting an Eastern European one. But we can learn from these extremes how important the impact of social security on the economy is and vice versa.

Impact of social protection on jobs

Even among countries at similar levels of development there is plenty of evidence that different social security systems have markedly different economic and social consequences. For example, different philosophies towards helping the unemployed and preventing unemployment have been pursued on either side of the Atlantic.[4] In most European Community countries benefit levels have become relatively more generous – help is available however long the period of unemployment – and employment protection laws have been progressively tightened. In the United States of America unemployment benefit is less generous relative to earnings and ceases entirely after six (or at most nine) months. There is no equivalent of Income Support (except for those – usually lone mothers – with dependent children). There are few restrictions on employers' freedom to hire and fire. In 1973, the year before the oil crisis, a similar number of people were at work in the European Community and in the United States. Since then, the number of people in work in the United States (excluding any unreported illegal immigrants) has increased by 35 million, of which 30 million are in the private sector; unemployment has risen from 5 per cent to 7 per cent; the average duration on unemployment benefit is three months; and around 6 per cent have been unemployed for more than one year. By contrast, since 1973 the number of jobs in the European Community has increased by only 8 million, of which 5 million are in the public sector; unemployment has risen from under 3 per cent to nearly 10 per cent; and almost 50 per cent who are unemployed have been so for more than one year.

Until the mid 1980s the United Kingdom was following a path similar to continental Europe with similar results. Above all we were paying unemployed people to spend longer and longer on benefit. Arrangements for payment of benefit had been divorced from job search. Rules requiring people to look for and accept available work had been enforced with declining vigour. Between the early 1970s and mid 1980s the number of people referred for refusing available work declined by two-thirds and the proportion who were then denied benefit fell from 80 per cent to 33 per cent. Since the introduction of the Restart programme in 1986, successful efforts have been made to keep unemployed people in touch with the world of work. During the 1980s the government also sought to lighten the obligations imposed on employers. It was felt that rather than protecting jobs such burdens discouraged employers from taking on extra staff. As a result of these changes Britain had markedly greater success in generating private sector jobs in the 1980s upswing than previously or on the continent. The more rapid moderation in pay settlements during this downturn and the recent four months decline in unemployment, unexpectedly early in the recovery, may owe something to our measures to make benefits for the unemployed conditional on remaining in touch with the job market.

The lessons from continental experience are clear – good intentions are not enough. Social measures designed to alleviate or prevent a problem may not merely damage the economy but actually exacerbate the very problem they were intended to solve. Generous, unconditional help for the unemployed sounds humane. But if it discourages job search and prolongs unemployment it damages the chances of the very people it is intended to help. It would be unthinkable in the United Kingdom and most European Community countries to terminate all help to the unemployed after a given time – certainly we are not considering it. But we have shown the value of making unemployment benefits conditional and providing active help to people to return to work. Beveridge himself foresaw making receipt of benefit 'subject to the requirement of attendance at a work or training centre after a limited period of unemployment'.

UK experience

So, what role does social security play in Britain's economy? I propose to publish shortly an analysis and projection of our social security expenditure[5] which I hope will stimulate an informed debate on this area.

Size

It will show that the DSS budget is huge, has grown rapidly and is set to continue outstripping national income in the future. This year we expect to spend over £80 billion. That is twice as much as the next biggest department, Health, more than eleven times as much as either Education or Transport – equivalent to the turnover of British Telecom, Unilever and BP combined. It means that to finance social security, every working person now effectively pays, on average, over £13 every working *day*.

Growth

Far from having been cut back (as a decade of media references to 'the cuts' might suggest), spending on social security has increased massively under this government. It is up two-thirds in real terms since 1979. And, since 1949 when the welfare state was first fully up and running, spending on social security has risen sevenfold in real terms. It is up from 18 per cent of government spending to 31 per cent now and from 4.7 per cent of GDP to 12 per cent now. The underlying trend in social security in recent years is obscured by the impact of the economic cycle. This particularly affects spending on unemployed people. However, even if expenditure on the unemployed is taken out, the rest of social security spending has still been growing at 3 per cent per annum in real terms since 1979.

Outlook for future growth

Moreover, the projections I shall be publishing suggest that, in the absence of reforms, underlying growth would continue at at least as high a rate into the next century. Indeed, excluding unemployment, the trend growth in social security spending over the rest of this decade is put at 3.3 per cent per annum in real terms. Success in reducing unemployment will of course dampen that growth. If, for example, unemployment were to fall by a quarter by the end of the century, total growth in the budget would still be 2.6 per cent per annum. So by the year 2000 we would be spending £14 billion more in real terms than now. If the level of unemployment were halved to 1.5 million spending would still grow by an average 1.7 per cent per annum to the end of the century. These projections show that on current policies there is a strong underlying growth in the social security budget which is faster than the likely increase in national income and considerably faster than our planned growth in General Government Expenditure.

We should look at the underlying rate of growth when considering how social security spending can be financed, not take comfort from the temporary moderation which a cyclical reduction in unemployment would bring. Indeed spending on unemployed people is excluded from the government's New Control Total for public expenditure. That is sensible because it is right to accommodate the cyclical rise in spending to help unemployed people. So it would be wrong to take credit for a cyclical decline in unemployment and relax restraint on public expenditure during the recovery. It is clear that the underlying position of spending outstripping national income cannot be sustained indefinitely. Britain is not alone in this experience or prospect. Country after country is grappling with the problem of social security spending outstripping national income. That is especially true in Western Europe where state welfare provision has been particularly extensive – and expansive. Only this week (21 June 1993) France announced that state pensions will have to be frozen in July.

The increase in dependency on benefits

Yet it is a paradox that social security spending should rise even faster than national income. It is true that as a country gets richer it ought to be able to afford better provision for those in need. But, other things being equal, one would expect that as a country gets more prosperous, *fewer* of its people would need to depend on state benefits and *more* people would make an increasing share of provision for future needs directly out of their own resources. If we are to understand why this has not happened, let alone address the daunting welfare problems of the next century, we need to analyse what has caused the growth in Britain's social security budget. Where has the money gone, and why?

Sources of growth

We already know in broad outline to which groups the money has been going. Total benefit spending last year was £74 billion – 67 per cent more than in 1979.

Nearly half of this spending – £34 billion – went on elderly people, by far our largest client group. Yet spending on this group has risen by not much more than a third – 38 per cent, since 1979. The growth in numbers of elderly people has been partly offset by rising private provision floating people off income-related benefits. It should be noted that this big total conceals one of the most rapidly rising elements in government spending – support for pensioners in residential and nursing care homes. This has jumped from a mere £10 million in 1978–9 to £2,500 million last year – a 250-fold increase! The new system of Community Care introduced in April will not only allow better control of this spending but also make better use of the available resources.

The next largest component in the social security budget is the £15 billion spent on long-term sick and disabled people. This has trebled in real terms since 1979. Since then, the number of people claiming Invalidity Benefit has more than doubled from 600,000 to 1.5 million, at a time when the nation's health is improving.

The third major group of recipients is families with dependent children. Since 1978–9, expenditure has risen by three-quarters to nearly £13 billion. Almost all that growth has come from the rapid increase in spending on single parent families which has nearly trebled to over half the total expenditure on families. There are now 1.3 million lone parent families in this country. Less than one in three receive any regular maintenance from the absent father. So nearly one million lone parents depend on benefits. Hence the establishment of the Child Support Agency which has just begun its work helping secure payment of maintenance.

The fourth largest group is unemployed people. At over £9 billion last year spending was 2½ times as great as in 1978–9. But this is the one element which goes down as well as up. It last peaked at over £10 billion in 1986, falling to half that level in 1989–90.

One benefit which straddles all those client groups is Housing Benefit. That has more than trebled since 1979 to nearly £7 billion. A large part of that growth reflects the rise in rents in the local authority, housing association and private rented sectors. There has been a move away from rent controls and subsidising bricks and mortar to subsidising the tenant.

Future sources of growth

As for the future, the projections which I shall publish shortly show four main sources of growth in spending. Almost a third of the projected increase between now and the year 2000 will come from sickness and disability benefits including Invalidity Benefit, Disability Living Allowance and Attendance Allowance. Approximately a quarter arises from Housing Benefit. Nearly a fifth of the increase arises from Income Support for non-pensioners largely going to the rising number of single parents. Most of the remainder arises from the build up of State Earnings Related Pensions.

Why does spending grow?

If we are to influence the growth of social security spending in future we need to know not just where the money is going but why expenditure is increasing. Growth in benefit expenditure can be the result of an increase in the amount of benefit per recipient or an increase in the number of recipients.

In practice most benefit rates are now uprated in line with inflation. The most important single spending decision in recent decades was the decision to link the basic retirement pension to prices rather than earnings. To have retained the earnings link would have boosted spending by £8 billion per annum already and set it heading remorselessly upwards. Instead we have been able to channel extra resources to pensioners in greatest need – by increasing the premiums on Income Support. Indeed – according to a recent report by the Social Security Select Committee – we have enhanced Income Support levels for beneficiaries of all ages by an average 15 per cent in real terms above the old Supplementary Benefit level prevailing in 1979. The only benefits which now automatically increase by more than inflation are those containing an earnings-related element where individual entitlement is linked to an employee's earnings record. The major earnings-related benefit is now SERPS. The earnings-related element in Invalidity Benefit has been somewhat curtailed and that in Unemployment Benefit has been abolished.

The amount of benefit per head can increase even where rates are held steady as a result of people receiving more than one benefit, upgrading to a higher benefit or through the introduction of new benefits. All these factors gave rise to some increase in benefit per recipient during the 1980s. Nonetheless the major source of the growth of expenditure has been the increase in the number of claimants.

The growth projections for the rest of this century assume no increase in benefit rates above inflation and no new benefits. The projected rise in Housing Benefit mainly reflects rising rents which will increase benefit per head as well as growing numbers receiving this benefit. And the maturing of SERPS and the Additional Pension in Invalidity Benefit will also raise benefit per head. So all the remaining growth is attributable to a projected increase in the number of invalidity and disability benefit claimants and single parents partly offset by fewer unemployed people.

The growth in the number of recipients can be due to more people coming on to benefit or to people staying on benefits longer. The latter was a powerful factor during the last decade. The inflow of people onto Unemployment Benefit follows the economic cycle but was not markedly higher in the 1980s than during the 1970s. However, people were staying unemployed for increasing lengths of time at least until the Restart programme and other measures I mentioned earlier. Inflows to Invalidity Benefit have been more stable but again the length of stay has steadily increased, boosting numbers. In the case of lone parenthood, the number coming onto benefit each year has increased over the decade. So has the length of time lone parents remain on benefit. The number of people reaching State pension age has been declining slightly since the mid 1980s. But the gradual increase in life expectancy is more or less offsetting this. So the total number of elderly is likely to remain stable for the nest decade or so. Growth will then resume as the 1940s baby boom retires.

Does it matter?

There are those who suggest rising social security does not matter. It is simply a transfer payment, they argue, with no net effect on activity. It must be said that this is not a view any longer held by any government of any complexion in any country I know of. It is certainly not my view. Quite apart from the financial arguments the prospect of a growing proportion of the population of working age becoming dependent on the state cannot be a matter for complacency. Still less can we welcome the prospect of an increasing proportion of the next generation being reared in dependency. On the contrary, as the national income rises we should be hoping to see an ever growing proportion of the population making provision for their own lives and tailoring that provision to their own needs. In any case it is clear that social security spending cannot be allowed indefinitely to outstrip the nation's ability to pay. The problem is a long-term one and can only be tackled over the long term – hence our current Long Term Review.

What then is to be done?

We need a constructive public debate on the reform of our social security system. Debate, I accept, implies disagreement. And of course there is scope for legitimate differences about priorities, how much can be afforded, etc. But it is usually best to begin with points on which we can all agree. We all want to make the system *better*. We all want to safeguard, in particular, the position of the most vulnerable. We all want to ensure the system does not outstrip the nation's ability to pay. And we all agree a system designed for yesterday requires updating to reflect contemporary human needs . These are the reasons why the government is undertaking its Long Term Review and the Labour Party has established its Social Justice Commission. So it ought to be possible to go beyond party political point scoring. And we must certainly not allow scaremongering to choke off any radical thinking. Radical ideas will often prove impractical or unattractive in themselves. But they are worth voicing since they often highlight strengths or weaknesses of the system and so help generate more modest but practical proposals. I hope, therefore, that this audience will not hesitate to contribute radical thinking to the debate. Meanwhile I will spell out a number of cautious propositions which I hope will help focus discussion.

First proposition

First, **there are no easy solutions**. That should be self evident, since if there were, I or my predecessors would have adopted them. Nonetheless people do suggest we can somehow side step the need for structural reform of social security by reforming the environment in which it operates. Usually they invoke more economic growth, training and investment in the infrastructure. These things are all desirable in themselves. They would all have desirable consequences for social security. We should certainly continue to foster them by all means. But on any reasonable prospect, these cannot be a substitute for structural reform of social security. Indeed if social security spending continues to grow too fast it will throttle economic growth and pre-empt both private and public resources needed for training , investment in infrastructure and other desirable programmes. Moreover, we start with a £50 billion deficit. It is cloud cuckoo-land to suggest we can add to it by major expansion of public spending in other departments in the hope that this will reduce social security spending some time in the future. There is no escaping the need for structural reform of the social security system – both to contain spending and to ensure that the money is spent to best effect.

Another attempt to escape this imperative is the claim that merging the tax and benefit systems would generate sufficient administrative savings to obviate the need to reform benefits. The fact is the benefit and tax systems each do essentially different things, in different ways, over different timescales. The benefit system is designed to alleviate need. Of necessity it works on a weekly or even daily basis, it assesses needs and it takes into account other household income and savings. The tax system looks at income on an annual basis, assesses individuals, usually ignores savings and relies on the co-operation of employers. Few benefit claimants have employers. So there is far less scope for administrative synergy than many suppose. To the extent that benefits are replaced by tax credits they would need to ignore savings and short-term variations in need. So they would be *less* well targeted and therefore more expensive than the benefits they replace.

Tax credits might be a good or bad thing – but they are not a potential source of savings. It is true that in the past the combined effect of taxation and benefit withdrawal as earnings rose could impose effective tax rates of over 100 per cent. That problem was resolved in the 1988 reforms by relating benefit to income net of tax. There is no reason to suppose further reduction in disincentives would arise from merging the Inland Revenue and the Benefits and Contributions Agencies. The one area in which these parallel systems cause problems – to employers – is the remaining differences in definition of income for the purposes of tax and national insurance. I have set up a Working Group with representatives of industry, small businesses and the self-employed to seek ways of eliminating these differences.

Second proposition

My second proposition is that **any effective structural reform must involve either better targeting, or more self-provision, or both.**

Third proposition

Most discussion of targeting centres around the relative merits of universal and means-tested benefits. Proponents of means testing benefits emphasise the fiscal savings but tend to ignore the disincentives on claimants. Proponents of universal benefits emphasise that they impose no disincentive on claimants but tend to ignore their huge fiscal cost. Yet the fiscal cost, of course, requires higher tax and greater disincentives on taxpayers. My third proposition is therefore that **disincentives are inherent in statutory benefits.** Where there is a choice between universal and means-tested benefits there is a trade-off between imposing disincentives on the claimants or on taxpayers. Usually the choice will be between a small extra disincentive on a very large number of taxpayers or a larger disincentive on a smaller number of claimants. A judgment will have to be made in each case as to which does the least economic harm relative to the social good. There can be no general rule as to which is best in all circumstances.

Fourth proposition

My fourth proposition is that **means testing is not the only way of targeting benefits more closely on need.** There is a variety of other methods. For example:

Categorisation. It may be possible to define by some factor not directly related to means, a category of people who are disproportionately in need of help. The main criterion Beveridge used was age. In his day most elderly people were poor. Nowadays there seems to be a far greater dispersion of circumstances in society whether by age or any other objective criterion. So selecting categories which coincide with inadequate means is not easy. But existing categories can be defined more tightly. For example when equalising the State Pension Age one option would be to equalise at 65.

Defining need. It is also possible to target benefits on those with objectively defined needs (rather than testing their means). For example, Invalidity Benefit is intended to be directed to those unable to work because of sickness or disability. We are examining the possibility of a more precisely defined medical test of inability to work.

Tighter enforcement. Parliament may define the broad circumstances under which a benefit may be available. But the extent to which it is actually focused on that group will depend how tightly the rules are defined in regulations and enforced in practice.

Conditionality. Conditions may be imposed as a quid pro quo for a benefit. I described earlier how the Restart programme reasserted the conditional nature of unemployment benefits – to the great advantage of those encouraged back into work.

Finally, the **Contributions test**, required for all National Insurance benefits, itself focuses benefits on those with contribution records. To abolish the contributory principle and make those benefits available regardless of payments would increase public spending by somewhere around £5 billion.

Fifth proposition

My fifth proposition is that **the existing array of benefits – contributory, universal and income-related – are rather more targeted than some comment suggests.** In aggregate, about 70 per cent of benefit goes to the 30 per cent of the population with lowest pre-benefit income. This proportion has been fairly steady over the last decade or more. Within the total there has been some compensating movement and some benefits are more targeted on means than others. The least well targeted on income are Child Benefit, Widows Benefit and Industrial Injuries Benefit of which 30 per cent, 40 per cent and 55 per cent respectively go to the 30 per cent of the population with lowest incomes. However these benefits are intended to help people cope with the costs of rearing children, the loss of a husband and the loss of faculty through injury.

Sixth proposition

Some people receive far more than they contribute. Some recipients will never have earned enough to make full provision for their current needs. For them the social security system provides an essential transfer from the better off. Others will previously have had reasonable earnings. The contributions they make may be greater than the benefits they receive over their lifetime. My sixth proposition is that **no one has the right to opt out of contributing to help those who cannot provide for their own needs. But there is no reason in principle why people should not (in addition to contributing to others) opt to make provision for themselves privately rather than through the State system.** There may, of course, be practical reasons why this option cannot be made available.

Seventh proposition

My seventh proposition relates to benefits where we do give claimants the right to opt out, using their contribution to make private provision as in the case of the State Earnings Related Pension Scheme (SERPS). The proposition is that **contracting out inevitably involves a switch from pay as you go to fully funded provision.** State schemes use this year's contribution to pay this year's benefit. Nothing is saved and set aside for the future. Private schemes save this year's contribution and invest it in industry to create the assets which are invested and will generate the income to pay for, for example, personal pensions in ten, twenty, thirty years' time. This is excellent for the economy. It means a stream of committed long-term savings available for British industry. But it also meanwhile leaves a gap in the public finances until pension policies mature. This would be true of contracting out of other benefits unless they mature on a shorter timescale than pensions.

Eighth proposition

My eighth proposition is that **the more the provision for needs and risks is monopolised by the state the less the incentive to work and save to provide for them.** Ultimately, people do not work for money itself, but for what money can buy. If they do not need to make provision for retirement, job loss, etc. and they cannot make any supplement to state provision in these key areas, they have less incentive to earn more or save more. People will only make a second rate effort to provide for second order needs. Consequently, the greater the extent to which people can make private provision for their own security (even if only at the margin to supplement a minimum state benefit), their incentives to work and invest are enhanced.

Ninth proposition

My last proposition is that **reform of something as vast as the social security system is best carried out sector by sector rather than by the 'big bang' approach.** Comprehensive 'big bang' reforms invariably result in imposing elegant intellectual and bureaucratic structures on the inconvenient diversity of the real world. I am much more attracted by the approach we adopted to tax reform in the 1980s – Lord Lawson's most lasting achievement. Each year one or more sectors were tackled. First, corporate taxation. Then taxation of husband and wife. Then the simplification of personal tax – and so on. Common principles underlay the reforms. But there was no attempt to subordinate all taxes to a preconceived master plan. I propose to adopt a similar approach to the reform of the social security system.

Conclusion

Reforms of our welfare state are essential. They are essential above all in the interests of those who most depend on the welfare state. Beveridge largely destroyed the evil Giant of Want. The only thing which would bring it back to life would be a system which both outstripped and undermined the nation's ability to pay. To allow the system to collapse under its own weight would be the greatest betrayal of Beveridge's ideal and of the most needy who would risk losing their protection. So failure to reform is unthinkable. By contrast successful reform will guarantee the position of the most vulnerable. It will reduce dependency, encourage self-reliance, harness popular energies, give people greater control of their own resources, boost savings and strengthen the economy on which the material well-being of all of us depends.

POSTSCRIPT

Since my Mais Lecture, the debate on social security has moved to the centre of the political stage. People now debate not *whether* reform is necessary, but *how* it should be reformed. A broad cross-section of the political spectrum now accepts that higher spending is not a panacea but a problem. The debate so far has focused on four main points.

First, more people recognise the immense and growing cost of the current system.

Second, there is growing concern about welfare dependency. More people accept that dependency on benefits can be debilitating, and that benefits can become a trap. So reinforcing incentives to work, save and take control of one's own life was a central objective of my reforms.

Third, more people now share my view that reform is not just about saving money. It is about creating a *better* welfare system, which certainly means a more affordable one, but also one that restores incentives, reflects modern needs and focuses help where it is most required.

Finally, there is wider acceptance that taxpayer-financed welfare places a burden on the economy, destroys jobs, and discourages work. By contrast, private provision can strengthen the economy. Private provision reduces the need for taxes. It also enhances incentives to work and boosts savings and investment.

How have the reforms worked in practice? Better than I expected. After fifty years in which social security spending grew twice as fast as the economy, that growth has been reined back. Indeed in 1997 there was actually a real reduction in spending. More important, the underlying growth has been curbed. And because most of the changes I introduced affect future claimants, their impact is still building up cumulatively.

Strong economic growth has also contributed to curbing the 'demand' for social security. But a prime thesis of the Mais Lecture was that economic and social policies interact. Social security reforms have, I believe, contributed to the more efficient working of the economy as well as vice versa.

This is not the occasion to review Labour's record on social security reform. Clearly they have accepted the bulk of my reforms that they criticised in Opposition. They have also adopted much of the Mais rhetoric if not its substance.

It is, however, debateable whether their first two major policy innovations have had a net positive or negative impact. The Welfare to Work scheme, which is budgeted to cost over £5bn, has had no appreciable effect on speeding up the numbers getting jobs. And redefining benefits as negative taxation (renaming Family Credit as Working Families Tax Credit) smacks of tricks with mirrors concealing a substantial increase in the fiscal cost of the enhanced benefit.

Whoever takes up the mantle of welfare reform in future will find it is a task which is never complete – like repainting the Forth Bridge. New needs will emerge. Old problems will diminish. And people will gradually find new ways of exploiting and misusing even what seem the best targeted benefits.

Notes

1 Beveridge, W. (1942), *Social Insurance and Allied Services*, HMSO.
2 OECD (1992) *New Orientations for Social Policy: Selected background statistics for the meeting of the employment, labour and social affairs committee at ministerial level on social policy*, December.
3 Lindbeck, A. (1993), *New Conditions for Economics and Politics*, Report by the Economic Commission to the Swedish Government, Stockholm.
4 OECD (1993), *Employment/Unemployment Study: interim report by the Secretary General*, Paris 1993.
5 Department of Social Security (1993). *The growth of social security*, HMSO.

12 The changing world of work in the 1990s

The Rt Hon Kenneth Clarke QC MP

(UK) E24 030 J65 J68

I take as my theme the world of work and the human as well as the economic challenges posed by the rapidly changing nature of employment and unemployment. I intend to extol the virtues of both a flexible labour market and a strong welfare state. I believe that both are essential for the quality of life that we aspire to in Britain. I believe that, properly directed, the two complement one another. I shall therefore argue that right of centre politicians should seek to create the right combination of the two to pursue the aim of full employment in a successful modern society.

Unemployment has been falling now for over a year. But at a time when recovery has taken us back to pre-recession levels of output, it still stands at almost 10 per cent of the British labour force. This compares to only 2 per cent twenty-five years ago when I first entered Parliament. Some unemployment will disappear as the recovery continues. But structural unemployment has been growing for the last four decades – an experience shared by the rest of Europe.

1944 Employment White Paper

Unemployment must therefore be the main preoccupation of economic policy makers in the 1990s. Nothing is ever entirely new, of course. This month marks the 50th Anniversary of the Wartime Coalition Government's famous White Paper on Employment. That had a clear diagnosis of the problem: inadequate demand. And it had a remedy: demand management through the levers of fiscal policy.

The White Paper is remembered chiefly for the first sentence which committed the government to 'a high and stable level of employment after the war'. That was a worthy commitment. But it needs putting into its proper context. The White Paper gave repeated warnings of the dangers of inflation 'bringing with it social injustice and economic disturbance'. There was a commitment to sound public finances 'such as will maintain confidence in the future which is necessary for a healthy and enterprising industry'. And there was recognition that employment cannot simply be 'created by Act of Parliament or Government action alone'. These cautionary words are all just as sound and sensible today as they were fifty years ago.

But the White Paper's main diagnosis of unemployment, and the principle remedy it proposed, are of little relevance to our problems today. No serious policy maker thinks today's problem is solely one of inadequate demand. Few would disagree with the importance that needs to be attached to keeping inflation down and cutting public deficits. But there is a general consensus that these measures by themselves will not be sufficient to tackle the problem of unemployment in the 1990s.

The UK approach

Current problems in the labour market are not unique to the UK of course. In many respects we have faced up to them rather earlier than other European countries. Our aim from the 1980s onwards has been to get the labour market functioning more efficiently. We believe that more jobs will be created if wages and working practices respond quickly to market pressures. Firms will be more likely to take on extra workers if they know they can do so without risking excessive hiring or firing costs or industrial disruption. The United States has a less regulated labour market than European countries and enjoys much lower levels of unemployment.

Some have argued that we face a simple choice between the American and European approaches. Most free-market economists would expect the American labour market to work well. There are few regulations or controls. Wage bargaining is highly decentralised. Trade unions are weak. Standards of social protection are also comparatively low. In European countries generally the opposite is true. Wage bargaining is more centralised. Unions are strong. Unemployment benefits are more generous. And there is a large and interventionist public sector.

The American approach has certainly been very successful at generating employment. Thirty-four million new private sector jobs have been created in North America in the last twenty years, almost matching the growth in the number of people seeking work. By comparison Europe, faced with the number of people available for work expanding by over twenty million, has created only 2.5 million private sector jobs. And European unemployment has risen greatly as a result.

But the low level of welfare support and coverage in the American system results in poverty and a miserable standard of life for a significant minority of the population. The American approach results in unacceptably low levels of social support across the range for those not in work, as well as those employed. The European approach goes too far the other way, by trying to use regulation of the employment market to redistribute income.

I have always proclaimed my belief that our objective should be to combine the best aspects of the two approaches: American enterprise and free-market efficiency with the European commitment to the welfare state. I have never believed that the two are incompatible.

Combining these two approaches, and taking the best of both, means leaving the labour market to work as freely as possible, while using government policies to deal with not only alleviating need for those who cannot work but also easing social problems for the working population as well. Of course governments should only intervene where the market does not work properly, and where intervention can make a positive difference.

The rise of structural unemployment

Before looking at how best European societies can tackle the problem of structural unemployment, I would like briefly to consider its causes. The long, relentless rise in unemployment from the 1960s to the 1980s was structural. The upward trend may now have been reversed. The last cyclical peak in unemployment was lower than that in the previous economic cycle. But unemployment now rises and falls around an average that is far too high.

Why is structural unemployment so high? There are some mistaken explanations. One is that unemployment is caused by stronger global competition from low-wage economies. I could not disagree more.

Greater openness and competition does not of itself create labour market problems or raise structural unemployment. Indeed, it channels our resources into activities where they are most productive and raises real incomes. But new patterns of foreign competition lead to structural shifts of demand to which we must adjust. The protectionist mistake is to argue that it is impossible to compete with low-wage economies and that European jobs can only survive with government support and protection. That argument denies the experience of the last hundred years. The protectionist option simply delays and ultimately increases the short-run costs of adjustment.

Technology and employment

Another myth is that technological change is responsible for unemployment. There have been hang-ups about technology since the Luddites. Technological change and innovation is an important creator of economic growth. It is not just about new labour-saving processes, but about new products and new services. In other words, new jobs. Higher productivity from the new processes increases real incomes available to spend on the new jobs. The available evidence actually suggests that the recent wave of technological change might have had a positive, if small, effect on employment overall.

But the combination of modern technology and free trade causes rapid and massive changes to traditional patterns of employment. Countries like ours see our wealth rise and the prosperity of people in work increase mainly as a result of modern technology and the growth of world trade. It is our failure to adjust to the changes quickly enough that causes joblessness to increase as the overall wealth of the nation increases. Governments must ensure that employers and employees continually make the required adjustments themselves as quickly as possible.

To take the simplest example we have lost for ever hundreds of thousands of low-skilled jobs in production-line operations. We have lost for ever skilled and high-paid jobs in products where we cannot be competitive or where the product is obsolete – we had 750,000 coal miners after the war and we have 15,000 now. But there is a growing demand for better-skilled technicians, multi-skilled staff, and people trained in information technology and financial management. We all know that to exploit these new job opportunities, our labour force must have the mobility and skills to move from old jobs to new ones.

We all know that full-time work in one job throughout life has ceased to be the normal expectation of today's young people.

As these truths have been borne in upon us, I believe that politicians across Europe have been far too slow to face up to the fundamental cause of structural unemployment. Structural unemployment arises from rigidities in our labour market. These impede adjustment to shocks, such as oil prices rises of the mid-1970s and early 1980s when unemployment first rose especially sharply, and to the continual shocks of ever more rapid structural and technological changes which face us now.

It is a mistake to view the shocks themselves as the cause of the rise in structural unemployment. Rather, it is the failure of the economy effectively to respond to these shocks that is the fundamental cause. And that failure primarily lies in rigidities in the labour market.

The role of the government

What role can the government play during this period of enormous change in the employment market?

Aside from the well-accepted need to keep inflation down and ensure sound public finances, the government can help in four important ways:

- Ensuring a flexible labour market.
- Helping individuals to adapt through active labour market measures and training.
- Helping those who are out of work by providing an adequate social safety net.
- Continually seeking to improve incentives to participate in the labour market.

Market mechanisms are the key in the economic world. Alleviating the needs of those who cannot work should be addressed by the Welfare system. Attempts to redistribute income through interfering in the labour market will ultimately lead to more, not less, misery.

Minimum wage laws are a notorious example of this in practice. Inflexible wages price people out of work. Needless regulation also traps people in uneconomic jobs and prevents new jobs becoming available. Clearly we need a strong body of regulation, on essential matters such as safety and discrimination. But unnecessary legislation that adds costs on the creation of employment damages the interests of the very people it is intended to protect.

Flexible labour markets

Our programme of labour market reform is already well developed. Rigidities in wage determination have been reduced by curbing the excessive powers of trade unions, breaking down national and centralised wage bargaining and modernising industrial relations. Deregulation and privatisation have encouraged competition in other markets, accelerated the spread of new technology, and encouraged more efficient use of labour. And reforms to the housing market have encouraged labour mobility.

We must win the battle to prevent the European Commission re-regulating our labour market, so increasing structural unemployment. We must avoid throwing away the gains of the free movement of goods, capital and labour, only to increase employers' costs by imposing unnecessary, Community-wide labour market regulation.

Encouraging small businesses has also played an important role. The Enterprise Initiative put together a package of measures to help small firms. And the new Enterprise Investment Scheme and Venture Capital Trusts will help to attract equity investment into unquoted companies, giving potential for a legion of firms to tap previously unaccessible sources of long-term private capital.

We should not let the economic cycle mask the underlying improvements in our labour market that we have already achieved. There is now a great deal of evidence that the British labour market is working better.

The improvements are most obvious at the micro level. Strikes are at their lowest level for a century.

Wage bargaining is much more flexible and decentralised so that pay is now increasingly market-determined. I am delighted to say that the latest data show that the proportion of employees covered by collective bargaining has fallen by a third.

The demise of centralised bargaining has placed pay determination firmly onto a market footing. There is less talk now of a 'norm' for wage growth. The 'going rate' became established at a time when governments believed that they could control inflation by controlling wage growth. That view was rejected in 1979. But the legacy of the 'norm' has survived the days of incomes policy. It has taken over a decade for both employers and employees to accept that an annual pay rise need not be inevitable.

As soon as the idea of 'the going rate' becomes firmly established as a thing of the past, then so should the idea of an annual pay round. Wages should be based on the economic success of the enterprise that provides the employment. Wage levels must also reflect supply and demand for the quality of the workforce required by that enterprise. They should only be changed when supply or demand changes, not according to some arbitrary time schedule for some notional wage round.

The government has been extremely successful in encouraging the development of profit and performance related pay. More than 50 per cent of firms now have performance related pay schemes in place. Profit related pay has also been encouraged, through the extension of tax relief. Participation in profit related pay schemes has grown as a consequence, from a quarter of a million employees in 1990 to over one and three quarters of a million today.

Performance and profit related pay encourage productivity gains, by increasing worker motivation. And there is some evidence to suggest that profit related pay helps reduce the volatility of employment, by allowing labour costs to adjust downwards when demand falls and profits are squeezed.

We have also seen some less comfortable but equally inevitable and probably desirable changes. In many developed countries in the west, pay differentials have widened in the 1980s. This is a direct result of the change in market demand for high performance and skills. This has occurred while the real earnings of the lower paid have continued to rise but no one knows how far the gap between the highest paid and the lowest paid will continue to widen. In my opinion, any political attempts to narrow this gap would damage performance and create more unemployment.

As a consequence of this greater wage flexibility earnings growth has slowed down sharply, and in recent months has been at the lowest levels for twenty-five years. At long last, the need for pay increases to be earned by enhanced productivity and performance is now widely appreciated on both sides of industry.

Helping the unemployed

Against this background, the focus of help for the unemployed must also change. The emphasis must be to focus on the supply side, improving the chances of the unemployed to find jobs at competitive rates. And the more successful we are, the more this helps to contain wage pressure, as well as helping individuals. Let us reflect on how far we have got so far.

The Employment Service now concentrates on keeping the unemployed in touch with the labour market by providing help with job search, work experience and training. And at the same time, eligibility for benefits has been made increasingly conditional on active job search.

The biggest supply-side challenge facing the British government is to raise the standards of general education. But the private sector has the major responsibility for training. Training is an area where indiscriminate state investment is not the answer. For a start we wouldn't know what skills to provide. That doesn't mean the government can't help. It means helping those who will benefit to help themselves. The government can provide the necessary infrastructure – which we have done for example by the establishment of TECs, new apprenticeship schemes, and a comprehensive system of vocational qualifications. The government's main emphasis in the longer term in my opinion must be in improving the attractiveness of training those whom employers might initially hesitate to employ – the below average achiever at school and the poorly motivated. This must be a key objective of government intervention in the field of vocational training.

There are definite signs that, as a result of the progress we have so far made, the unemployment position is improving. Unemployment has responded faster to changes in output, both in the down-turn and the recovery. In this cycle, unemployment started to fall less than a year after the recovery got under way. It fell in 1993 by nearly quarter of a million, and is continuing to fall this year.

The message from academic studies is that structural unemployment started to fall in the second half of the 1980s, after rising steadily for two decades. And if we press on with the policies to create a better trained and motivated workforce and a modern flexible labour market, there is every reason to believe that this downward trend will continue.

Perhaps the most encouraging improvement is what has happened to employment. We are now creating new jobs at a much faster rate. Following the sharp shake-out of labour in the early 1980s, we saw a period of dramatic growth in employment and self-employment in the second half of the decade. Of course some of those extra jobs have been lost during the recent recession, but employment is still 1.25 million above the level of the early 1980s.

Where did all these jobs come from? There have been major contributions from the growth of small businesses and the service sector. Small firms, those employing 100 people or less, accounted for 4 out of 10 jobs outside central and local government in 1979; now it's 5 out of 10. That may not sound a lot – but it translates into an extra two and a half million people now working in small firms.

Small firms proved remarkably resilient even during the recent recession. Job creation in an efficient market economy depends on people looking for the rewards from success and willing to run the risk of failure. Last year 400,000 new businesses accepted this challenge.

There are a lot of myths, for example, about the growth of employment in services. It is often argued that service jobs are predominantly low paid, raising the spectre of an economy based on menial 'McJobs'. But it is simply not true that most service jobs are poorly paid. The service sector provides a huge variety of work with a huge range of skill requirements and rates of pay. On average, weekly full-time wages are actually higher in services than in manufacturing. About 80 per cent of service workers are professional or skilled, and it is these occupations which have enjoyed the fastest employment growth over the past ten years. A growing share of service employment is the norm in advanced countries.

It is also said that we cannot rely on service jobs because they do not enable us to compete effectively in international markets. But services are increasingly traded internationally – partly because of the opportunities created by the IT revolution. Our exports of financial and other professional services grew by nearly 10 per cent last year – a net contribution of £11.5 billion to the current account and a remarkable performance given the weakness of many of our key export markets.

Other people talk about there being no hope for the unskilled, and about a loss of low-skilled jobs. But in fact in the 1980s low-skill unemployment remained broadly stable in absolute terms. The important thing is for people in unskilled work not to feel stuck there, and we must help them find ways into better paying jobs and provide them with the incentives and the means of acquiring skills.

Another strand of criticism has focused on the growth of part-time jobs, and again there are a number of misconceptions. Part-time working is an important source of flexibility for both employers and employees. The vast majority of part-time workers are working part time not because they couldn't find a full-time job but because they want to. It fits in better with their own personal circumstances. And there are many full timers – one survey suggests over a third – who would like the opportunity to work shorter hours. The growth of part-time working undoubtedly reflects a desire for more jobs of this kind. It certainly doesn't mean poverty pay, and is often an important second source of household income.

It's amazing that some countries effectively prohibit part-time work. We are much less wedded to the idea of a standard 40 hour week than many in Europe. In Spain, for example, 70 per cent work no more and no less than 40 hours in a normal week – here the figure is only 10 per cent. It is this flexibility that allows us to match the needs of employers with the preferences of an ever-changing workforce.

And there has been rapid growth in self-employment and in female employment. Self-employment has grown by 21 per cent since 1984, an extra half a million jobs. Female employment has risen by nearly one and a half million, or 15 per cent, since 1984. Women now make up 46 per cent of those in work.

The human dimension

The Euro-jargon of the social space, the social partners and the Social Chapter are indeed a throw-back to the British disease of the 1970s. But the resistance to change is not just political. The pace of change has created fears and uncertainties amongst men and women in every walk of life. Families need a sense of security in the personal finances, their home ownership depends on mortgage finance and their old age requires adequate pension provision. No individual will see any advantage in a flexible labour market unless he or she sees how career prospects and life-cycle finances can be enhanced by it.

We must not allow the political left and those who oppose market economics to claim to be the only people who understand these very real human concerns. Many people worry that making industry and markets more efficient can only come at the expense of social justice. I do not agree. I believe that a strong welfare state can complement, not hinder, more flexible markets by reducing fear of change and opposition to it. These fears provide a fertile breeding ground for protectionist sentiment and resistance to change. Not only adequate state welfare provision but a whole range of other social policies should alleviate such fears, and offer a sense of security in a world where retraining and changes of job are becoming necessary events in most people's working lives.

We have a huge advantage in Britain in having a free National Health Service and a free education service paid for out of general taxation. A better National Health Service and better schools will give a greater sense of security to British workers in a rapidly changing world than American workers have ever been able to have. I have devoted a great deal of my political life to strengthening our systems and I would never support any attempt to dismantle them.

It is important that the social security system complements an efficient labour market. And it is of course essential that welfare provision is affordable, by keeping control of the ever-increasing demands on the social security budget. We should not lose sight of the basic objective of ensuring that hardship is mainly alleviated by sustainable private sector employment growth. The government is looking not only at the cost of welfare provision but also at the extent to which the welfare system distorts work incentives at the lower end of the income scale.

I tried to make some progress in my November Budget to minimise such distortions. National Insurance contributions for lower paid employees were reduced by 1 per cent, and the 20p income tax band was widened. The government is looking at means of ensuring that the welfare system *encourages* the low paid to find employment. Sustainable employment, not permanent dependence on welfare payments for doing nothing, is the means by which the needs of the able-bodied of working age should be addressed.

The challenges ahead

I believe that we now need to make much more progress over the next few years in facing up to two major challenges, over and above continued progress, in creating an ever more flexible labour market:

- Overcoming the fear of change that the rapid developments in the employment market will inevitably bring about;
- and ensuring that the growth of prosperity is extended to all, by bringing the disadvantaged into the mainstream of economic life in a prosperous economy.

The way in which employers create work is set to undergo fundamental change over and above simple changes in the labour market. Production is being divided among smaller and smaller units, forming a network of suppliers with no concern for international boundaries. At the touch of a button, designers can transmit their ideas through the airways – using virtual reality they can demonstrate their products to potential customers thousands of miles away – and send instructions to turn out the finished product anywhere in the world. The service sector is certainly not immune from the challenges of globalisation. Routine audit work is already being done at low cost by skilled auditors in India – their work transmitted by fax back to headquarters.

But elsewhere technology has brought production closer to home. Car manufacturers, for example, now hold very few stocks – taking advantage of 'just-in-time-technology'. When a car gets to the point where it needs to be fitted with seats, an order is triggered automatically to the supplier. I know of one example where the time taken to produce the seats and get them to the factory is less than two hours – just in time to meet a car without seats at the right point on the production line.

Technology will continue to change the way we work even more dramatically.

Teleworkers – people working from home using information technology – are now an established feature of the British labour market. Eleven per cent of employers are already employing workers based at home – a further 8 per cent expect to introduce teleworking in future. They can be found in virtually all industries and for a huge range of occupations; including translators, trainers, journalists, designers, consultants, accountants and secretaries. And the employers of teleworkers are generally enthusiastic about the benefits – from the saving in office space to better recruitment and retention of skilled staff.

All these changes in technology provide enormous opportunities for British business. But they also present the ordinary man and woman with major challenges. We can no longer expect to leave school or university and join a firm for life. Lifetime in the same occupation will become increasingly less widespread, as technological change renders skill obsolete. People will have to face up to the fact that they will be likely to undergo several changes of occupation, if not employer during their working life.

Such a change in employment will affect the way in which we all organise our personal finances. A steady stream of income, gradually increasing over the course of an individual's working life-span can no longer be relied upon. People are likely to face greater volatility in their wages, with intermittent periods out of employment becoming more commonplace.

This greater volatility in earnings will have implications for our expenditure habits. It will affect, particularly, the way we plan for large purchases. And the greatest single item out of any household's budget is, of course, their home. The provision of mortgages, therefore, will increasingly have to take into account variable income streams.

The huge growth of private provision for retirement, pensions, savings and insurance against unexpected personal crisis must also reflect the realities of the flexibility of our labour market. For example, if people are going to move jobs more frequently, it is essential that their pension plans can move with them on terms which are fair, acceptable and affordable. The government has already made much progress in increasing the portability of pensions, and intends to increase it further next year.

These are the problems that individuals face. The challenge faced by governments is to ensure that the fear of change does not impede that change. A strong welfare state has an important role to play in reducing these fears – the knowledge that a period out of employment will not necessarily mean hardship. Such knowledge would almost eliminate resistance to the necessary change in the employment market. And another priority for government is to ensure that incentives are in place for all individuals to participate in the labour market. This is the route to prosperity for all.

Underclass

The policies that I have outlined are, I believe, the best ones for ensuring the future well-being of this country. Low inflation, sound public finance, a deregulated private sector free from unnecessary government interference and an effective welfare state provide the best environment for future prosperity.

But it is important that this increased prosperity be enjoyed by all members of society. I never have believed that sustained economic growth will automatically trickle down into the pockets of every citizen and it becomes ever more certain that it will not in the future. We need actively to create the conditions in which everyone has the chance to share in the wealth of society. One approach is to attempt to achieve this worthy objective by using a range of policy instruments to directly redistribute income and wealth. This approach is misguided and needs to be abandoned. The distortion to incentives and impediments to the workings of the market ultimately serve to hinder efficiency and reduce productivity. Living standards fall for everybody.

What then do I believe we should do to create the conditions that will ensure a spread of wealth and therefore social stability in a competitive free market economy?

My approach is not to limit the spread of the market but to expand it. This means ensuring that opportunity and incentives to participate in mainstream society are available in every nook and cranny of our inner cities.

The urban underclass is a major plague on American society. It is thanks to our Welfare State that an underclass on this giant scale has not yet developed in Britain. The government has made a determined effort to provide real economic assistance to many of our most-afflicted regions. Urban and regeneration expenditure is now more than £1 billion per year. We have made steady progress in ensuring that expenditure is better directed to making a real difference to many people's lives. When I was Inner Cities Minister I produced a pamphlet on *Free Markets and the Inner Cities* and we have made a lot of progress since then.

Expenditure alone is not the solution. We must also look more closely at how those on the fringes of mainstream society can be brought back in. And, I cannot repeat this enough, this means ensuring that they do not get trapped in a web of dependency and exclusion from economic activity.

Conclusion

Let me conclude. Economic success depends on our ability to increase jobs and productivity through innovation, competition and change. International competition has increased, and traditional patterns of world trade are changing as a result. Working methods and skill requirements are changing with the diffusion of new technologies and pressure on firms to adapt to international best practices.

The pace of change is quickening all the time. And the challenge is to achieve the flexibility we need to adjust successfully. The adjustment process can never be entirely smooth and painless, but it is essential if we are to continue raising living standards and compete effectively in global markets.

We certainly can't afford to be complacent about our record. While the labour market is clearly becoming more flexible, unemployment is still far too high.

Progress must be based on harnessing market forces. The answer is not just flexible wages – though they are essential. The aim should be to remove barriers to employment wherever they exist. We have to look further at excessive costs imposed on employers. We must continue to address the continuing lack of skills, and continue to encourage risk-taking and entrepreneurship.

Harnessing market forces does not mean abandoning social protection and the Welfare State. On the contrary, we must strengthen them. But we must not do so in a way which damages employment and the creation of wealth. That is the trap which many European countries have fallen into, and Britain is climbing out of. In the past fifteen years we have achieved better living standards, more new jobs, high standards of health and safety, and a better Welfare State. We have to continue on this course if the employment objectives of the 1944 White Paper can become a reality. I am as committed as the author of that paper to a 'high and stable level of employment': we shall get there not by pursuing simply a flexible labour market or simply a strong welfare system, but by recognising that the two must reinforce each other. Both are essential in the world of work in the 1990s.

POSTSCRIPT

The only postscript that I can add is that I am pleased that the lecture has stood the passage of time so well. I continue to stand by all the views that I set out in the lecture, which really sets out the philosophy behind the welfare to work policy of the last Conservative government. This also has really been pursued by the present government. The only passage of the speech which could not be adopted by Gordon Brown is the paragraph where I warned of the dangers of minimum wage laws, and the government has actually avoided the worst problems of a minimum wage by setting it at a very low level.

Unemployment has continued to remain low by European levels and now that it is below 6 per cent it becomes even more difficult to move towards the aim of full employment which I set as my aim in 1994. We have been lucky to have an unprecedented period of sustained growth with low inflation, and the real test will come when the economic cycle turns and we experience any period of recession. It is then that we will discover whether our labour markets have remained sufficiently flexible and our policies of positive encouragement to work are strong enough to maintain progress.

I hope, therefore, that we continue to pursue the twin objectives of a flexible labour market and a strong welfare state, and I continue to believe that both are essential for the quality of life that we aspire to in Britain.

Part IV

13 Some presumptions of economic liberalism*

Sir Samuel Brittan

Introduction

Economic liberalism is a convenient name for one family of ideas. It is based on a wider ideal of personal freedom of which the economic aspect is only part. The ideal certainly derives from the classical liberalism of the past. 'Classical liberalism' may conjure up a picture of high-minded people in frock coats. But its modern extension covers the revolt of the young in the 1960s in favour of 'doing their own thing', the enjoyment of alternative lifestyles, including that of hippies, MPs with exotic sexual tastes, and flower children, as well as that of bond dealers in the cities of London and New York.

A liberal in my sense does not have to pretend to derive all public policy from one stated goal. If he calls himself an *economic liberal*, he must obviously attach some importance to prosperity and living standards as well as freedom. Moreover, economic liberalism is not and cannot be a rigorous set of deductions from some ethical theory combined with already established causal relations. (Nor can any other set of beliefs meant to guide action.) Economic liberalism is best seen as part of a tradition encompassing figures such as Richard Cobden and John Stuart Mill, or Ludwig Erhard in our era. It can only be fully understood in the context of specific events and developments. No liberal could have had anything to do with the ill-fated 1993–4 Back to Basics campaign of the UK Major government, which, whatever its original intentions, soon became an exercise in Grundyism.

One cannot pretend that the economic liberal tradition is in good shape. If we tried to find the present-day successors of Cobden, Mill, or Erhard (themselves of course rather different individuals), it would have to be mainly among academics on the American side of the Atlantic – and not all that many even among them.

Indeed, I must admit to not having been much impressed by the claims to a wider belief in personal freedom of the pro-market economists whom I first encountered. They were alive to the denial of choice arising from restrictions on

---

* This version of my Mais Lecture is based on the revision I made for my book *Capitalism with a Human Face* (Edward Elgar 1995, paperback edition, HarperCollins 1996). But I have brought back a few paragraphs from the original which were omitted from the later version for lack of space.

imports of cars and textiles, but took as a fact of life much greater invasions of liberty such as peacetime conscription. (I refrain from anecdotes about purely university matters, except that one well-known 'liberal economist' played a key role in sending down an undergraduate before he could take his degree, for publishing an allegedly blasphemous poem.) It was not until I came across Milton Friedman, and learned that he had spent more time in lobbying against the 'draft' than any other policy issue, that I began to take seriously the wider philosophic protestations of the pro-market economists.

In the political world, there has developed a tragic chasm between the two sides of the liberal tradition. Those who care most about civil liberties, open government, limitation of police powers and similar matters have drifted to the left, while those who have been most concerned with economic liberalism have drifted to the right. Both sets of ideas have become impoverished as a result.

To an economic liberal, what has gone wrong with the movement to market economics in our day is not that it is too extreme or not extreme enough, but that it has been divorced from a wider commitment to personal freedom. Unfortunately, it is often just those political leaders who claim to be most against state control of economic life, who have most reservations about freedom of personal and artistic expression. But because the main political outlet for the explicit expression of market ideas has been among conservative politicians, free-market supporters have too often turned a blind eye to the total package offered by the latter.

The morals of markets

The greatest obstacle faced by the market economy throughout recorded history is the belief that it is based on, or encourages, selfishness, materialism or acquisitiveness.

We know that the self-interest doctrine is an over-simplification. Institutions concerned with health and education are usually non-profit-making even when their services are sold for cash; and there are good reasons why this should be so. (Even so, those who run those institutions know if they ignore the self-interest of the staff and pay less than the going market rate, they will lose valued members – not only caretakers and cooks, but scientists and physicians.)

Nor do we need to play down professional motivations. A great musician or surgeon will often have a strong sense of vocation and not just play or operate for the money. A doctor or teacher should have some responsibility to his patient or pupil over and above the search for fees, and so on. Market rates of pay have their effects at the margin. They bring in the less dedicated who might otherwise have chosen a different field of endeavour, and they affect even the dedicated in their choice at the margin between work and leisure. (X might be a surgeon even if he were not paid for it. But he would perform fewer operations.)

Thus the 'Invisible Hand' is pretty pervasive, even though it does not explain everything. It upsets more people by its apparent sanctioning of greed than by its economic reasoning. Their worries will need to be tackled if a modern form of economic liberalism is ever to establish its moral legitimacy. There are numerous ways in which market economics can be presented without overemphasising the greed motive. Self-chosen aims can be emphasised at the expense of merely selfish ones. We can say, as Denis Robertson once did, that the economist economises on love: that is, he has to make it go the furthest possible way without wasting it in spheres where lesser or baser motives would serve. We can point out that the altruistic businessman should strive harder than his rivals to make profits and differentiate himself by what he does with his gains. Finally, we can point to specific examples. For instance, it would have been the height of social folly to have sold coal or oil at artificially low prices during the energy shortages of the 1970s.

Here we reach the heart of the matter. We do not always have the *knowledge* to assess the effects of our actions on other human beings, especially those more remotely affected by them. For this, if for no other reason, we need *prima facie* rules of conduct. Examples are: 'Don't tell lies', 'Do not steal', 'Keep promises' or, in the public sphere: 'Observe international treaties'.

The Adam Smith self-interest doctrine takes its place as one of the more surprising *prima facie* subordinate maxims of conduct in a broadly utilitarian system of public morality. Its essence is that, *in some areas and under certain conditions*, the use of markets avowedly based on self-interest will prove more beneficial than an overt attempt to achieve the public good directly. The suggestion is that in matters such as buying and selling, or deciding what and how to produce, we will do others more good if we behave *as if* we are following our self-interest rather than by pursuing more altruistic purposes.

In the remainder of this paper I intend:

- to defend the morality of economic liberalism;
- to explain its relation to mainstream economics;
- to differentiate it from mere pro-business policies;
- to attempt a few provisional conclusions;
- to take them further forward with the aid of new-style social contract thinking and say something on the Welfare State; and to try to provoke a little on financial markets and currencies.

My hope of persuasion, as distinct from a summarising statement, lies in your looking into my book, *A Restatement of Economic Liberalism* (Macmillan, 1988).

Neither Adam Smith nor any of his successors (with the unconvincing exception of a few modern American 'anarcho-capitalists') believed that the whole of public activity should be left to the market place. A functioning market presupposes a basis of trust (which is itself a form of social capital), a legal system and an apparatus of law enforcement. Smith did not believe that police and defence should be left to private armies.

Certain background conditions are necessary for the market to produce, not an optimum, but even reasonably satisfactory results. For instance, there needs to be a way of dealing with the more blatant spillovers or externalities – that is, costs imposed on others which do not appear as financial expenses to those who perpetrate them, or as benefits for which no reward is received.

The background economic condition and policies, required for the *Invisible Hand* to operate have been much elaborated upon by Smith and his successors to the present day. There are also numerous other unstated provisos. The shooting of one's competitors is not an acceptable way of maximising profits or even minimising losses. Nor is the bribery of legislators.

The full set of assumptions, side-conditions and constraints required for the pursuit of market gain to yield beneficial results can never be fully written down. Many of the most important rules are not formulated explicitly until a specific problem arises.

It will therefore often be uncertain how far the background conditions are even approximately satisfied. There will be occasions when the normal citizen will suspect that the *Invisible Hand is* giving the wrong signals, even in spheres where he might expect it to apply. No maxims of political economy can then absolve him from exercising his own moral judgment. Let me take an analogy from a different sphere. Freedom of the press is a good general maxim and part of our basic freedoms: 'Publish and be damn'd!' But this general presumption does not absolve the newspaperman or television reporter from examining carefully the possibility that a particular act of publication could be so damaging to specific human beings – for example, information that would interfere with a hi-jack rescue – that the general presumption must in this instance be overthrown.

A similar story applies to the pursuit of profit maximisation of personal gain in a competitive market economy. The absence of effective legislation should not excuse a chemical company for polluting the air – although the competitive advantage to be gained over others by an unscrupulous firm suggests that the law should be put right soon, so that the public-spirited firms are not forced out of business.

These common-sense qualifications do not destroy the presumption that, by following the profit motive, subject to the written and unwritten rules of society in which he lives, a businessman will also best serve the interest of his fellows. Similarly a worker by hand or brain can normally follow with a good conscience his own self-interest in his choice of occupation or place of work.

But I have been too pious so far in my treatment. I would rather end this section by laying on the line my personal conviction that people in the grip of greed do much less harm than people in the grip of self-righteousness, especially when that righteousness is harnessed to the supposed needs of a collectivity or given some theological or metaphysical justification. The most unscrupulous property dealer is much less of a threat than the Grand Inquisitor in the Schiller/Verdi *Don Carlo* who brushes aside Philip II's scruples about killing his own son by sonorous declarations about Faith, God, and the safety of the State.

Like Bertrand Russell (1954):

> I do not deny that there are better things than selfishness, and some people
> achieve these things. I maintain, however, on the one hand that there are few

occasions upon which large bodies of men, such as politics is concerned with, can rise above selfishness; while on the other hand, there are a very great many circumstances in which the population will fall below selfishness if selfishness is interpreted as enlightened self-interest.

And among those occasions on which people fall below self-interest are most of the occasions on which they are convinced that they are acting from idealistic motives. Much that passes as idealism is disguised hatred or disguised love of power. If men were actuated by self-interest, which they are not – except in the case of a few saints – the whole human race would co-operate. There would be no more war, no more armies, no more navies, no more atom bombs.

Relation to mainstream economics

There are distinguished economists who reject the 'Invisible Hand', not because it is immoral but because they believe it impossible to say very much in general terms about either the working, or the desirability, of a market economy.

Consider for instance the summary by a modern general equilibrium theorist, Frank Hahn, of what he believes can be rigorously demonstrated. There must be an economy of many rational agents. All production must be under constant returns to scale. There must be no externalities or public goods or other complexities or complications. In addition there must be available binding contracts stretching indefinitely ahead even for goods which will only be available in the future, including conditional contracts. (For instance, I will deliver fifteen bales of hay on 1 October in ten years' time, but only if rainfall that summer has not exceeded the average.)

Then, and only then, there exists an allocation of present and future goods on which no agent can improve without making others worse off, and there also exists a set of prices at which this allocation would be achieved and clear markets. (This statement is sometimes called the Fundamental Theorem of Welfare Economics.) In any case the required conditions are clearly not fulfilled in reality. There are, for instance, too few markets stretching far enough ahead.

This kind of analysis may throw doubt on markets, but does not tell us how governments could improve on markets or even the direction which intervention should take. The rigorous study of the optimal allocation of scarce resources among a known present or future population with given tastes employing known techniques may have its value as a mathematical research programme. But, unfortunately, it bypasses the most important role of markets as evolving institutions reacting to unforeseen change.

By contrast economic liberals put more emphasis on markets as a discovery procedure in a world where tastes and techniques are changing and information scarce and expensive. (That this view is still often described as 'Austrian', as if it were something foreign and exotic, is itself revealing.) Markets are means of disseminating information diffused among millions of human beings (who will not be conscious of all the information they possess). This information is transmitted in the form of signals – price changes in flexible markets, but also shortages and surpluses where price changes are delayed by habit or law. These signals provide an incentive to meet unsatisfied needs and to move resources from where they are no longer required. Wants, techniques and resources are not given, but are constantly changing in part due to the activity of entrepreneurs who suggest new possibilities (whether digital records or cheap stand-by transatlantic flights) which people did not previously know existed.

The view of markets as a discovery procedure and co-ordinating mechanism is now common property to many economists, irrespective of their politics, especially in the United States (away from the eastern seaboard). But it is still 'double Dutch' to large numbers of Oxbridge graduates who have been brought up to suppose that they have only to diagnose a departure from perfect competition for the case for the markets to collapse; and that they are then free to propose any ingenious intervention that occurs to them, or just follow their general political predilections.

To be fair to Hahn, he is well aware of the signalling and discovery aspects of markets and gives full credit to Schumpeter and Hayek for insisting upon them. But because there is no rigorously formulated body of knowledge concerning 'the behaviour of a market economy when it is not in a coherent state which we call equilibrium or, nowadays rational expectations equilibrium', he prefers to call these contributions 'political economy', to distinguish them from 'scientific economics'.

Market failure

A shift to the discovery procedure view of markets by no means establishes a case for *laissez-faire*. Just like language and law – those other products of social evolution with which Hayek compares it – the transmission and incentive mechanism of the market can be improved. So shifting attention from the static allocation of resources to the market as a discovery procedure does not remove the issue of intervention.

And of course we have always known of many cases where the 'Invisible Hand' did not work or required supplementation. Many were cited by Adam Smith himself. Externalities have long been known. There are costs and benefits which do not appear in the profit and loss accounts of those responsible. A familiar negative example is the damage caused by a smoking chimney. A positive externality or spillover is the benefit from training a person who then leaves to join another firm. Another related example is that of public goods, such as defence or pleasant urban vistas, which confer indiscriminate benefits. In other words, one person's consumption does not diminish that available to another. A less-familiar example is television transmission.

The old term for most of these examples is 'market failure'. A modern label which captures most (but certainly not all) of the relevant cases is the Prisoner's Dilemma.

This is based on a classic example where two prisoners, who follow their own narrow private interest and confess, receive a harsher sentence than if they had stood by their thieves' code of honour and followed the rule 'Never confess'. How does one decide whether Prisoner's Dilemma aspects – suggesting either public intervention or moral restraint – or 'Invisible Hand' ones – suggesting leaving matters to market forces – are more important in particular instances?

Defects of the political market place

Mainstream economists differ from market liberals in remaining content with a case-by-case approach. But even on that basis it is necessary to compare like with like. Too often the case for intervention is made without asking whether the human beings who will have to carry out that intervention have the knowledge or the motivation actually to improve matters. The defects of real markets are implicitly compared with the hypothetical actions of a benevolent and omniscient dictator (as frequently in the more technical writings for reasons of mathematical convenience as from deeply held convictions).

Research into the political economy of government (sometimes called public choice) has highlighted various likely governmental shortcomings. One particular distortion has recently come to the fore. If there are no constraints on state action, individuals have a much stronger incentive to invest resources in political activity and to try to use the state machine to supply them with goods (or contracts on favoured terms). The activity is now called 'rent seeking'. People vote to obtain a government that will favour either council tenants or private home owners; managers of enterprises divert their efforts into keeping on good terms with ministers and officials, or sitting on time-wasting committees and keeping *au fait* with the latest governmental fads and fashions; and, at local level, find it wise to keep in with the authorities who dispose of the more desirable school places or subsidized homes.

The idea that politicians and officials are themselves in a market place, like oil salesmen and car salesmen, has taken an astonishingly long time to penetrate the British economic establishment. (One British official to whom I pointed out the existence of the economic analysis of political behaviour replied that he was very sorry but he was not up on psychoanalysis.)

Many of the defects of the political approach appear not only in specific acts of intervention, but in the cumulative effects of many such acts in enlarging the political sphere. *To a liberal the market is not just a piece of machinery to manipulate but a device that has evolved – imperfect and capable of much improvement though it may be – which reduces the number and range of decisions which have to be taken by coercive organs after a struggle for votes, power and influence.*

The biggest disease of the modern extended state is that it becomes neither a provider of public goods which cannot easily be provided by the market, nor a vehicle for redistribution to the less fortunate, but an engine for the provision of private benefits to interest groups. Political pluralism, seen as a struggle and compromise between interest groups, was a harmless doctrine – even a benign protection against more ambitious ideas of the state – when government controlled a small proportion of resources, but becomes extremely harmful when government has a major say in the disposal of around half of the national income.

The reason for this degeneration is well known – namely, the concentration of benefits from intervention among specified and loud-voiced groups and the dispersal of losses among the mass of consumers and voters. What is less well known is that many major interest-group benefits do not appear in public spending or taxation figures. The main cost of the Common Agricultural Policy is not the budgetary transfer to Brussels, but the imposition on the consumer of food prices far above world levels. The cost of mortgage interest relief, or relief from capital gains tax on owner-occupied residences, appears only as allowances against tax, and buried away in a subsidiary table in the British *Public Expenditure* documentation.

The American economist Mancur Olson has pioneered the analysis of the pernicious effect on economic growth of interest-group privileges in mature democratic countries. But even more important has been the corrupting effect (sometimes corrupting in the straightforward sense of temptation to bribery) of the state as feeding-trough, rather than umpire or keeper of the rules. The ultimate danger is of a Hobbesian state of nature at the collective level in which we all have to join aggressive interest groups for our own defence, and in which the absence of rules or norms provides an incentive to predatory raids.

A few guidelines

There is no philosopher's stone: no simple criterion for distinguishing between government interventions which improve the functions of a market economy and those that take us a few steps further along the road to serfdom. But it is possible to state a few presumptions or guidelines or maxims which, taken together, give a few clues:

1   (a) *Non-paternalism*. Individuals should be treated as if they are the best judge of their own interests.

    (b) Desires that individuals have to coerce or down-grade other people (*negative interdependence effects*) should have no weight in public policy.

2   *General rules* should govern policy, with a minimum of discretionary power for publicly appointed officials – or private bodies engaged in backstage pressure – over their fellow men and women.

3   Where possible *market remedies* should be used to treat market distortions. This implies not only a preference for price mechanism remedies, but also where necessary for the assignment or modification of property rights.

4   We should try to *limit the domain of political activity*, even though we cannot make out the exact circumstances in advance.

These presumptions interact with and qualify each other.

The first set can be skipped because most mainstream economists claim to hold at least 1(a) (non-paternalism).

The second presumption, in favour of general rules, needs a little more elaboration. F.A. Hayek, who called it the rule of law, argued that it would be sufficient to eliminate intervention harmful to personal liberty or a market order, and I can claim to have examined the contention more thoroughly than many professed Hayekians. Unfortunately, it does not succeed in doing this. There can be coercive general rules – for instance, a ban on any criticism of the principles of Marxism-Leninism. Nor would general rules prevent a great deal of oppressive economic intervention, such as exchange controls or foreign travel bans.

But although it is not a cure-all, the concept of a government of laws rather than of men is one of humanity's greatest discoveries and perhaps the most important single protection of freedom. The case for general rules is partly one of efficiency and good government. At best, the official using his discretion will play safe and back the respectable and the well known. At worst, there will be widespread corruption. But much worse is the subjection of one human being to the arbitrary power of another. *The greatest argument for the European Union is that, for all its maddening aspects, it is firmly based on the rule of law – an aspect to which many so-called market economists remain blind.* I have already touched on the case for my third maxim, the use where possible of market and price mechanism-type remedies. But an economic liberal will put a different slant on such remedies to a mainstream economist. The latter will generally put the case for paying the market rate to recruit members of the armed forces, or for financial measures to protect the currency instead of foreign travel controls, in terms of efficiency. The liberal will be most concerned to recapture freedom, with any gain in efficiency seen as a bonus.

Similar considerations apply in the environmental field. The great advantage of road pricing over licensing of cars in urban areas, or of selling fishing permits at a price high enough to prevent overfishing, is that the choice of how far to pay the charge, and how far to cut down the activity in question, is left to the individual or firm – within a framework that ensures the desired overall result is achieved.

We can often go one stage further. Many adverse externalities or Prisoner's Dilemma cases arise because property rights are insufficiently defined. The principle 'polluter pays' is an attempt to redefine a property right so that the owner of a chemical plant that emits pollution into a stream has to pay for the damage he inflicts downstream.

New and redefined property rights are also relevant to 'macro' problems, such as whether it is possible to have a 'soft landing' after a period of inflation and excess demand without too great a check to output and employment. Earnings increases are notoriously resistant to downward pressure; and the conventional response to a demand squeeze, especially when profits are starting from a high level, is to slow down recruitment and as a last resort dismiss non-hard-core workers. Matters could be different if wage contracts were to contain a large profit-related element so that adjustment to squeezes can be more through pay and prices and less through output and employment than in the past. Insiders who have property rights to jobs may be more willing to accept profit-related elements in pay if recently hired outsiders are excluded from the bonus element.

The fourth and most important guideline – the need to limit the domain of the political – is the most difficult to state precisely. For there is no sphere of human activity that can *a priori* or forever be removed from political responsibility. The nearest I can approach to a general maxim is that whenever one new sphere of activity is brought into the political sphere we should seek to remove another from it. The inherent bias of a democracy is to expect too much from government action. But such action is likely to be more effective if limits are placed on what it can be expected to achieve. If ministers and officials are made to feel responsible for everything, their feelings of responsibility for tasks that are indisputably theirs – whether safeguarding the currency or removing unnecessarily harsh prison regulations – are diminished to vanishing point.

One reason for trying to limit the economic role of government may surprise some fellow economic liberals. This is that there is for the foreseeable future going to be such a large role for government in what is now called the welfare state area that there is no room for any avoidable load elsewhere.

I can best explain my contention by saying that there is no established liberal position on the distribution of income and wealth. We cannot just dispose of the matter by showing, as we easily can, that complete equality even of opportunity, let alone of outcome, is on close examination deeply unattractive, if not intellectually incoherent. Nor is it enough to point out that the wealth of the rich is not necessarily the cause of the poverty of the poor. Neither proposition establishes the desirability or even legitimacy of any particular distribution of entitlements to wealth and income.

Revival of the social contract

The revival of social contract theory is the most promising foundation for a new liberal theory of entitlements. Although John Rawls's version is the best known, it is part of a larger family of contractarian doctrines. In place of the historical social contract of seventeenth- and eighteenth-century writers, the modern idea is to work out the principles on which free and rational persons, concerned to further their own interests, would desire their community to be run if they did not know their own social or economic place, the market value of their own talents and many other key features of their real situation – what Rawls calls the 'veil of ignorance'.

A major advantage of the new social contract approach is that it precludes the potential oppression of the minority which follows from uninhibited majority voting. Contractarians place less reliance on majority voting than the conventional democratic theorists. Representative institutions and majority voting are simply possible decision procedures which may be laid down at the constitutional stage as the way to take second-order post-constitutional decisions.

The contractarian assertion is that everyone would gain from some restraint on the power of the majority of the moment to do what it likes, including even those who for the moment belong to that majority. The gains would come from greater security and predictability. The implicit bargain is a trade-off in which the affluent agree to a reduction in their property rights (in both their nonhuman capital and the earnings from their own talents) in return for a limit on state redistribution. The better-off make a sacrifice in previously held wealth in return for more certain enjoyment of the remainder. As for the worse-off: in return for a limit on the amount of redistribution that they could obtain via the ballot box, they become more secure of the redistribution they already have.

Nor can one claim that contractarian thinking has reached the stage where it could form a basis for either the reform or the entrenchment of different parts of the welfare state. In *A Restatement of Economic Liberalism* I simply accepted that economic liberals could and did have different attitudes to redistribution and asked how much redistribution and of what kind was compatible with basic freedoms. The analysis, written when egalitarianism enjoyed more support than it does today, could become relevant once more.

I highlighted two very pernicious forms of redistribution. One was attempts to control specific prices and wages, which could, if pressed too far, lead to the direction of labour. The other was what I called specific redistribution, which derived its appeal from plausible slogans such as 'Nobody should be able to buy privileged education for his child or better medical treatment simply because he has more money'. (The right of the citizen to buy private health or education was under fundamental challenge in the 1970s and could be so again.)

Some of the support for such statements is based on a simple mistake of economic analysis: the belief that educational, medical and similar services are in inelastic supply – which they may be in the short run, but not in the long – and hence that 'queue-jumping' by those prepared to pay fees deprive others of vital services. But beneath the mask of social concern is a use of state coercion to limit freedom of choice.

By contrast there is no way of ruling out on liberal grounds generalised fiscal action to affect the distribution of income and wealth, although, if pushed beyond a point very difficult to define in advance, efficiency and prosperity could suffer so badly that governments are tempted into illiberal expedients.

No dismantling the welfare state

These statements are essentially defensive. On the positive side, the usual market liberal view is that redistribution in cash is preferable to services in kind, because it respects individual freedom of choice. But I have never seen the welfare state as a promising area for large reductions in public spending. Let us look at them briefly in turn.

Housing is clearly a private, not a public, good in the economist's sense; and there is nothing to be said for expensive state intervention. But by the early 1990s housing policy had little direct public expenditure cost in the UK (if we treat Housing Benefit as basically social security).

Health is a much more difficult area. There are technical reasons, due to the economic characteristics of insurance, why privatisation is unlikely to provide effective or adequate health care.

Similar 'moral hazard' reasons apply to basic *pensions*. I am not persuaded that the same technical reasons apply to *education*.

Social security is in most advanced industrial countries much the largest sector of public spending. But it is already paid by definition in cash rather than kind. And although I favour dropping the fiction of national insurance and moving as far as possible towards integrating tax and benefit, it is a snare and delusion to suppose that such a reform offers an easy way of reducing the social security bill.

By placing too many hopes on reforming the welfare state, free-market radicals are letting the interventionists get away with too much perverse interference in what used to be the heartlands of the market economy: trade, industry, agriculture. Even after the experience of the 1980s in which many governments professed devotion to competition, we have a full enough agenda in these areas without entering the much more complex emotive area of privatising the welfare state.

Businessmen's economics

This is a good place to introduce what I call 'businessmen's economics', which is often a much greater threat to economic liberalism than anything of a more left-wing flavour – if only because market economics and pro-business policies are so often confused in public discussion.

But an equally important reason for highlighting them is that if many kinds of state activity and intervention are either unavoidable or extremely difficult to run down, it is all the more important – for much wider reasons than the narrowly economic – to avoid overloading the political agenda with policies based on these fallacies.

Here are a few examples of the kind of fallacy I have in mind:

1   The idea that a country or group such as the EU must be a key producer or exporter of products in areas such as aerospace or nuclear arms. It does not have to be so at all.
2   The view that some sectors of economic activity are inherently superior or inferior; for example, 'I really don't believe myself that the USA is going to become a nation of hamburger stands, Chinese restaurants, laundries, banks and computer operators. I think we have to have some sort of manufacturing sector.' The relative role of these different sectors is better determined by the most distorted and imperfect of markets than by the instincts of the self-important.
3   The view that an increase in exports or reduction in imports must always be to a country's advantage. This is just plain wrong.
4   The assertion that 'we', meaning governments, have to decide, for instance, what to do 'when UK oil runs out', whether to be self-sufficient in coal or allow imports. Again, there are available self-adjusting mechanisms, highly imperfect, but upon which it is most unlikely that government will improve.

All the above are primitive fallacies which one does not have to be a *laissez-faire* fanatic to reject. Why, for instance, should the British or French Cabinet determine the size of the nuclear power programme, the choice of reactor or the structure of the nuclear industry? In the much smaller Swiss electrical power system, the choice of reactor is made by the utilities concerned and two different systems are in successful operation. Other examples of misplaced energy include the arm-twisting of motor companies to buy national components. Then there is the strong preference for home-made products in the public sector or, worst of all the 'Voluntary Export Restrictions', forced on Japanese and developing country exporters of cars, consumer electronics and textiles to the USA and the European Union.

The most ridiculous aspect of the whole debate is that businessmen argue that market economists are cynical and myopic and that they are the long-sighted statesmen. My examples are mostly drawn from an excellent exposition of common fallacies by David Henderson. But whereas he calls them 'do it yourself economics', I prefer to call them businessmen's economics – for two reasons. First, it highlights the difference between market liberalism (or the social market economy) and mere pro-business policies. Secondly, there is no fallacy, however pernicious, that has not been supported by some highly sophisticated economists. In the academic world demand for a certain type of product creates its own supply, and many highly trained economists in Cambridge (Mass.) are engaged in rationalising the business demand for protection under slogans such as 'the need for an American industrial strategy'. Here is an area where the USA could learn from European experience, but is determined not to do so.

Developments in financial markets

I cannot end without a few remarks on financial markets. These have always provided some of the most controversial aspects of capitalism in practice. If we are to have dispersed ownership, there has to be a secondary market in paper titles to business property and less-tangible assets such as government debt. The speed and ease with which such titles can change hands are important for efficiency and the freedom of action of citizens with even the most meagre financial holdings.

There is nothing to regret in the disappearance of cartel arrangements, such as fixed commissions in the London Stock Exchange or other restrictive practices, including the enforced separation of trading from brokerage – akin to the distinction between barristers and lawyers and many other arcane procedures and restrictions inside the legal profession. Nor is it such a bad idea that banks or building societies should have to pay competitive rates of interest on depositors' money, including the accounts on which cheques can be drawn.

There is much to be said even for the unpopular activity of take-over battles. A widely recognised problem of modern organisational theory is that of the 'principal-agent'. How does one find incentives for a senior civil servant, health service manager, head of a monopolistic public utility or managing director of a private-sector corporation to act in the interests of those to whom he is responsible – in the latter case the shareholder – rather than to follow his own goals? To secure the maximum return on shareholder's assets is normally in the interest, not merely of the shareholders, but also of the nation. It is not in the interest of the poor or the unfortunate that assets should be inefficiently or under-utilised. The reformer may wish to change the distribution of equity ownership, but not – if he is sensible – to hold down the return on capital.

On the other hand corporate managers left to themselves may well follow objectives such as a quiet life, or profitless growth, or – at the other extreme – safety-first cash mountains. Without the threat that in the last resort underperforming management will be replaced by a more successful one, a vital incentive to performance is missing. In continental Europe the role of keeping management up to scratch is often played by large banks. But is this closed-door method of decision really preferable? And does not the close connection between banks and corporations provide large concentrations of power at least as objectionable as American or British corporate conglomerates?

We need not so much 'takeovers' as 'take-over battles'. (Monopoly and merger law must of course always be there as a long-stop to prevent business concentrations which threaten competition.) Those of us who favour decentralisation and are suspicious of big battalions will be happiest when the outcome of a takeover fight is an internal revolution in the threatened company, which is then able to repulse the bidder. But unsuccessful take-over bids cannot exercise their galvanising role if there is not at the time a threat of success. The first takeover fight I remember was when ICI made a bid for Courtaulds in the early 1960s. The bid was unsuccessful; but it did succeed in shaking up the Courtaulds management and led to the emergence of the late Lord Kearton, who had a thoroughly beneficial effect there before he decided to venture elsewhere as an industrial statesman.

To the extent that financial institutions do take too short term a view, a likely reason is that they are too managerial. Much financial business is now carried on by salaried employees, often young, ambitious and energetic, but who are judged by their performance over three-month periods – or, in very liberal establishments, perhaps over a year. Most of the traders and principals today are employed by institutions such as pension funds, protected by tax privilege, which are under no pressure to act as profit maximisers, but merely not to do conspicuously worse than their peers in any period.

Stabilising speculation is more likely if many participants are using their own money and can decide for themselves whether to back a longer view. It was the old-fashioned capitalist, with ample personal resources of his own, who could afford to take the long view. The suntraps of the world are full of prematurely retired, cantankerous characters who backed their own long-term judgments against the fashions of the moment.

This is a problem with which we may just have to live. The spectacular increase in the number of private shareholders associated with privatisation has been in individuals holding a handful of shares, who can hardly be expected to play the role of stabilising speculators. In any case, large fluctuations in financial asset values have been characteristic of the history of capitalism and indeed of all systems with a market-related sector.

Obviously speculative bubbles and overextended or imprudent credit expansion can occur. The job of central banks, which now have to act together across frontiers, is not to 'know better', but use their lender-of-last-resort power to ensure that failures of particular institutions or markets do not spiral into a general contraction of money, credit or purchasing power, as Bagehot taught several generations ago. But Bagehot did not explain how the problem of moral hazard could be resolved without keeping people guessing which institutions will be rescued and on what terms. The occupational temptation of central bankers is to rescue too many rather than too few, both of institutions and countries.

As a cautious risk-averse person, I welcomed the emergency packages that the IMF and the central bankers put together in 1982 and immediately afterwards to avert country default in the Third World debt crises of that period. Market prices, however shadowy, eventually came to exist for most Third World debt; and the time came for the banks to make their own deals with the debtors, with some degree of write-off and without calling on the taxpayer for a contribution.

Money and currencies

Unfortunately, those on the free-market side have not presented a very happy spectacle either. They put too many of their eggs into two baskets: the belief that there was a stable predictable relationship between something called money and the price level or the national income; and the view that floating exchange rates were the best way for different national currencies to co-exist.

Neither doctrine is an essential part of market economics of any variety. It would, of course, be convenient if all we needed to cope with the world's macro-economic problems was a monetary constitution in each country instructing the central bank (a) to increase a defined measure of the money supply by a pre-determined percentage amount; and (b) not to intervene in the foreign exchange markets. But it would be astonishing if the world were so kind to us; and it is sad that the free-market economists allowed themselves to be identified so exclusively with these two doctrines.

The defects of monetarism, in the narrow sense, are that it concedes too much power to government policy, underrates the influence of competition in providing monetary substitutes, and takes official statistics far too much at their face value. None of this should have been surprising. The invention of new monetary instruments to replace old ones – and competition between currencies – was bound to become more important as communications improved further, capital markets became even more closely linked, and controls on both financial institutions and on currency movements across frontiers were abolished.

Floating exchange rates were probably the least bad method of weathering the decade or so after the collapse of Bretton Woods in 1971, a period which also saw two oil price explosions, and two waves of double-digit inflation. Nevertheless, the combination of national economic policies hardly led to a harmonious development of exchange rates. The dollar doubled against the German mark in the five years up to March 1985. Then in the subsequent two years it halved. One did not need to have a view of the *right* exchange rate pattern to conclude that if the 1980 and 1987 dollar rate was right, then the rate of 1984–5 was absurdly high. The unsustainably high dollar of the middle 1980s had longer term ill effects, as it put immense commercial pressure on the sectors of the US economy involved in exports or subject to import competition. But as the very high dollar did not last, any adaptations which were made proved to be a mistake. American producers of traded goods had to rebuild market shares after their overseas competitors had entrenched themselves and were prepared to see their margins squeezed.

Unfortunately, it is a big leap from recognition of exchange rate misalignments to devising an improvement. Many of these problems were tackled automatically under the gold standard, and we may have yet to return to some kind of commodity-related standard. We cannot pretend that such a standard is around the corner. In the meanwhile market liberals should not sneer at the groping and often fumbling attempts to evolve a world or European monetary order. Stable money in the broadest sense has always been regarded by the wisest economic liberals, from Hume and Smith onwards, as a vital background condition for the operation of markets and it is a legitimate sphere for official action, even of an imperfect kind.

Exchange rate objectives are unfashionable at the time of writing. Rather than try and guess if and when they will become fashionable again it is more important to reiterate the lesson that *on their own* they will never be enough. When such targets are under strain, should the onus be on strong currency countries to loosen their internal policies or on the weaker countries to tighten theirs? The world rate of inflation and demand growth become indeterminate if exchange rates are the only guide.

One suggestion, worth repeating, is that the level of nominal world interest rates might be adjusted upwards or downwards if aggregate national income in money terms (combined nominal GDP) in the participating countries threatens to exceed or fall short of objectives. The distribution of national interest rates around this average would then be adjusted to help the key currencies to stay within their target zones.

Conclusion

Important as these arguments on financial strategy are within the liberal camp, they are often overrated. They would certainly be the wrong note on which to conclude. I am more concerned by a wider issue.

In 1973 I wrote a book to persuade the open-minded reader that the right kind of market economy could be an instrument of human freedom as well as a way of satisfying human wants. Since then, a strange paradox has arisen. The case for the market is now more widely accepted politically; and it is less of a lonely, although it is still a minority, voice in intellectual circles. The virtues of decentralisation, deregulation and dispersed ownership – not only of personal property but also of the means of production – have become almost an orthodoxy.

Yet something vital is missing. The market case is now almost always put forward in terms of prosperity, efficiency or 'accepting hard realities'. The discussion about the bearing of different forms of economic organisation on freedom has all but disappeared. Moreover, a great deal of present-day capitalism is not based on liberal-individualist values. Many commentators have noted that the successful capitalism of East Asia is based on a very different Confucian tradition. Thus, while in the early 1970s one of the main tasks of economic liberals was to put the case for competitive capitalism to supporters of 'permissiveness' (a derogatory name for freedom), their task now is as much to explain to upholders of the market the role of personal freedom.

The movement of institutions and technology has been favourable to market liberalism. The movement of ideas has been much less so. There is understanding of markets as a form of co-ordination superior to collectivist compulsion. But belief in personal freedom, on which the whole approach rests, has taken some knocks, which I trust will prove temporary.

The most realistic hope is not that one political party will be captured for classical liberalism or the social market economy, but that different aspects will be advanced by different groupings. Although we need to think of how to put together the political coalitions which will advance liberal ideas in practice, this cannot be a substitute for much-needed further thought on the content and development of the ideas themselves.

People may make many mistakes in the use of freedom, and nature or society may hold many unforeseen snags. But in the end the dangers from freedom are far, far less than the dangers from those on the left and right alike who deign to tell fellow citizens how to live. The absurdities produced by the moral authoritarians and the economic collectivists alike will always provide the supporters of freedom with a chance, so long as their supporters are prepared to meet the challenge.

POSTSCRIPT

There have obviously been major developments since I last revised this lecture early in the 1990s. They include the emergence of 'globalisation' as a hot topic for debate; the development of the Internet; the ferocious British argument about the euro and the advent of a new Labour government in Britain led by Tony Blair.

To cover these adequately would require another essay or lecture at least the length of the above. But I feel absolved from this task because some of the ground has been covered in a later book of essays (*Essays, Moral, Political and Economic*, Edinburgh University Press 1998.)

This is as well. For as Chou En Lai said when asked what he thought of the French Revolution, 'It is far too early to tell.' It is tempting to dismiss globalisation as nothing more than the extension of free capital movements, aided and abetted by the worldwide movement to decontrol and technical improvements in the transmission of information.

The Internet, of course, comes under the information category. I feel inclined to regard it as just another development in the speeding up of the transmission of information from one place to another, rather like the transatlantic cable in the mid-nineteenth century, although not quite as important. But there are people who believe that it will bring a technological revolution on the scale exceeding anything since the invention of the steam engine. Enthusiasts also claim that it can abolish boom and slump, or bubble and burst, and permit rapid growth to continue without interruption or inflationary overheating. These claims are made most frequently in relation to the 'New Economy' which is supposed to exist in the USA. At this stage the best response is to introduce a note of caution or even scepticism, but await events.

Similarly, I am not among those who believe that the decision about British entry to the euro is one of the great events of either constitutional or economic history. The main economic reason for joining was that it seemed at one time by far the most likely route to an independent central bank. But since the Labour government surprised financial opinion, when it came to office in 1997, by giving the Bank of England operational independence, this case is now much weaker.

References

Bagehot, W., *Lombard Street*, original edn, London, 1873.

Brittan, S., 'Capitalism and the Permissive Society', 1973; the main parts are reprinted as the first three chapters of *Restatement* (below).

Brittan, S., *A Restatement of Economic Liberalism*, London: Macmillan, 1988, pp. 80–111 and 138–43.

Hahn, F., 'Market Economics', in R. Skidelsky (ed.), *Thatcherism*, London: Chatto & Windus, 1988, Ch.6.

Henderson, D., *Innocence and Design*, Oxford: Basil Blackwell, 1986.

Olson, M., *The Rise and Decline of Nations*, New Haven, Conn.: Yale University Press, 1982.

Peacock, A., H. Willgerodt and D. Johnson, *Germany's Social Market Economy: Origins and Evolution*, London: Macmillan, 1989.

Peacock. A. *et al.*, *German Neo-Liberals and the Social Market Economy*, London: Macmillan, 1989.

Rawls, J., *A Theory of Justice*, London: Oxford University Press, 1972.

Russell, B. *Human Society in Ethics and Politics*, London: George Allen and Unwin, 1954.

14 Markets, governments and virtues

Chief Rabbi Jonathan Sacks

The story is told of an English philosophy professor who was invited to deliver a lecture at the University of Beijing. Not being able to speak Chinese, he was provided with an interpreter. The day of the lecture arrived, the professor delivered the first sentences of his talk, and waited for the interpreter to translate. The interpreter, however, told him to continue. He would, he said, signal when he wanted him to stop.

After fifteen minutes, the interpreter signalled a break, delivered a brief sentence to the audience, and gestured to the professor to continue. The same thing happened after thirty minutes, and then after forty-five, and again at the conclusion of the talk. As the audience filed out, the English academic went over to the translator and expressed his amazement. 'I am astonished at your power of compression. I have just given a complex lecture on metaphysics, and yet you managed to translate it into four sentences. What did you say?' 'Simple,' replied the interpreter. 'After fifteen minutes I said, "So far, he hasn't said anything new." After thirty I said, "He *still* hasn't said anything new." After forty-five, I said, "I don't think he's going to say anything new." And at the end I said, "He didn't."'

One of the advantages of being a religious leader is that no one expects you to say anything new; in fact, the older, the better. Today I want to take a look at economic systems – specifically the market economy – from a distance in time, the distance lent by a religious tradition, one of whose roles is to view the present from the perspective of past and future. Not the least of religion's tasks is to initiate a dialogue between immediacy and eternity, something necessary at times of great change. From this perspective, it may be possible to gain a clearer picture of some of the wider issues involved in an economic order, especially in the way a market interacts with a culture, shaped by it, and shaping it in turn.

To give an example: The Harvard economic historian David Landes poses a fascinating question in his book, *The Wealth and Poverty of Nations*.[1] In the Middle Ages, China was far in advance of the West in many aspects of technology. It had been the first country to invent printing, paper, porcelain and explosives. Why then, asks Landes, did the Industrial Revolution take place in Europe, not China? He suggests several explanations, but they have one thing in common. They have to do with culture, specifically with what we call today the Judaeo-Christian ethic. The Hebrew Bible, for example, is marked by a revolutionary concept of time –

time as a journey toward a destination. This, known as 'linear time', is in marked contrast to the *cyclical* time of other ancient civilisations. To make progress, in other words, a culture has to contain the *idea* of progress. It needs a linear concept of time.

More broadly, Landes argues, the key factor Europe had, and China did not, was a market economy, one that encouraged free enterprise, rewarded innovation, and protected private property from seizure by kings, emperors or governments. That ethic has its origins in the Hebrew Bible, and the renewed Christian encounter with the Bible as a result of the Reformation. Why then did Judaism value the market to the extent that it did, in both biblical and post-biblical times?

The answer, I believe, is to be found in the two epoch-making journeys with which the faith of Israel begins: Abraham and Sarah's journey from Mesopotamia in the east, and Moses and the Israelites' exodus from Egypt in the west. Strikingly, Judaism begins with a rejection of the two greatest civilisations of the ancient world, Mesopotamia with its city-states, and Egypt of the Pharaohs, two cultures which, even today, remain awe-inspiring in their technological achievements. Mesopotamia witnessed the invention of the wheel, the arch, writing and astronomy. Pharaonic Egypt produced architecture on the most monumental scale. What, from a Jewish point of view, was wrong with these social orders?

The answer lies in four explosive Hebrew words in the first chapter of Genesis: *na'aseh adam be-tsalmenu ki-demutenu*, 'Let us make man in our image and likeness.' What is revolutionary about these words is not that a human being can be in the image of God. That was an idea familiar to the ancient world. Sumerian kings and Egyptian Pharaohs were precisely that, gods, or representatives of the gods, in human form. What was new was not that *a* human being can be in the image of God, but that *every* human being is. From its inception, Judaism was a living protest against hierarchical societies that give some, but not all, dignity, power and freedom. Instead it insisted that if any individual is sacred, then every individual is, because each of us is in the image of God.

It is a measure of how profound this idea was, and how long it took before it was translated into political structures, that it was not until 1776 that the American Declaration of Independence, largely drafted by Thomas Jefferson, declared: 'We hold these truths to be self-evident, that all men are created equal, that they are endowed by their creator with certain unalienable rights, [and] that among these are life, liberty and the pursuit of happiness.' These truths, of course, are anything but self-evident. They have been implicitly denied by most societies at most times in history. They are self-evident only to someone steeped in the Hebrew Bible. Indeed it is worth noting that of the three great political revolutions of modernity, the American, French and Russian, only the American was driven by religious values. The other two were inspired by philosophical values, those of Rousseau in the case of France, Marx in the case of Russia. Precisely these two, inspired by visions of a secular utopia, ended in bloodshed and the suppression of human rights.

To return, then, to Judaism: the central question is, how do we build social structures that honour and sustain the freedom, integrity and creativity of the individual? The brief answer is that the Hebrew Bible is an extended critique of what we would now call big government. At one extreme we have the biblical portrait of ancient Egypt, a nation which builds extraordinary buildings but at the cost of turning human beings into slaves. At an opposite extreme we have the justly famous eighth chapter of I Samuel, in which the people come to the prophet and demand a king. On the instruction of God, Samuel tells them that if they appoint a king, he will eventually seize their sons and daughters, their fields and vineyards, and a percentage of their harvests and cattle. Even constitutional monarchy, in other words, will involve a sacrifice of rights of property and person. 'When that day comes, you will cry out for relief from the king you have chosen, and the Lord will not answer you on that day.'

We can summarise the classic Judaic view as follows: Governments are necessary for defence and the maintenance of social order. As a rabbinic teaching of the first century CE[2] puts it: 'Pray for the welfare of the government, for were it not for the fear of it, people would eat one another alive.'[3] But state action always stands in need of justification, because any government, however democratically elected, *ipso facto* represents a curtailment of certain fundamental rights such as the right to enjoy the fruits of one's own labour. It can only be justified on the grounds that secure possession of those rights depends on the existence of a central power that defends individuals against lawlessness on the one hand, foreign invasion on the other. Long before Hobbes, Locke and Jefferson, therefore, biblical Judaism is a theory of *limited government*. This principled insistence on the moral limits of power is the only secure defence of the individual against the collective, whether it be the tyranny of kings or what John Stuart Mill, following Alexis de Tocqueville, called the 'tyranny of the majority'.

Let me use a personal example. From time to time, Elaine and I invite politicians to dinner – from all parties, I hasten to add. When we have finished eating, we say Grace after meals, and I am always anxious in case any of our guests should take the grace (at least 2000 years old in its basic formulation) as a party political statement, containing as it does the sentence, 'We ask of you, God, not to make us dependent on the gifts of men' – a line that could have come straight from the pen of Milton Friedman or Charles Murray. This is not because Judaism is intrinsically opposed to a welfare state, but because it places a high, and specifically religious, value on economic independence as a component of individual liberty.

The most famous example of this is in Moses Maimonides' list of the eight rungs of charity.[4] Of these, the highest but one is where an individual gives generously, without having to be asked, and where neither the giver knows the identity of the recipient, nor the recipient the identity of the giver. Even this sublime form of altruism is, however, only the penultimate achievement. The highest is to provide someone with a job or the means to start his own business. How so? Unlike all the other forms of charity, this involves the donor in no financial loss and the recipient in no unearned gain. On the face of it, there has been no act either of giving or receiving. Why then is this the highest form of charity in Jewish law? Because through it, we give someone something more precious than money. We give him back his dignity. In Judaism there is no higher dignity than in enjoying the benefits of our own work, our own creativity. As we say at the beginning of each working week, quoting Psalm 128:2, 'When you eat of the fruit of your labour, you shall be happy and you will prosper.'

Looking back, then, with centuries of hindsight with which to test the Hebrew Bible's foresight, we can say that the market economy did deliver in terms of higher living standards, and no less importantly, in liberating energies and fostering human creativity. As a result, the average citizen of the liberal democracies of the west has, in an average supermarket, a range of choices that would have been, only a century ago, beyond the dreams of kings. He or she can travel the world and communicate globally at speeds unimaginable then. We have better health, longer life expectancy, more access to education and information, than any generation since life first stirred on earth. Above all, despite its inequalities, the market economy is the best means we know for fostering the freedom, dignity and moral responsibility of the individual, as opposed to a privileged elite. At its best, it gives us *equal access to hope.*

However, I cannot end there, because the human story – as opposed to fiction – never ends with the words, 'And they all lived happily ever after', not least because the human story never ends. There is always another chapter; always what economists call 'the law of unintended consequences'. At this point I turn, not to the market economy *per se*, but to that stage of its development known as late capitalism, which is to say, the present.

One of the turning points of economic history was the justly famous observation of Adam Smith: 'It is not from the benevolence of the butcher, brewer or baker that we expect our dinner, but from their regard to their own interest. We address ourselves not to their humanity but to their self-love.'[5] What made the market so potent was that it turned self-interest into collective gain, through the working of what Smith called an 'invisible hand'. Out of the seemingly disconnected efforts of myriads of people, each pursuing their own advantage, the market created something vast, unintended and benign, namely economic growth. The Internet represents another graphic example. The product of thousands of separate initiatives, it has turned into an extraordinary collective resource from which each of us can benefit.

In the course of the twentieth century, however, an intellectual discovery threatened to challenge the central premise of Smith's argument. In 1944 John von Neumann invented a branch of mathematics designed to shed light on decision-making. It was called Games Theory, and its most famous paradox, formulated in 1950, was the Prisoner's Dilemma.

The Prisoner's Dilemma imagines the following scenario: Police arrest two men on suspicion of a serious crime. They do not have enough evidence to convict them; at most they have evidence sufficient to prove them guilty of a lesser offence. Their aim is to get them to inform on one another. They therefore put them in separate rooms, with no possible communication between them, and offer them a deal. If one informs and the other stays silent, the informant will go free, and the other will receive a jail sentence of ten years. If both inform, they will be sentenced to five years each. If both stay silent, they will be found guilty of the lesser offence and be sentenced to a year in prison.

It does not take long to work out that for each, the optimal decision is to inform. The result, however, is they both receive a five-year sentence, whereas if they had both stayed silent, they would have received only one year. The Prisoner's Dilemma may seem no more than a curiosity, but it is not. It establishes the paradoxical, but deeply significant, fact that two people, each pursuing their own self-interest, generate an outcome which is bad for them, both individually and collectively. Smith's Law is defeated by Murphy's Law.

The solution, when it emerged, was equally fascinating.[6] It came in the late 1970s, as the result of a convergence between two disciplines, socio-biology and computer science. What people suspected, and were eventually able to prove, is that the Prisoner's Dilemma yields its paradoxical result only if it played once. If it is played over and over – the so-called 'Iterated Prisoner's Dilemma' – the parties eventually learn that they are doing themselves, as well as the other person, harm. Once they discover this, they learn to co-operate.

At this point, Games Theory provided socio-biologists with an answer to a question that had long puzzled Darwinians, including Charles Darwin himself. In the struggle for survival, the fittest wins. Despite this, all human societies value altruistic behaviour, and some forms of it can be found in non-human species. What evolutionary advantage could there be from the sacrifice of one's own interest to the interests of the group? One biologist, Robert Axelrod, had the insight to sense that an answer could be found in the Iterated Prisoner's Dilemma. This was a schematic way of representing action – human or animal – under conditions of uncertainty. In 1979, he announced a global competition to find the computer programme that performed best in repeated encounters with itself and all other programmes.

The winning programme (incidentally also the simplest and shortest) was called 'Tit-for-Tat'. It consisted in being nice on the first encounter, and then repeating the previous action of its opponent. If it was aggressive, so was Tit-for-Tat. If it was co-operative, Tit-for-Tat was likewise. The programme, in other words, was the computer equivalent of what the Bible and Shakespeare called 'Measure for Measure'. No less fascinating was the discovery in the late 1980s of a programme that beat Tit-for-Tat. The work of a Polish mathematician, Martin Nowak, it was called 'Generous'. Generous overcame the one weakness of Tit-for-Tat, namely that when it met a consistently vicious opponent, it was drawn into an endless and destructive cycle of retaliation; a computer simulation, in other words, of a phenomenon all too familiar from the politics of Bosnia, Northern Ireland, the Middle East and Rwanda. Generous was similar to Tit-for-Tat with one exception: randomly but regularly it broke the cycle by forgetting the last move of its opponent. It embodied, in other words, the computer equivalent of forgiveness and reconciliation.

I find this an utterly fascinating chapter in the history of thought, and one that has huge implications. Against everything I was taught at university, it now seems that we can establish a rational basis for ethics, indeed a specific form of ethics.

What Tit-for-Tat and Generous show is that those populations survive and thrive who practise the two fundamental ethical principles of the Judaeo-Christian tradition – reciprocity and forgiveness, or what used to be called justice and mercy. It is no accident, therefore, that these two faiths have survived while so many other civilisations have disappeared.

In addition, we are now better able to understand why *Homo sapiens* – i.e. us – have an evolutionary advantage over all other species. It lies in our ability to co-operate. Set one man against one lion, and lion wins. Set ten men against one lion, and lion loses. The secret of evolutionary success is co-operation, and the basis of co-operation is trust. So important is this phenomenon that economists have now given it a name. They call it *social capital*, meaning the level of trust in a society.

What is crucial, though, is to remember how trust is created, namely by the Iterated Prisoner's Dilemma, in other words by people repeatedly interacting with one another. That, for example, is why crime rates are always higher in inner cities than in villages. Someone is more likely to take advantage of you if you are never going to see him again (the single Prisoner's Dilemma) than if you are going to meet him in the street tomorrow and the day after. Habits of co-operation depend on the existence of long-term relationships.

I now need to take the argument one stage further. Imagine you are taking a child, a nephew or niece for example, for a ride on the London Eye. As you rise, you see the Houses of Parliament, and you explain to the child that these buildings are the seat of government, the home of politics, and that politics is about the creation and distribution of power.

Next you point out the offices and shops, and in the distance, the Stock Exchange building. You explain that these are the homes of the market, the domain of economics, and that they have to do with the creation and distribution of wealth.

Finally, the child notices the steeples and spires of London's churches and the great dome of St Paul's. What, she asks, are they. You reply that they are houses of worship. 'And what do they create and distribute?' she asks. It's a good question. Perhaps we would be inclined to say that they are not that sort of thing; in which case, we would be wrong. Houses of worship, congregations and communities, do create and distribute something, but it is a special kind of thing.

We can see what this is by a thought experiment. Imagine that you have total power, and then you decide to share it with nine others. The result is that you now have one-tenth of the power with which you began. Now imagine that you have a thousand pounds, and then you share it with nine others. Again, you have a tenth of what you had before. The reason is that power and wealth are, at any given moment, zero-sum games. The more I share, the less I have. That is why governments and markets are arenas of mediated conflict. That is why we need them.

Now imagine that you have a certain quantum of love, or friendship, or influence, or loyalty, and then you share it with nine others. Do you have less than when you started? No, you have more. I am going to call them *social goods*, and they have this characteristic in common, that the more I share, the more I have.

For this, there is a simple reason, namely that they only exist in virtue of being shared.

The question now is: where are such goods created? Where do we acquire love and loyalty, friendship and trust? The answer is: in families, communities, neighbourhoods and congregations – the places where the 'We' takes precedence over the 'I'. We can now say, in quite unmystical terms, why. These are the homes of the Iterated Prisoner's Dilemma, where we form long-term relationships with other people and interact with them repeatedly over time. They are the environments in which we learn the grammar of reciprocity and the vocabulary of forgiveness – the essential habits of co-operation. They are places where we are there for other people, knowing that they are there for us. We can now say what they create and distribute: *social capital*, meaning, relationships of trust.

This brings me, finally, to the great tragedy of late capitalist societies. For at least the past half-century, public debate about society has revolved around two institutions: governments and markets, the domains respectively of politics and economics. The great argument has been which to prefer. The Left tends to favour government action, the Right, the workings of the market. Recently a Third Way has been proposed as a synthesis between the two. The taken-for-granted assumption has been that these are the only options. The State represents us in our collective capacity. The market is us as individuals, making choices. What else is there?

The answer is that there is a *third sector*: the domain of families, congregations, communities, neighbourhood groups and voluntary organisations, all of which are bigger than the individual and smaller than the state. My argument has been that they play a vital role in our social ecology because they are where we learn the habits of co-operation without which the rational pursuit of self-interest fails to produce optimal outcomes. If there is one thing clear about the present condition of liberal democracies throughout the west, it is that these institutions are in disarray. Why is this?

Consider, as an example, the institution of marriage. Let us hear two imagined but typical voices, one from the Right of politics, the other from the Left. The voice from the Right says this: In the past, people married because, in most cases, they had to. There was no one else with whom to share the burden of bringing up children. Today there is. It is called the government. It provides resources in terms of social security, welfare benefits, child-care, social workers and schools. The State has, in effect, become a surrogate father. The result is that it is possible now to sustain a single-parent family, whereas in the past it was not. The State has weakened the family because, while it has privatised much else, it has effectively nationalised paternity.

The corresponding voice from the Left says this: What has destroyed marriage has been the mentality of the market. In the past, virtues such as fidelity, loyalty and respect for the common good were salient forces in society. Today those values have been eroded by a consumer society whose creed includes such axioms as, 'Buy it, use it and throw it away', 'If you find a better deal, go for it', and 'Life is a supermarket. All you have to do is choose.' Those values are incompatible with marriage, which depends on steadfastness and a willingness to sacrifice. A world driven by market values would be one of temporary and provisional loyalties, serial relationships without commitment. That is the world we have.

The Right blames the State, the Left blames the market, and both miss the point, which is that marriage belongs to a realm which is neither State nor market, where relationships are built on trust and not on transactions of power or monetary exchange. The sheer dominance of State and market are slowly but surely driving out of existence those institutions which Burke called the 'little platoons', sociologists call 'mediating structures', and which we know as families, communities and congregations. What is damaging is neither the State nor the market but the slow attrition of the humanising, virtue-inculcating institutions between.

Why should this matter? Firstly because economic systems are not ends in themselves. They are means to advancing what the American Declaration of Independence called 'life, liberty and the pursuit of happiness' and Bentham spoke of as 'the greatest happiness of the greatest number'. If I were to ask you what are the sources of your own happiness, you would be unlikely to say, 'My BMW, my Armani suit and my Rolex watch'. You are far more likely to say, 'My wife or husband, my children, my reputation, my friends'. As the third sector institutions of family and community erode, so too do the sources of our happiness; which is precisely what has, in fact, occurred. For the past fifty years, while average incomes have steadily risen, so too has the incidence of depressive illness, stress-related syndromes, suicide attempts and drug and alcohol abuse, especially among children.

Secondly, our age is one of epoch-making change. Globalisation and the information age, while they will bring huge benefits, will also intensify the strain on our social structures. Employment will become less secure as production, and even clerical tasks, are switched around the world in response to wage rates and currency fluctuations. Communities and neighbourhoods will become even more attenuated as high street shops give way to e-commerce, and face-to-face encounters are increasingly replaced by mobile phones, e-mail, and Internet-based video-conferencing. Wage differentials will continue to rise as we move more deeply into a world dominated by intellectual capital, which favours the gifted few. The social bond will become ever more tenuous. In medieval times the local squire had a real interest in the welfare of those who worked his land. In the nineteenth and twentieth centuries, industrialists had a similar interest in their employees. To be sure, it was not always exercised generously or imaginatively, but it existed. The new economy, by contrast, is for the most part not based on long-term relationships with people to whom you can put a face or whom you know by name.

We are, in other words, moving at great speed into an age of rapid and accelerating change with few of the traditional resources that gave people a sense of stability and security – a marriage, a career, a neighbourhood and friends, that stayed with you for life. These were the things that gave us an identity, a set of values and a sense of being at home in the world. Their loss will make change far more unsettling. Presently we are being cushioned from the effects by the longest peacetime boom in living memory. But what will happen if we hit recession, or even if we don't, but just keep going in the present direction?

It was the unlikely figure of Bertrand Russell who offered a warning. Speaking of his two favourite periods of history, he wrote:

> What had happened in the great age of Greece happened again in Renaissance Italy. Traditional moral restraints disappeared, because they were seen to be associated with superstition; the liberation from fetters made individuals energetic and creative, producing a rare florescence of genius; but the anarchy and treachery which inevitably resulted from the decay of morals made Italians collectively impotent, and they fell, like the Greeks, under the domination of nations less civilized than themselves but not so destitute of social cohesion.[7]

That is our clear and present danger, that we too are becoming destitute of social cohesion. I remain, though, an optimist. I believe in free will. As the Yiddish novelist Isaac Bashevis Singer put it, 'We *must* believe in free will. We have no choice!' And because we can choose, we can change.

I believe in the market economy, not simply on economic, but on moral grounds. It is our best guarantor of human freedom and creativity, of technological progress and the fight against poverty. But the market depends on virtues that are not produced by the market, just as the State depends on virtues not created by the State. Those virtues – the habits of co-operation which constitute social capital – are born and sustained in families, communities and friendships, that third sector of society in which relationships are built not on power or exchange but on loyalty, reciprocity, forgiveness and trust. That is why Adam Smith wrote not one book but two. One he called *The Wealth of Nations*. The other he called *The Theory of the Moral Sentiments*. He remembered what we, at times, forget, that societies need more than governments and markets. They need virtues, moral dispositions, 'habits of the heart'. We need them now.

If, then, we care for the market and for the personal liberties it creates and protects, we will have to work harder in the future to champion and defend those institutions – marriage, the family, community and congregation – which are the seedbeds of the virtues on which the market depends. I believe we can do it. I pray we will.

Notes

1 David Landes, *The Wealth and Poverty of Nations*, London: Little, Brown, 1998.
2 That is to say, first century common era, the beginning of the Christian era.
3 *Avot (Ethics of the Fathers)*, 2:2.
4 Maimonides, *Laws of Gifts to the Poor*, chapter 10.
5 Adam Smith, *The Wealth of Nations*, London: Penguin, 119.
6 The full story can be found in Robert Wright, *The Moral Animal*, London: Little, Brown,

1995; Matt Ridley, *The Origins of Virtue*, London: Viking, 1996; Francis Fukuyama, *The Great Disruption*, London: Profile, 1999.

7 Bertrand Russell, *History of Western Philosophy*, London: George Allen and Unwin, 1962, 18–19.

Appendix: list of Mais Lectures 1978–2000

Index